YOUR GARDEN SHOULDN'T MAKE YOU CRAZY!

Also by C.L. Fornari

The Cape Cod Garden

Your Garden Shouldn't Make You Crazy!

C.L. Fornari

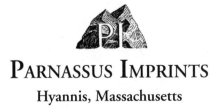

PARNASSUS IMPRINTS
Hyannis, Massachusetts

First Edition

ISBN 0-940160-72-2
Library of Congress Catalog Number 97-66085

Text Illustrations by E. Paul Oberlander
Cover art courtesy of C.L. Fornari

Back Cover Photos: *Top:* June bloomers in the author's garden. *Bottom:* Brick patio in Sue DiMartino's garden (C.L. Fornari).

Parnassus Imprints
30 Perseverance Way
Hyannis, MA 02601

Manufactured in the United States of America

For my father, James H. Albertson, who is greatly responsible—either through genetics or by example—for my sense of humor.

ACKNOWLEDGMENTS

In addition to friends and family who are constantly supportive, my thanks go to all the fellow gardeners who welcome me into their gardens and their hearts. Your gardens and your generosity always inspire me.

As I worked on this book Alan Gelb's comments were especially helpful. I value his advice as well as his friendship. Thanks to: Carol Perfit and Sue Swanson for giving me feedback and help from other planting zones; Karen Levine, Susan Halpren, and Sheri Brown for their good ideas; and Dale Gelfand and Roberta Clark for their help and expertise.

I continue to appreciate working with all the good people at Hyannis Country Garden, as well as the employees and other volunteer Master Gardeners at the Barnstable County Cooperative Extension. I could fill an entire book with the names of all who have my gratitude, and for that alone I am truly blessed.

CONTENTS

INTRODUCTION

The day we moved from Manchester, Massachusetts to Cape Cod, my friend Sheri Brown arrived to deliver a gift. She squeezed her car into our driveway, parking it next to the numerous boxes, furniture, and appliances that waited to be crammed into the moving van. Sheri then began to add some heavy-looking plastic bags and garbage cans to our piles. "It's compost!" she explained when I gave her a questioning look. "Your moving gift is two yards of the best compost . . . I found a man in Ipswich who makes it."

I will admit that at the time I thought she was nuts; the last thing I wanted to deal with at that moment was plastic bags filled with decayed organic matter. But I also understood the wonderful meaning of the gift. Enriching the soil of our new location with organic matter from the old was a touching idea, not to mention a practical one . . . the sandy soil of the Cape can use all the amendments it can get!

The present also told me that my friend, who was new to gardening, already had one of the traits common to most gardeners: they love to share. Very early in our friendship I gave Sheri clumps of perennials from my old garden, and now she was passing on some great compost she had discovered.

Gardeners everywhere are eager to share; they tell each other about a plant which is especially lovely, or an ingenious technique for outsmarting pesky wildlife. Perennials are divided, seeds gathered, and cuttings are rooted, all to be passed on to friends and strangers alike. Time saving strategies, flower bed disasters, and successful plant combinations are traded over backyard fences, in the aisles of garden centers, and over cups of tea.

It is in this spirit that I write this book. My goal is to help people get as much pleasure from their gardens as I do from mine. I want gardens to be a source of inspiration and meditation, not places of worry and guilt. Many gardeners lead such busy lives that they don't have hours and hours to spend on their plants. When the time to garden is limited, it is important that people both enjoy the garden and feel satisfied with their efforts; our gardening can bring rewards far beyond the abundance of plants which grow there.

Every day at the garden center I speak to people who feel overwhelmed and mystified by what is happening in their yards and gardens. Their frustration is usually caused by lack of knowledge about the basic care which is necessary for growing healthy gardens. In general, the more we know, the less overwhelmed we feel; whether we are buying a car or a tree for our property, we feel more sure of our choices when we are making informed decisions.

Even in those times when "expert advice" is contradictory, knowing the pros and cons of a situation helps us to decide what makes the most sense before we take action. And when a plant dies, it is helpful to know if our actions as gardeners prolonged its life, contributed to its decline, or were inconsequential one way or the other. It is important to remember that sometimes plants die despite our care and intervention.

Information alone does not create happy gardeners, however; it is my opinion that successful gardening is a combination of technique *and* attitude. The Norwegians have a saying: "There is no such thing as bad weather, only bad clothing" which is another way of saying that it is pointless to fuss about situations we can't control. Many things are outside of our control in the garden, and we are often better served when we "change our clothing" rather than fight that which we cannot alter.

The Norwegian saying also reminds me that Nature is what Nature is, and we are well advised to work with the natural processes whenever possible. Throughout this book I have tried to stress the wisdom of looking to Mother Nature as our primary instructor in the garden.

Observant readers will note that the chapters containing information about soils, soil amendment, and the overall treatment of the ground in our gardens are the longest in the book. Another avid plant person once told me that she has a sign above her garage which says "Under all is the land." No matter how pressed for time we are, taking care of the soil is a necessity. Successful gardens begin and end in the dirt, and good gardeners know that proper attention to the earth will be returned several fold.

Plants also receive a great deal of coverage here, and although I have tried to recommend those which are suitable for many areas of the country, the plants listed cannot possibly grow in all zones, soil types, and climates. Plants are not "one size fits all" and we should rejoice that this is so. Although it would be convenient to be able to list fifty plants that will thrive in all areas of the country, imagine how boring it would be if the gardens of Los Angeles, California; Saint Louis, MO; Charleston, North Carolina; and Burlington, Vermont all looked the same. Gardeners should consult knowledgeable personnel at their local garden centers, extension services, or regional reference books when choosing plants that will thrive in their area.

When talking about plants I usually refer to them by their Latin names, which are italicized. Because I did not study Latin in school, the use of Latin (and its pronunciation) is often more of a struggle for me than for many others, so I sympathize with readers who moan when they see lists of italicized words. The common name is always given in parentheses after the botanical name, except in those few blessed cases where the common and Latin names are the same.

Having worked in a garden center, I have come to see the importance of these Latin names, even for home gardeners who are not particularly plant-crazed. When my customer requests Snow-on-the-mountain, does she want the tidy, annual *Euphorbia marginata* or the highly invasive *Aegopodium podagraria*? Several plants may share the same common name, but because every plant has its own botanical name, using Latin names can prevent misunderstandings. (Usually.) Just as there are plants such as *Forsythia* for which the common and Latin names are the same, there are also plants whose common name is identical to the Latin name of another that is completely unrelated. *Catharanthus roseus* is a small flowering annual which is often called Vinca, even though it bears no relation to the evergreen groundcover, *Vinca minor* or *Vinca major* . To confound things even further, sometimes both of these plants are also called periwinkle!

Added to this muddle is the fact that every year some Latin names are changed, leaving all of us in the perennial section, shaking our heads at the *Leucanthemum* (Shasta daisy) which used to be a *Chrysanthemum*, and wondering where it will end. As much as I believe that we all need to accustom ourselves to the Latin names, I realize that there are times when the common name is so familiar, and the botanical label so seldom used, that using the familiar designation makes the most sense. Dave Lane, my boss at Country Garden, keeps it all in perspective for me. If I ask him if we have ordered more *Physostegia virginiana* his reply is likely to be "Gesundheit!"

In gardening, a light approach often serves us well. As much as I have tried to give practical, factual advice, I recognize the value of just plunging into your garden and *doing it*. The Nike approach to gardening? Sheri (my compost-sharing friend) told me recently that as a new gardener she was timid about digging beds and placing plants for fear that she would make a mistake. It was at this point that I invited her to come to my garden for plants. We tromped through my perennials with the requisite "shovels, rakes, and implements of destruction" (so well described by Arlo Guthrie), popping up plants, splitting clumps with shovels, and generally ignoring proper dividing times and methods in our eagerness.

Sheri tells me that as we worked she realized that although she had more to learn about gardening, it was not something that she needed to be afraid of. In the garden, enthusiasm goes a long way. Although I can't invite everyone to come dig perennials with me, I hope you will consider this book another garden of sorts. Here is some of the information I have found useful, some of the plants which I love, and a few of the lessons I have learned from my gardening. Grab a pencil instead of a shovel and dump your fear in the compost . . . let's get into some dirt, spend time with the plants, and celebrate gardening together.

YOUR GARDEN SHOULDN'T MAKE YOU CRAZY

Recent surveys show that gardening is now the number one leisure activity in the United States. Being a fairly plant-obsessed person myself, I think that this is a good thing. Gardening puts us in intimate contact with the natural world at the same time that it beautifies the landscape around us. How could this be anything but wonderful? Gardening, like other positive things we do in our lives, is a problem only if it becomes a pressure. Faced with demands of work, family, and household maintenance, gardening can become one more thing that we *should* be doing.

When you look at your yard or garden, do you see the beautiful plants that are, perhaps, growing against the odds? Or do you see the weeds that need to be pulled, the bare area waiting to be planted, or the shrubs that need pruning? When planning a new flower bed, do you approach the task with enthusiasm or does your desire to do it right find you paralyzed every time you visit the garden center? In August, do you notice how much the annuals that you planted in May have grown over the past three months? Or do you think only of how you will plant them differently *next* year?

We all want our gardens to be as beautiful and as healthy as they can be, and we should, of course, notice when a plant isn't looking well or when our gardens need weeding. But we should also be able to see the tremendous beauty that is always there, in the plants we have placed in our gardens and perhaps in the weeds as well! Our gardens should be places of refuge and not just other items to add to our daily lists of "things to get done today."

Gardens make people crazy when there seems to be too much to be done in the time allowed. Plants that die, or just look sickly, make gardeners feel frustrated, as do those that don't grow or bloom as they should. Sometimes the unexpected in a garden throws us for a loop. Attacks of insects, disease, and wildlife can make us mad, and spending time and money on young plants, only to have them die, can drive even the most patient person nuts.

If it were up to me, I would make sure that any national health insurance includes the help of a gardener, once a week, for every household. This in addition to a weekly massage and two years of therapy for everyone over thirty. At this writing, however, it is *not* up to me (and considering the national debt, this may be a good thing), so most of us bumble along doing the work ourselves with the assistance from family members and an occasional hired hand. But without such regular help, is it possible to do our jobs, maintain friendships, be there for family members, squeeze in some time to exercise every week, *and* have a beautiful garden? And is it possible to have this garden and not feel pressured by it? Our gardens shouldn't make us crazy.

WORKING AGAINST YOURSELF

Most people don't spend six hours a day tending the plants on their property, or have the means to hire full-time gardeners. For most gardeners, working with their plants is a weekend activity, or one that takes a couple of hours per week. Such gardeners don't have time to make mistakes, yet many of the difficulties that people encounter may be self-created, or perhaps self-exacerbated. Gardeners often choose the wrong plants for the wrong reasons, then find themselves having to spend time dealing with a garden that is not doing well. Similarly, the right plant may be planted in the wrong location.

The publications that we turn to for help, those beautiful full color books and magazines that fill every bookstore, inspire and educate us about plants and gardening techniques at the same time that they can leave us with inappropriate desires. Who has not seen pictures of gorgeous perennial borders and not come away with a serious case of garden lust? I know that *I* am not immune . . . *I* see a picture of a huge arbor dripping with wisteria in full bloom, and I want one! Never mind that I don't have the space for the arbor, or the sunshine required to make the wisteria bloom.

Plant lust isn't all we are left with after seeing those lovely garden pictures; we are also left with a wheelbarrow full of unreal expectations. Photography can be remarkably deceiving. I can take a photo of a garden that hides the bare spots, hoses, and the mildew on the zinnias. Shot from the right angle, you would never guess that the Nippon daisies get bare, brown stems by the beginning of August, or that the garden pictured will soon be overrun with self-seeded rose campion. Pictures can educate and inspire us, but just as air-brushed photos of models give us unrealistic expectations of how human beings should look, garden photos can lull us into thinking that the plants and gardens we see look picture perfect all the time.

We also forget to put those photographed gardens in their proper perspective. Perhaps that luscious perennial border was created with the help of a garden designer, planted by a landscaper, and maintained by team of twice-weekly garden helpers. Even if a flower bed or landscape is planned and maintained exclusively by the owners, they may be hopelessly obsessed plant fanatics who are pulling up weeds as they sip their morning coffee, and dividing their perennials by the light of the moon.

My point is not to make you so jaded that you no longer enjoy the magazines and picture books. One of my great pleasures is to sit in an overstuffed chair with a cup of tea and a new issue of a gardening magazine. (Believe me, I subscribe to them all!) I am in no way disparaging those beautiful gardens pictured, or the means by which they are planted and maintained; many of the gardens and plant combinations pictured in books and magazines would be appropriate for the average gardener. I am merely reminding you that in addition to leaving us with a craving to grow the plants pictured, we can also be left with unreal expectations of what we have the time, space, climate, or ability to achieve.

IF YOU DON'T HAVE THE TIME TO DO IT RIGHT, WHEN WILL YOU FIND THE TIME TO DO IT OVER?

It is not necessary to be skeptical about inspiring photographs or feel defeated by seeing a garden maintained by a team of groundskeepers. It is only necessary to do a bit of research when planning your own gardens, so you will know which plants, gardening practices, and garden layouts will work *for* you, not against you. The amount of time that it takes to learn a few basics will pay off tenfold in hours saved later.

A brief example: I spoke to a woman who came into the garden center where I was working. She was there to buy another *Andromeda polifolia* (bog rosemary—not to be confused with *Pieris japonica*, which is often called andromeda, or the herb rosemary—this is a different plant all together) because the plant that she planted the previous year died. It turned out that the plant that she had planted the year before that had died too, and she was very disappointed but was determined to plant a third because she loved how the bog rosemary looked. When asked where she had planted it, she said it was on a sunny, sandy slope on the side of her house. I explained to her that the *Andromeda* loves damp, peaty soil; it's common name, *bog* rosemary, is a clue to the growing conditions needed to keep it happy. A sunny slope in sandy soil would not retain the moisture needed to have such a plant thrive.

This woman, like many of us, was choosing a plant because she liked its appearance, but she kept having to spend the time and money to buy another, and the time to replant it and baby it along once planted. Instead of getting pleasure every time she looked at it, she felt frustrated as she watched it decline throughout the season.

Some advance research would have saved this woman time, and spared her the aggravation. She would have learned how to make the bog rosemary happy, or which plants would provide a similar look in that location. A *Lavandula* (lavender) or *Calluna* (heather) would be close in appearance but would love the good drainage that her location provided. If nothing but an *Andromeda* would do, she could consider planting the shrub in a location that routinely got regular watering—under a birdbath for example—knowing that she would first need to dig a large quantity of peat into the soil where a bog rosemary was to be planted.

Had this customer taken the time to learn about the *Andromeda* plant before she purchased and planted it, not only would she have saved time and money, but she would have had a plant that would be three years along in its growth, instead of a small, newly planted one every year. Most importantly, she would have had three years of enjoyment and pleasure when she looked at this garden, not three years of worry and frustration.

CHOOSING THE RIGHT PLANT

It is possible to choose flowers, shrubs, and trees that aren't prone to problems and will therefore require less time to keep them looking their best. Some plants need a certain amount of moisture, or a particular type of soil in order to grow well. Others are not as fussy. Many plants grow best in full sunlight, others will do well in sun or part shade, and some plants prefer full shade. There are plants which are especially subject to insect and fungus attacks, or are otherwise more prone to diseases. And some plants are more difficult to grow because they have a delicate constitution, or are, perhaps, determined that no mere *human* should be telling them what to do.

Other plants seem so willing to grow in even adverse conditions that trifles such as drought, poor light, or even cement don't stop them for a minute. In my yard there is an *Agastache foeniculum* (Anise hyssop) that seeded itself next to the house. This would be unremarkable in that this *Agastache* is famous for self-seeding, except that in this part of my property there is asphalt paving right up to the cement foundation. The plant is growing out of the half-inch crack between cement and asphalt, and against all odds it thrives under an arbor on the north side of the house. I leave it there, not only because it is a pretty plant, but because I value its *willingness*.

While not all have the tenacity to grow through cement, it is possible to choose plants that are not prone to many diseases, are not *too* fussy about their soil, and are not considered five star meals by the local insect populations. Such plants should be called something saintly, but in actuality they are most commonly referred to as "low-maintenance" plants. Choosing such plants (discussed in detail in Chapter 4) can prevent headaches and heartaches for the gardener.

CHOOSING THE RIGHT LOCATION

Where a plant is placed is as important as the choice of the plant itself. Even a plant considered "low-maintenance" will shrivel and die if planted in the wrong location. At the very least, the wrong site will prevent a plant from doing its best. A sun-loving *Perovskia* (Russian sage), for example, may live if planted in the shade, but it would grow spindly and may flower sparsely.

Sometimes the plants that are already thriving in a location can give you a clue to the conditions there. If the area is filled with the sorts of plants that love good garden soil and full sun, then you know that another plant that thrives in such an atmosphere will also grow there. If the area has a rich carpet of moss that seems alive and well, you know that other plants that like damp, shady, or compact soil will also grow there.

You may not know ahead of time which plants like rich loam and sun, or which grow well in moist shade. There are any number of books or knowledgeable garden center employees that can supply that information. But the experts and resources *can't* tell you what the growing conditions are in the various locations on your property. This is information that only you can supply, and all that is required is that you take notice. Look at your property over a period of time; notice all the nooks and crannies or broad expanses throughout the day. Study the soil in a dry spell and after a heavy rain.

Sounds time-consuming? It does not have to be. It might only take a few minutes for you to stroll, coffee cup in hand, around your yard on a Sunday morning. But what *is* called for is some concentration. If you are wondering if you remembered to pay the telephone bill, or rehashing the error you found in your credit card statement, you will either finish the walk with little information, or it will take twice as long to collect the data you need. In most cases, learning about the growing conditions on our properties is simply a matter of giving it our full attention.

CULTURAL PRACTICES

The methods we use to plant our gardens, and how we take care of them on a routine basis, are called cultural practices. We might dig a large amount of composted manure into the soil before we plant a shrub, or we might dig a hole just big enough to slip the plant in the existing soil and call it planted. A tree might get planted too deeply, or the roots may stick too far above the natural soil line. It might be your habit to water your plants with a quick squirt of the hose in the morning, or by setting an automatic sprinkler to water every fourth day. These are all examples of various cultural practices, and they can all effect the health and happiness of our plants.

Cultural practices that keep our gardens growing well mean less time spent in the garden. (Chapters 2 and 3 detail such practices.) Healthy plants don't have diseases that need to be treated, and properly planted shrubs and trees will not have to be replaced the following season. Giving plants proper care means less work for the gardener.

TOP TEN GARDEN MISTAKES AND
MISUNDERSTANDINGS

1. *Mistake: Planting large growing shrubs or trees around foundations.*
   That shrub that seems so cute and compact in the nursery can grow to four times its size in, perhaps, ten years time. In their desire to have their homes look landscaped as soon as they put in the foundation plantings, most people forget that a shrub which is the right size now

will soon grow to be too large, and will become a nuisance shortly thereafter. Find out how large a shrub will grow before you consider planting it under your windows, and be willing to have plantings that may seem too small at first. (See the discussion of foundation plants in Chapter 4). Planting shrubs that won't outgrow their place also eliminates the necessity of shearing them into shapes in order to control their size.

2. *Mistake: Buying only plants in bloom*

While it is understandable that people want to see the color of the flower on the plant that they are buying, the blooming plant may not be the most healthy one available. When choosing any plants—shrubs, trees, annuals, or perennials—pick a plant that looks healthy and has a good shape, not necessarily the one that is in full flower.

3. *Mistake: Cutting the top off a tree*

Trees should never have their tops cut off, except if this part of the tree has been cracked off in a storm, or has died because of the presence of a borer. Lateral branches of the tree can be removed to make space around power lines or to open a view. Topping a tree robs it of its natural shape, and exposes it to insect attack and disease.

4. *Mistake: Planting invasive plants*

Beware of any plant which is described as a "vigorous grower." Just as "garden apartment" is a euphemism for a less-then-desirable basement dwelling, "vigorous grower" usually means invasive. Such plants will quadruple in size after their first year, and crowd out neighboring plants in the years to come. This may be desirable if you need a fast growing groundcover, but such plants should be avoided in mixed borders or small gardens. Be especially careful when considering invasive plants for small lots. One neighbor's lovely groundcover is another's call for Agent Orange.

5. *Misunderstanding: Hills are not hills*

Packages of cucumber and squash seeds will often instruct gardeners to "plant several seeds together in hills." Most people dutifully pile up a small mound of soil and stick their group of seeds on top of it, never really understanding why. In many cases, this hill of soil prevents good germination because the water runs down off of the dirt and away from the seeds and seedlings. A hill does not mean an actual mound of earth, but merely a group of seeds. In areas where drainage is good, but moisture is often lacking, it may be more prudent to plant such a group in a depression rather than on a mound. In most areas, the level surface of the garden will do.

6. *Misunderstanding: Tree roots don't grow as deep as you think.*
Somewhere, somehow, on some forgotten day in the distant past, all of us were shown a picture of a tree's root system that portrayed said system as being a mirror image of the canopy of branches on top. We were all left with the impression that the roots of trees are deep, deep in the soil, and we are all mistaken. Most tree root systems are in the top 18" of the soil. They do extend out as wide as the canopy, and often grow wider, but they grow near the surface of the earth, not way below it.

This makes perfect sense if we give it some thought. Because smaller plant roots take up much of the water in the first foot of soil, it would need to rain excessively and consistently to keep earth wet so far below the surface. Trees compete with the understory plants for available water. . . if they depended on having enough rain to feed those smaller plants, and then continue to soak down deeply, they would have died out long ago.

Nutrients too, many of which come from decaying organic matter on the earth's surface, are in the top few inches and the trees are in competition with other plants for these as well. Mixed in with the minerals, organic matter, and water are many organisms such as beneficial fungi and bacteria that help make the nutrients available to plants. All of these, including the roots, need oxygen, and where is that the most plentiful? Near the surface, of course.

Now why am I taking the time to rob you of this lovely mirror-of-the-branches image you have held dear? Because knowing that most tree feeder roots are in that upper 18" can affect how you garden. You will realize that anything that you do in (or on) that upper section of soil under a tree —whether planting flower beds and small shrubs, or driving heavy machinery to build a house—affects the roots of the tree. What affects the roots has consequences for the health of the whole tree.

Your financial health may be affected by this knowledge as well; keep a tight hold on your wallet if anyone tries to talk you into paying for a "deep-root feeding." For most trees (a very few do have tap roots), fertilizer that is pumped three feet or more under the soil's surface may as well be poured into the storm drain. Say no to the deep-root feeding and treat yourself to a nice meal out with the money.

7. *Misunderstanding: Raised vegetable beds don't have to be raised.*
Just the mention of raised beds puts us all in mind of tidy boxes made of wood or stone which neatly contain the vegetable plants. It is possible, and from an aesthetic point of view perhaps desirable, to build your vegetable garden in this manner. But raised beds don't have to be raised.

A raised bed is an area of soil that you do not walk on, or till with heavy machinery. The idea is to keep the soil as rich, loose and deep as possible in order for the roots to penetrate the earth easily. In places where the drainage is poor, raised beds provide a way to fill a vegetable patch with soil that drains well, and a bed raised to double or triple heights makes the garden accessible to a wheelchair-bound gardener.

Those who don't need the added height, drainage, or formal appearance that raised beds provide can achieve the benefits of rich, loose soil without the bother of building containing walls. It is helpful to mulch the paths between the designated bed areas with a material that is different from that used on the beds themselves. Stone, shredded bark, or hay laid down in the walkways announces clearly that people should "walk here." The bed itself should be narrow enough so it may be easily tended from the path, eliminating the need to walk on the soil. Such beds can be thickly planted so that the vegetables shade the soil sufficiently to hinder the growth of weeds.

8. *Mistake: Mulch piled high around shrubs and trees*
The benefits of mulch are many but like vitamin A for humans, some is good but too much can be fatal. Many people think that if three inches of mulch keeps weeds from growing, think of what six or ten inches can do! In their zeal to defeat the demon-weed they pile the mulch right up against the stems of the perennials or the trunks of the trees. By doing so, they create a cozy place for critters and diseases to call home and perhaps, a place for them to dine while doing so. Keeping the moist mulch so close to the plants allows any fungi that like such moist environments to flourish there. Like most people, plants like "some space," and leaving three to six inches of bare ground around their stems and trunks gives it to them.

9. *Mistake: Plants placed too closely together*
It's too bad that we can't time travel. Not only would it be immensely entertaining and educational (read the history book . . . then go visit and see for yourself!), but it would help when planting the garden as

well. We could place our plants in the garden, zip forward five or six years and take a look. Yikes! What were a few skimpy perennials planted a foot apart have become an overgrown jungle of a border; the tiny shrubs that looked like small sticks near the front of the house have grown so close together, you can't see where one stops and the other begins.

Plants that are placed too close together need much more attention, and they need it sooner than those that are planted further apart. Perennials will need dividing sooner, shade one another, or get their roots so grown together that they will be hard to separate. Spacing them out and filling in the bare spots with annuals for a couple of years will save work later.

10. *Misunderstanding: Every bug is a bad bug*
The sight of an insect crawling over the plants sends many people to the garden shed for a can of insecticide. In our rush to be helpful to our plants we forget that most insects are beneficial, or at least harmless in the garden. Insects pollinate our flowers and make it possible for us to eat the fruits and vegetables we grow in our gardens. Many bugs eat other bugs, keeping those that are garden pests under control. If we kill "the good guys" because of guilt by association, we upset the natural order that keeps our gardens in balance. By being too zealous in the protection of our plants, we often end up wasting time and money treating something that isn't really a problem at all.

The following chapters will go into detail about the many ways that gardeners can help themselves in the garden. The plants are already willing to do their utmost; given the slightest bit of help in the way of amended soil or water during a drought, most plants will knock themselves out at every opportunity.

Q & A: THESE THINGS ARE MAKING ME CRAZY!

Q.   *I purchased two matching shrubs and planted both in my back-*

yard only eight feet from each other. One has been growing gangbusters, and the other hasn't grown much at all. What could be the problem?

A.   This is a puzzle that makes many homeowners nuts. You plant two shrubs, apparently identical, and one grows well while the other just sulks. This can be particularly annoying when they are planted on either side of a front door, or in another location where symmetry counts. The reasons for the disparity can be many and varied, but following are a few possibilities.

Although it may, on first glance, seem that both plants are planted where the growing conditions are the same, in actuality they may be in two separate microclimates. All properties have areas that are warmer or colder, wetter or drier, sheltered or more exposed than the rest of the area. Sometimes it is the man-made features that create these micro climates, and sometimes they are created by natural landforms or waterways in the area.

Perhaps the roof drains on one side of the front porch and not the other, causing one plant to be watered more frequently. The placement of the house may shelter one particular spot from the prevailing winter winds, or expose another place to extra wind that is funneled between two buildings.

The house where I live, for example, has a small U-shaped cutout that faces west. The small garden there is bordered by the house on two sides, and a cement and stone path across the front; it is warmed by the strong afternoon sun, sheltered by the house, and the soil is kept warmer at night from the radiant heat stored in the dark walkway stones. Every spring the plants in this garden are always three times bigger than those in the rest of the garden.

Underground features, which we are often unaware of, can also affect how a plant grows. Large rocks can influence the temperature or drainage in an area, or provide barriers to good root growth. Deposits of clay may be preventing good drainage, or small underground springs might be keeping the soil moist. Conversely, an area where the soil seems moist on the surface may have a large deposit of sand or small rocks a foot below the surface which causes any water to drain quickly away. Would that we all had Superman's X-ray vision, and could see what is going on where our plants' roots grow!

X-ray vision would also help us to check out the roots themselves, and this might give us a clue as to why a particular plant is not growing well. If a plant's root system has been damaged, the plant will not put on much growth. Perhaps the roots were cut when the plant was taken from the grower's field, or they might have been damaged in the planting somehow. Maybe an animal is eating the roots below the surface, or perhaps the root system has dried up or rotted.

When two shrubs look identical when they are planted, but one of them fails to grow, there is something different about them that is influencing their growth. It may be that one is simply a healthier plant. We all know some people who are never sick and others who catch every virus that comes their way. Plants have different constitutions as well. But before I would assume that one plant is just "sickly," I would carefully check to see if there are cultural conditions that are affecting them differently.

Q.   *I bought a hanging basket with a lovely impatiens in it. A few weeks later it started to look wilted so I started giving it more water. It got worse, not better, so I took it back to the place where I bought it and they said it had rotted. A plant that is wilted is thirsty, right? How could this have rotted, and if this is the case, how can I know in the future if the plant wants water?*

A.   Was the plant too wet or was it thirsty? Who is right, you or the person who sold you the plant? Well, you are both right. The plant was thirsty, but the reason it was wilted was because the roots had rotted and were no longer there to send water up to the stems and leaves of the plant. When an entire plant wilts, it means that it is not getting the water it needs. Any number of things can cause this condition, including drought, rotted roots, a disease that collapses the plant's vascular system, and insects or animals eating the roots.

If the hanging basket was healthy when you bought it, the cause of the wilting may be too much water. Perhaps the first time it was wilted the soil really was dry, but later, in your zeal to keep it well watered, you may have started *overwatering* which resulted in root rot. The test to see if a plant needs water is very simple—stick your finger in the dirt. If the soil feels dry, water the plant. If the soil feels moist you should wait until it has dried out before watering again.

Because they are small and filled with lightweight soil, hanging baskets require frequent checking. Remember that a good portion of the pot is filled with roots, not potting soil. The lightweight potting mix holds only so much water, so hanging pots tend to dry out quickly. A quick way to tell if you need to feel the soil for moisture is to hold the bottom of the pot firmly with your fingers and lift slightly, feeling the pot's weight as you do so. A dry plant will be very light. If the pot is heavy, you don't need to bother feeling the soil—you will know from how heavy it feels that it still has plenty of water.

Q. *I tore out some old, overgrown foundation plants, and I want to replace them with some shrubs and a few perennials. Any new shrubs that I look at seem so small that I am afraid that they'll look ridiculous. Are there any shrubs, perhaps ones that bloom, that will grow quickly but stay short enough so that they won't grow over the windows?*

A. If anyone ever develops a plant that grows quickly to a certain height, then stops growing and stays attractive, that person should take out a patent on it immediately and it will be better than winning the lottery. And as long as we're dreaming, let's make said shrub be evergreen *and* bloom all summer! Now I'm not making fun of your desire to have your foundations be perfect, but I am gently reminding you that a plant must be a plant. It would be unlikely for a plant that grows quickly to suddenly stop growing, although some do slow down after an initial growth spurt when young. A few shrubs bloom all summer, and some of these are even evergreen, but they grow in warm zones where it does not freeze in the winter.

I applaud your desire to be thoughtful about your foundation plantings. You are wise to choose plants that won't block the windows in a few years, and there are several of those. Realize though, that every plant has its fine points and its drawbacks. You wouldn't expect (I hope) to have a child who never got a virus, had a temper tantrum, or never needed help with homework. By the same token, plants have their problems and personalities too. Plants have preferences about growing conditions, they increase in size, and they sometimes die.

Replace your foundation plants with those well-suited to your soil, your climate, and the amount of light that side of the house gets. If you are restricted further by wanting an evergreen, or a shrub that blooms, choose one that won't outgrow the site knowing that you may have to compromise on its present size. Throughout life we usually have to compromise on *something*, and so it is in our gardens.

2

THE ESSENTIALS: GROUNDWORK

Faced with the myriad of plants, equipment, gardening terms, and tasks to complete, most gardeners can feel quickly overwhelmed. How can this garden be kept healthy? How can I do my best to see that my plants will do *their* best? Whether you have endless hours to work in your garden, or must squeeze your gardening into a very limited time period, there are certain basics that you need to know.

How the soil is prepared, and the plants are watered, mulched, and fertilized, can affect the long-term vitality of the garden. Knowing the essentials of these basic practices can, in the long run, save you time. A properly planted, well-maintained garden is a healthy garden, and healthy gardens need less attention.

START WITH THE SOIL

When talking about garden essentials we start from the ground up. Plants need a place to sink their roots. The root system delivers water and nutrients to the plant, and the roots hold the plant in place while it grows. So in essence, it all starts with the soil that the plants grow in. Paying attention to the soil both before you plant and on a yearly basis, yields long-term benefits whether you are planting shrubs, flowers, or vegetables.

Before deciding if your soil needs assistance, it is necessary to know what you already have; knowing what the soil is like to begin with will help you to determine what is needed to help it along. Begin by digging a small shovelful of dirt from several areas of your yard. Does it look or feel sandy? Or when you rub it between your fingers, does it feel like smooth, slippery clay? Perhaps you are lucky enough to have a dark rich loam which is a balanced mix of sand, silt, and clay. If there is organic matter mixed into the loam, it is even darker and softer . . . worth more to a gardener than gold.

SOIL TEXTURE

If your soil feels gritty, it contains a large amount of sand. Sand grains are the largest and roughest soil particles. If the soil is mostly sand, it may actually be sandy colored. If it contains some silt (the next smaller size of soil particle) and some organic matter, it may be dark in color but still gritty to the touch.

Clay soils are heavy. They feel smooth to the touch because the particles are very fine and flat. Clay particles stack up, one on top of another, leaving little air space between these flat particles. For this reason, water does not drain through clay quickly, and it is difficult soil to dig into.

Loam is a soil that is in between clay and sand in texture. A sandy loam will feel a bit gritty, but it will have smaller particles of minerals in it as well.

In addition to mineral particles, soil contains organic matter. This comes from dead plants and animals, and it is an absolutely necessary component for healthy soils. Organic matter decomposes first to ammonia, then to nitrites, and finally to *nitrates,* which are a nutrient for plants.

Beneficial organisms such as bacteria, fungi and molds thrive in this decaying matter and help it break down. Perhaps I should stress the term *beneficial*; when most people hear bacteria they think *E. coli* and when they hear fungus they think of Athlete's foot. But rest assured that there are many, many organisms at work that do no harm to humans; they do, however, help keep our gardens healthy. Organic matter and the various soil organisms it supports are a necessities for a good growing medium.

SOIL STRUCTURE

How the assortment of mineral particles and organic matter stick together is called structure. Now I can almost hear you wondering why anyone in their right mind would care how their soil sticks together. "Let it arrange itself however it wants!" I hear you cry. I assure you that this *is* important enough for me to spend the time writing about it and for you to spend a minute reading about it.

The structure helps determine how air and water travel through the soil. Plant roots need both air and water to grow well. Although there are plants that can live underwater or with their roots constantly submerged, the vast majority of plants that grow in the average yard and garden will not thrive in a bog; they need to drink, but they also need to breathe.

Sandy soils need organic matter to improve their structure because they have too much air between all those large particles, and water and nutrients rush right through. Organic matter acts like little sponges to hold onto the nutrients and the moisture. It provides the material necessary to stick everything together so the soil contains a mix of minerals, decaying matter, air and water.

Clay soils also need organic amendments to improve the soil structure. Clay holds water *too* well, and organic material provides air spaces that allow it to drain more quickly. Organic matter lightens clay soils, facilitating the movement of water and nutrients.

Even that ideal loam that I envy (I garden in a sandbox) needs to be continually amended with organic materials because organic matter continues to break down. Maintaining the health of your soil is like maintaining your own health; it is never possible to say "There! I worked out for the past year and I will now be physically fit for the rest of my life!" Would that it were so. Like it or not, some things are not permanent and can't be stored. Organic matter must be added to the soil regularly.

When you think about plants in the wild, you will see the beauty of this system. Plants die, but their death feeds the soil so that future generations of plants may thrive. Since most of us don't leave the dead plants in our gardens to feed our soils, we must add some composted organic matter back to the earth our plants grow in. And because we insist on growing things that may not be completely suited to the sand or clay that we garden in, we must improve the structure of the soils to make those plants happy.

Soil structure is also affected by activity on the surface of the garden. Anyone who is landscaping the yard around a new house needs to be aware that the heavy machinery used in construction packs the soil down tight. Garden beds will need to be tilled, and top soil and humus will most likely need to be added after what is there is loosened by tilling. Residents of older houses may need to do the same if their gardens have been trampled in the course of building a new addition or septic system.

Working the soil when it is very wet or dry will also damage soil structure. Digging in very wet soils will cause the ground to become more compact, and will reduce dry earth to dust. Resist the temptation to work in soil after a prolonged period of rain or drought.

Good soil structure is achieved by the addition of organic matter, the activities of earthworms, and a minimum of disturbance by the gardener. Disturbance includes digging and walking on the surface of the soil. Since low maintenance gardening means less time spent in the garden, it encourages good soil structure.

pH

What is meant by a soil's pH, and why on earth does it matter to the gardener? The pH stands for the concentration of hydrogen ions, which form one part of the soil's chemical composition. The pH scale measures a soil's acidity. It ranges from 0, which is the most acidic, to 14 which is the most alkaline. Soils that measure near the midpoint of 7 are said to be neutral. Gardeners need to know if their soil is acidic or alkaline because the soil's pH level can make a great difference in how, or if, a plant will grow.

The pH of a soil varies greatly from place to place. Local geology, the amount of rainfall and the acidity of that rain, and the plants that add decaying organic matter to the soil—all influence the pH of a region. To find out what type of soil you have in your area, call the nearest cooperative extension. A simple, inexpensive soil test will tell the pH of any specific area of your garden or yard. Home soil-testing kits are available, or the Extension office will be able to tell you how to have a sample tested.

A plant's intake of nutrients is greatly influenced by the pH. Potassium, phosphorus, calcium, and magnesium (as well as other minor nutrients) are made most available to plants when the pH is in the neutral range, between 6.0 and 7.5. If the soil is too acidic, those nutrients become less available. Some trace minerals and toxic elements (such as aluminum) become *more* available if the soil is too acidic. If the pH is too high, nitrogen becomes less available to plants; the beneficial bacteria that make nitrogen from organic matter obtainable for plants become less active in highly alkaline soils.

This does *not* mean that we should all be out there adding lime to acidic soils and sulfur to alkaline ones in pursuit of a constant neutral reading. Some plants have adapted to grow best in acidic conditions, and others thrive in neutral or alkaline ones. Rather than change the pH of the local soil willy-nilly, it makes most sense to be sure all large, permanent plantings are suited to the native soil's pH. This would include shrubs, trees, and wild flower gardens. The pH can be adjusted in smaller areas such as annual and perennial flower beds, or vegetable gardens, if needed.

The amount of lime needed to raise the pH of acidic soils will depend on the climate where you live and the type of soil in your region. Clay soils need more lime than sandy soils. Once your soil has been tested, ask your extension service to recommend the type of lime you should use and its recommended rate of application. Most places that test soils, whether an extension service or a private lab, will give a recommendation along with the test results.

Gardeners who need to lower their soil's pH will use either sulfur, aluminum sulfate, or ferrous sulfate. Sulfur is the most effective at lowering soil pH, and ferrous sulfate also adds iron to the soil. Aluminum sulfate should be used only for acid-loving plants, and then used with caution because it adds aluminum to the soil, which is toxic to plants that do not require acidic conditions. Sulfur is added at the rate of one pound per 100 square feet of soil. A pH test should be done the following year before any more sulfur is added.

SOIL TYPES

Every type of soil has its advantages and disadvantages, although those who garden in deep, organically rich loam will have to think long and hard to come up with any disadvantages, while the rest of us are dying with envy while they do so. Most soils do need improvements or present certain challenges. Once you have felt your soil and have more information *at your fingertips*, so to speak, you can decide what amendments your garden needs.

Sand has an insatiable appetite for compost, so if your soil is sandy, be prepared to amend, amend, amend. Sandy soils also need watering and fertilizing more often, since the moisture and nutrients tend to run through the soil so quickly.

Gardeners who have clay soil are spared the frequent watering and fertilizing, but they must also add organic matter, and it is not always a *simple* matter to do so. Clay is hard to dig into, so working those organic soil amendments in to the ground can be difficult work. Once a certain amount is turned into the clay, however, the earthworms can be counted on for assistance.

Loam also needs organic matter added, although gardeners who plant in loam don't have to be quite as vigilant about it. *All gardeners should try to put at least two inches of compost or composted manure on their garden beds every year.* In addition to two inches of top dressing, gardeners in clay or sand should add organic matter to the planting area every time an annual or perennial plant is put into their garden.

ORGANIC SOIL AMENDMENTS

The organic matter used to amend your soil can be in the form of homemade compost, composted manure, purchased compost, or other decaying plant matter such as leaf mold or seaweed. It is best to compost any manure or plant matter before you add it to your garden although fresh vegetable materials can be placed into the soil if the process of digging them in won't harm the roots of surrounding plants.

Fresh manure will burn or outright kill plants if you add it to a garden that is growing. Plant materials such as leaves or seaweed won't burn plants, but they will use nitrogen from the soil as they decompose, especially if they are dug into or under the soil. Since this can deprive growing plants of necessary nitrogen, if possible, let all plant materials break down in a compost bin before adding them to the garden beds.

SOURCES OF SOIL AMENDMENTS

Most gardeners have some form of compost bin, if for no other reason than their local landfills will no longer accept leaves and other yard waste. Even if you don't have the time or the interest to do what is necessary to make compost and spread it on your garden, you may want to build a bin to throw yard wastes into. A compost pile gives you a place to put kitchen scraps, grass clippings and plant trimmings where they will slowly decompose over time. Who knows? In a couple of years you may suddenly need some soil amendments when you are planting a shrub, and a poke at the bottom of that long ignored pile will reveal *black gold*, sitting right there!

Even gardeners who compost more actively find that their own home piles don't supply enough organic soil amendments. Some augment their piles with sawdust from nearby sawmills, coffee grounds from local restaurants, manure from a stable, or seaweed hauled off the beach. Collecting the material, hauling it home, and shoveling it into the compost bin takes time, however. Anyone who is squeezing gardening work into a weekend or a couple of evenings a week won't have the time to haul fresh compost materials around. Bringing in the finished product is usually necessary.

All garden centers sell bagged composted or dehydrated cow manure and peat moss. Some also sell compost and manure by the yard, delivered. Compost or manure by the load is less expensive, but requires more time to shovel it from the pile where it is dumped, into the wheelbarrow, and then onto the flower bed or around the shrubs and trees. Bagged manure can be placed in the car, transferred to the wheelbarrow, and rolled to the place where it is to be spread.

Many towns are now composting leaves and wood chips from municipal landscapes and homes in the area. This compost is often made available to town residents, either free or for a small charge. (You load it and haul it.) As awareness grows of the importance of adding compost to our gardens, commercial enterprises are following, and in many areas you can find composted plant material available by the dump truck load. Many of the businesses that sell top soil and mulch also sell compost.

WHEN TO SPREAD COMPOST

Organic matter can be added to the soil before any plants are placed in the ground; empty beds are easily amended. Once the perennials or shrubs and trees are planted, however, it would be unwise to dig organic soil amendments into the ground right next to them because you would disturb their roots. Once the garden is planted, compost can be placed on top of the soil. Our assistants in gardening, the earthworms, help spread it into the soil so that it affects the soil structure.

Organic matter can be spread on the soil at any time, but it is probably most convenient to do so in the late fall or early spring. At these times of year the previous season's plants have been cut down, so it is easy to see the soil around the shrubs or the clumps of perennials, and annual beds are bare. I think that the late fall is the best time to amend the soil; the weather is cool enough to make the work pleasant, and there aren't a zillion other garden tasks calling to you while you work. In the spring we often feel overwhelmed by the planting, fertilizing, pruning, and other chores that need to be done.

MULCH

Mulch is almost a necessity for low maintenance gardening. It keeps weed growth to a minimum and holds moisture in the soil at the same time. Mulching helps new plantings to look attractive and marks where a bed ends and a walkway begins. If the mulch is an organic material, it also amends the soil as it breaks down. I know that there are gardeners who believe that only vegetable gardens should be mulched, but I am sure that they are not trying to limit the time that they spend on garden work. For anyone who wants a garden but does not have endless time to tend it, mulch is essential.

Mother Nature, after all, uses mulch all the time. There is very little bare soil in the natural world, unless you are in an area such as a desert, where it is so inhospitable that even the hardiest of weeds won't grow. In most landscapes, leaves fall and plants die, thus covering the soil with organic matter. These not only become soil amendments, as we just discussed, but they also cover other plant's seeds and sprouts. Ah, those clever plants! They not only fertilize themselves with their castoffs, but they squash the competition at the same time!

SUPPRESSING THE WEEDS

Many seeds need light to germinate. The main reason that mulch suppresses weeds is that it covers weed seeds with a layer that the sunlight does not penetrate. It also covers any seeds that do manage to germinate, so that the sprouts don't get enough sun either; without light, the small sprouts won't live.

Weed seeds remain viable in the soil for many, many years. A seed may be laying there, four inches under the surface of the soil—a tiny time-bomb, waiting for its chance to sprout and grow among your perennials. You may give this seed the chance it has been waiting for when you dig a hole to place a new plant in your garden; you might even pull it to the surface as you yank out a weed that is already there! Weeding is never ending, and even a layer of mulch does not prevent all weeds from making an appearance where you do not want them to grow. (A weed, after all, is any plant that appears where you do not want it to grow.) A three-inch layer of mulch will prevent most of the seeds from sprouting, however, and in doing so will save countless hours of weeding in your flower gardens, shrub borders and vegetable plots.

CONSERVING MOISTURE

Mulch not only keeps the weeds out, it keeps the moisture in. All of us are aware that our water supplies are not unlimited; we want our gardens to have the moisture that they need, but we don't want to use more water than absolutely necessary. Those who have seen their water bills skyrocket in the past few years have a financial reason to be prudent with their watering in addition to an environmental one. A layer of mulch on the garden prevents the rapid evaporation of water from the soil.

Watering the garden is not only expensive, it is time-consuming as well. If you are using a standard hose and sprinkler system, lugging the hoses and setting the whole thing up, then moving it to the next location can take hours (it's a given that the first time you put the sprinkler in place it will water the driveway, your neighbor's yard, or your open car door). I garden on a very small piece of property, and when I used sprinklers it took an entire day to get all of the beds watered. Mulch can reduce the frequency of watering, no matter which method you use to deliver the liquid to your garden.

OTHER BENEFITS OF MULCHING

A garden that is covered with mulch has soil temperatures that are more even. This, along with a longer lasting period of dampness, means less stress to the plants, rapid change being just as disconcerting to plants, perhaps, as it is to people. In the vegetable garden a layer of mulch can slow the spread of disease; fungi that have overwintered in the soil can infect your current crops when rainwater splashes from the ground to the lower leaves of your plants. Mulch slows or prevents this earth-to-plant transmission of disease.

DISADVANTAGES OF MULCH?

Are there any reasons *not* to put mulch on your garden? I suppose if your garden is so damp that you don't want evaporation to be slowed, you might not want to cover the surface of your soil. But if an area is *that* wet, it would be better to place those plants that *like* it moist and boggy, mulch them to keep the weeds away, and enjoy the flowers or shrubs that love having their feet in damp soil. Low maintenance gardening is taking advantage of a given situation, in this case a damp area, rather than trying to change it.

Many new gardeners worry that mulch will invite molds, fungi, or other pests or diseases. While it is true that bugs and fungi live in decaying plant material, and that you are likely to have more of these if an organic material is used on your garden, viewing these as undesirable is a misunderstanding. Insects that feed on decaying organic matter help break these materials down, amending your garden soil as they do so. And as has been mentioned, many fungi are garden good-guys, helping in many ways to keep our gardens healthy. Providing such decaying-plant eaters such as earwigs with mulch to munch helps to keep them from eating seedlings in desperation.

There is often concern about the breakdown of the mulch using nitrogen from the soil. Any organic matter requires nitrogen to decompose, and mulch is no different from compost in this regard. If a fairly thick layer of mulch is put on top of a garden already low in nitrogen, some additional nitrogen may be required to meet the needs of both the de-composing mulch and the plants. Those who garden in sandy soils may need to supplement the nitrogen under a mulch since sand does not hold onto nitrogen well.

Nitrogen depletion is more of an issue if un-composted materials are dug into the soil rather then spread on top, but if a soil test shows low nitrogen levels a balanced fertilizer such as a 10-10-10, or a 5-10-5 or the equivalent can be used. It is not necessary to use a really high nitro-gen fertilizer such as a common lawn food. Those who prefer to use all-organic fertilizers can either apply an equivalent balanced, granulated brand, or use one of the pure sources of nitrogen such as bloodmeal.

TYPES OF MULCH

The type of mulch you choose depends on the type of garden you are spreading it on, the availability of the material, and how you wish the finished beds to look. Vegetable gardens which are traditionally planted in patches or rows, can be mulched with any organic material, or with rolls of plastic or paper.

Plastic and paper mulches

Many people favor black plastic because it is inexpensive and fairly easy to apply. Because the plastic is dark, it prevents the light from reaching the weed seeds. Plastic will also keep the ground warm by acting as a solar collector; in fact, those living in areas with very hot summers may find that black plastic keeps their soils *too* warm.

There are porous plastic mulches available which allow water to seep through to the plants. If a solid plastic is used, soaker hoses should be laid underneath to allow sufficient moisture to reach the roots of the plants. Most people who use plastic place it on the garden early in the season. The sheets are rolled out (*after* the soaker hose is in place) and either pinned to the ground or weighted with rocks, logs, or piles of dirt to prevent a strong wind from carrying the plastic into the next county. It is important to secure the edges of a plastic mulch well.

Once the sheets of plastic are in place, holes are then cut in the mulch where necessary to place the plants into the ground. It is impor-tant to get the plastic on the garden early in the season, before the weed seeds sprout. Once the weeds get growing—and this happens frighten-ingly fast—the plants may puncture the plastic as it's put in place. Any large holes in plastic mulch allow the sun to get to the weeds, creating an ideal place for them to grow.

The disadvantage of plastic mulch is that it must be taken up, usually every season, and it can be difficult to keep it in reusable condition. As gardeners, we know the importance of keeping our solid trash to a minimum, so it seems a shame to choose a mulch that will end up in the landfill instead of enriching the garden. Unlike organic mulch, plastic adds nothing to the soil.

Rolls of paper can be used in much the same way as plastic, and have the advantage of decomposing and amending the soil after life as a mulch is over. There are rolls of recycled paper made specifically for mulching. Newspaper can also be used and it is more cost effective by far. Both the newspaper and "store bought" mulch need to be covered so they do not blow away. The rolls of recycled paper can be held in place with other mulch materials such as wood chips or hay, or by placing large rocks or logs along the paper's edges. Newspaper needs to be completely covered with another mulch material such as shredded bark or grass clippings.

Plastic is less successful when used to cover the ground around permanent plantings such as perennials and shrubs. It must be cut to fit irregular beds and covered with something that looks good and will weight it down. Invariably the top layer of mulch is blown or washed aside in places and the plastic peeks through, getting torn or ragged in the long run. Pulling it up gets messy, especially if gravel was used to cover it. Landscape cloth and plastic covered with bark or gravel are best used in large unplanted areas such as a path or parking area.

Covered paper is a fine mulch for new beds, whether they are flower gardens or areas to be planted with shrubs and trees. Plants can be placed in the garden by moving the top layer of mulch aside and cutting through the paper.

If your soil is predominantly clay, or if the garden you are planting is damp, a thin layer of paper is better. Thick layers of paper covered with wood or other organic material will keep the soil damp. If your area is usually short of rain this might be a good thing, but if a lack of moisture isn't a problem, stick with only six layers of newspaper covered with two inches of organic materials.

Organic mulch materials

Many people automatically think of shredded wood when they decide to mulch their gardens. It is widely available by the bag or by the yard, delivered. But this is only one of a number of fine, organic mulch materials available to gardeners. Gardeners should investigate which materials are abundant in their local areas since the more abundant the material, the less expensive it will be. I would have to pay quite a bit for ground corn cobs, provided that I could even *find* a source of it on Cape Cod. If I were still living in the Midwest, however, corn cobs might be the most inexpensive mulch available.

Ask around to find locally available mulching materials that are inexpensive or free for the hauling. Be sure to check with your cooperative extension office to see if such materials have any drawbacks that you should know about. On Cape Cod, for example, cuttings from cranberry bogs might be available, and at least one of my gardening books lists this as an excellent mulch. Cranberry bogs may be filled with dodder, however, (a horrible, parasitic weed) so all plant material from cranberry bogs is best avoided. In addition to the possibility of containing weed seed, commercial crops might have been sprayed with chemicals, which home gardeners wouldn't want on their soils. Material from crops that have been recently treated with herbicides can have an adverse effect on the growth of plants.

Many towns now chip all municipal tree clippings, and the shredded leaf and wood mixture is available to town residents. Garden centers and others that sell landscape supplies and top soil offer a range of mulches as well.

Peat moss is best used as a soil amendment, not a mulch. If you have ever tried to wet a large amount of peat you will know why large quantities of pure peat seem to repel water. If used as a mulch, peat can form an impenetrable barrier on the surface of the soil, keeping the ground underneath dry. The peat will look moist on the top, leading you to believe that the water has soaked through. When the mulch is disturbed, however, it will reveal that the bottom of the layer of peat, and the soil under it, are still dry.

TOP TEN ORGANIC MULCHES

1. *Wood chips/Shredded bark.*
   Easily obtainable, reasonably attractive, and effective in both water retention and weed suppression. Large chips though less effective, are attractive and are best put over paper, landscape cloth or smaller wood chips.

2. *Hay/Straw/Salt marsh Hay.*

Usually used on vegetable gardens around plants and on paths. Salt marsh hay makes a good winter mulch because its light weight makes a covering that contains a great deal of air space. Make sure that the hay does not have seed heads in it, or you may be bringing more weeds (or oat seedlings) into your garden than you are keeping out.

3. *Grass clippings.*

When grass clippings are used as mulch they need to be spread in a thin layer so that the mulch does not smell as the grass decomposes. Keeping each application to one inch, and letting that layer dry well before more is added will prevent unpleasant odors. Clippings may contain weed seeds. Do not mulch with clippings from lawns that have been recently sprayed with weed killers; studies show that plants mulched with such clippings have depressed, stunted growth.

4. *Cocoa, buckwheat, or cottonseed hulls.*

All are attractive and small in size but they may blow away in gusty winds. Available by the bag in most areas, hulls can be expensive and might be best used in small spaces. Cocoa hulls smell like chocolate when spread, making the application of this mulch a very pleasant activity! Hulls make a good mulch for window boxes and other container plantings.

5. *Seaweed.*

Hauling may be a problem, and seaweed often comes with shells and sand attached. Seaweed does not have to be rinsed before you use it; the amount of salt that it contains is not a problem; it is effective but less than neat in appearance. Seaweed adds trace elements, such as magnesium and calcium, to the garden and is said to repel slugs. Check to be sure the removal of seaweed is legal where you live.

6. *Pine needles.*

Very attractive mulch, often available by the yard delivered, as well as free for the raking in some yards. A thick layer (five to six inches) may be needed to smother weed seeds. Pine needles do not encourage much earthworm activity but they make excellent mulch for strawberries, which need to be kept off the ground. The slight acidity won't harm plants.

7. *Leaves.*

Many of us have them in abundance in the fall, and they make good mulch if composted (leaf mold) or shredded. If they are used "right off the rake," they may first blow away, then pack into a thick cake which keeps water from reaching the plant roots. Composted leaves contribute valuable nutrients to the soil and earthworms love them.

8. *Compost.*

Usually used as a soil amendment, compost can also be used as a mulch. Home compost usually contains seeds from weeds, annual flowers etc. Compost made from leaves and chipped wood makes a better mulch.

9. *Paper.*

Effective, widely available, but less than attractive, paper is best used under another mulch. If you have to spread another material anyway, why use the paper at all? Newspaper is very effective in smothering existing lawn or weeds, and for improving moisture retention in perpetually dry soils.

10. *Manure.*

Fresh manure must be aged to remove harmful salts. Not the most attractive mulch in existence, it is better used as a soil amendment or added to leaves etc. in the compost bin before used as mulch. *Caution:* Fresh manure may contain many weed seeds. Bagged manure, composted or dehydrated, usually does not have this problem, but is much more expensive.

ESSENTIALS OF MULCH

Mulch is similar to fertilizers in that some is good, but too much can cause problems. A mulch layer more than six inches thick can keep the soil too moist, causing roots to rot. Remember that the roots of plants need air, and a thick application of mulch may trap too much water, which leaves no room for that air. Two to four inches of mulch is enough to keep the weeds at bay, conserve moisture, but let the soil breathe.

It can also be harmful to pile mulch up against the stems of plants and trunks of trees. The many fungi and insects that live in the mulch are fine when they are chewing up the mulch and helping it decompose, but you don't want all that activity on the base of your plant. Putting the mulch next to stems keeps them too moist, encouraging disease and rot.

Leave two or three inches of bare soil around each perennial and about six inches clear around shrubs and trees.

Winter mulch and summer mulch

You would think that it is enough of a bother that our wardrobe changes every season, must the mulch change as well? Most gardeners who live in a temperate climate have heard of a winter mulch, and wonder if, in addition to the weed-smothering mulch that is already on the garden, they need to put a special mulch over their plants to keep them cozy over the colder months. Although an explanation of winter mulches follows, I will say up front that it is one of the last things that a gardener with limited time needs to do. Do you *really* have several extra hours in between Thanksgiving and New Year's to get some special mulch and cover your beds with it?

A winter mulch is lightweight material such as pine boughs or salt marsh hay, which will form a layer of trapped air around and over the plants. The best winter mulch is a deep layer of snow because snow contains a lot of air spaces. If you live in an area where snow falls every winter and covers the ground until spring, you can skip the rest of this section and go make a cup of tea while the rest of us plod on. (Those readers who live in a warm climate have, of course, left at the first *mention* of winter.) A layer of trapped air accomplishes two things: it keeps the ground frozen at a constant temperature and keeps the area above ground a bit warmer when the temperatures dip to abnormal lows.

Once the ground is frozen, plants are best off if the earth around them does not thaw and freeze, thaw and freeze. Expansion and contraction of the soil can break off a plant's roots. Because one of the purposes of a winter mulch is to prevent this heaving of the ground, the mulch is applied *after* the ground is frozen. Delaying the application of mulch until early winter is also wise for another reason; if applied too early, a winter mulch is an attractive home for small animals such as mice and voles. They will bed down in your pine boughs and dine on your perennials while the snows fall on top of their snug mulch dwellings. If you wait until the ground freezes it is likely that the critters will have found winter homes elsewhere . . . hopefully, *not* in your garage.

The crown of a perennial plant is the part that is just at or below the soil line. A layer of air pockets over the crown acts a bit like a comforter, keeping the plant just a bit warmer when the temperatures suddenly dip. Such covering does not make it possible to grow tropical plants in areas where the winters are frigid, but a mulch layer *can* make a difference to a slightly more sensitive plant when there is an occasional night temperature that is lower than normal.

Evidence that a winter mulch keeps a plant warmer

If you live in an area where the winters can get quite cold, you might have observed something I used to see in the Berkshires. If we had gone through a winter with a deep snow cover, but the temperatures had gone down to about ten below zero, the following spring all the *Forsythia* would bloom in a very odd manner. There would be a layer of bright yellow blossoms right next to the ground, roughly corresponding with the height of the snow, while the upper branches of the bushes would be bare of blooms. *Forsythia* forms its flower buds during the previous growing season, and those buds that were insulated by the snow were protected from the sub-zero temperatures. The buds that were out in the open air got too cold and died.

Because winter mulches cover the tops of plants, they must be removed in the early spring when you *want* the soil to thaw. (If your winter mulch is snow, the sun handles this task quite nicely.) The straw, pine boughs or salt marsh hay can be used as a regular mulch elsewhere, or put into the compost bin. Does this sound like a great deal of work? Well, for those who have a great deal of time, it's not too bad. Garden work is a pleasant activity, and moving mulch around in the early winter and early spring gets you out in the garden when you might otherwise be indoors eating potato chips.

Just say no!

If your gardening time is limited, however, it is best to forego the winter mulching altogether. The layer of mulch that suppresses the weeds and keeps your soil moist in the summer will also help keep the soil frozen in the winter. If you have chosen plants that are perfectly hardy in your area, they won't need to have their crowns protected. Part of choosing the right plant for your location is finding plants that don't need to be coddled in your climate.

FERTILIZERS

At least once a week someone comes to me with concerns about a plant that is not looking well. A common first response to this problem is to reach for a fertilizer package, perhaps because the name of a commonly sold fertilizer seems to promise miraculous happenings. It is important to remember that even the best fertilizers are not medicines, and a plant may have a poor appearance for reasons other then a lack of nutrients.

Aside from trying to revive sickly plants, there are situations when gardeners might need to take the time to fertilize their gardens. The array of products to add to the soil is both confusing and overwhelming, however, and many people find themselves looking at a garage full of fertilizers, all purchased for different uses in their yards and gardens. Many customers come up to me in the garden center and ask "Can I use the lawn fertilizer on my shrubs?" "Can African Violet Food be used on any other plants, or just on the violets?" or "Is there any difference between all of these products on the shelves?" Clearly some general discussion about fertilizers is in order.

THE THREE NUMBERS ON THE PACKAGE

Every fertilizer package should have three numbers on it. These numbers are the first thing that you should look for, since they will tell you which parts of the garden will benefit from the use of that particular fertilizer. Some of the more popular brands of fertilizer place these three numbers in tiny type, almost hiding them on the label, but they should be there if you search for them. I am convinced that they do this because they don't want you to compare brands, either for contents or price. I urge you to look at all labels closely, and do compare fertilizers. You may find an equivalent product which is much less expensive, or one that offers something extra (micro-nutrients, for example) for the same price.

The three numbers on the fertilizer label stand for the percentages of nitrogen, phosphorus, and potassium that are contained in the fertilizer. These elements are sometimes represented by their chemical symbols—N, P, and K. They are always given in the same order, so when you look at a package of fertilizer you know that the first number given is the percentage of nitrogen, the second the percentage of phosphorus and the third the percentage of potassium. Potassium is also called potash, a term that came from the days when this fertilizer was made by steeping wood ashes in an iron pot.

NITROGEN

Nitrogen is necessary for vegetative growth—the leaves and buds—of all plants. Unlike other nutrients in the soil, nitrogen does not come from the mineral particles in the earth. Nitrogen must come from the air (made available to plants by specialized bacteria or in rain and snowfall), from organic matter which breaks down in the soil, or from fertilizers.

All plants need nitrogen, but those grown only for their leaves, such as grass, and those that must produce great leaf growth in one season, such as a cabbage, use even more than most. For this reason, fertilizers formulated for lawns have a very high percentage of nitrogen.

Organic forms of nitrogen fertilizers include blood meal, cottonseed meal, fish emulsion and manure.

PHOSPHORUS

The second number on a package of fertilizer is the percentage of phosphorus, sometimes called phosphate or phosphoric acid. Phosphorus encourages both root growth and the formation of flowers and fruits. Fertilizers for plants that bloom have a higher middle number for this reason.

Phosphorus does not travel as quickly through the soil as nitrogen does. This is good because it won't rapidly leach out of the soil and run away, but it can be problematic because the phosphorus will only reach the roots near the surface if it is placed on top of the soil.

If your soil is low in phosphorus, or if you want to help stimulate bloom on a plant that is not flowering, you will need to mix some superphosphate in the soil around new plants or use a liquid fertilizer that will travel down to the area around the roots of an established plant.

Bone meal has been the traditional source of phosphorus for organic gardeners, but it is said to be less effective now that bones are completely processed for other uses. Bone meal, like all organic fertilizers, does have the advantage of also adding organic matter to the soil.

Superphosphate may be used instead of bonemeal, but take care not too add too much of this concentrated fertilizer. Placing too much of any fertilizer in your garden can throw the balance all out of whack. It's bad enough that there are all kinds of people leading unbalanced lives, we don't want our plants to suffer this way too!

No matter which form of phosphorus you choose, it should be worked into the soil where the roots are going to grow. Because it does not leach out of the soil quickly, it will be there when the roots grow into that area.

POTASSIUM

Potassium helps stem and leaf growth in plants, as well as the production of flowers and fruits. Plants take more potassium from the soil than any other element, with the exception of nitrogen and calcium. Like phosphorus, it is most effective when present in the soil where the roots are actively growing. Potassium is present in the ashes of any vegetable material that is burned, so wood ashes are the most common organic form of potassium used in gardens.

COMPLETE FERTILIZERS

Fertilizers are most often sold in formulations that contain the three basic elements just discussed, sometimes with the addition of others that are called the micro-nutrients. A fertilizer that contains nitrogen, phosphorus, and potassium is called a complete fertilizer. In general, a complete fertilizer is the best to use. If you suspect that your soil might be deficient in one nutrient or another, have your soil tested before putting any amount of a single nutrient on your plants. Your cooperative extension service can tell you where you can get a local comprehensive soil test.

A fertilizer intended for plants that are grown only for foliage, such as some house plants and lawns, usually has a percentage of nitrogen (the first number) that is as high as or greater than the other two numbers. Those products that are formulated for blooming plants have a lower percentage of nitrogen and higher second and third numbers. Because phosphorus encourages flower and seed production, fertilizers intended for annuals, perennials, and blooming house plants have a high middle number.

You shouldn't use a lawn fertilizer on any other plants; too much nitrogen will make blooming plants produce a lot of leaves and will stimulate too much tender, weak growth on shrubs and trees. A fertilizer containing equal percentages of nitrogen, phosphorus and potassium can be used on all of your gardens, provided it is sparingly applied. Those with higher levels of phosphorus and potassium can be used on all plants as well, and they are especially well-suited for bloomers.

GRANULAR OR LIQUID

Fertilizers are available in granular products that are spread dry, powders that are mixed with water before applying to the garden, and liquid concentrates that are diluted before using. It does not matter which is chosen as long as the product is used according to the directions.

A powder that is meant to be mixed with water should *not* be dumped on the ground and then watered in with the hose. This is not the same as mixing it first and then pouring it on. Because you can't be quite sure what concentration you are applying, some areas will get too much fertilizer since the first mix to enter the soil is bound to be more highly concentrated than what follows.

The most important thing to know about fertilizers

Fertilizers are like aspirin or vitamin A . . . a little can be a good thing, but too much can be fatal. People who would never think of swallowing a handful of aspirin because a few *more* just might cure their headache *faster*, think nothing of throwing three or four extra handfuls of fertilizer on their gardens, or mixing in so much blue powder into the watering can that it looks positively electric. Don't do it. Too much fertilizer is usually worse than none at all. *Think of fertilizer in the same way you do dessert or makeup: show restraint.*

Recent research shows that plants given supplemental fertilizers are often more prone to disease and insect attacks. Fertilizers stimulate new growth, and plants that are artificially pumped up produce fewer defensive chemicals and tend to have reduced root systems. While this might not be as much of a problem for annuals and vegetables which grow in one season, perennials, trees and shrubs need to be as resistant as possible to diseases and insects.

Clearly, anyone interested in low maintenance gardening does not want plants to be more prone to attack then they would naturally be. Our intention in fertilizing our plants is to create a garden that is healthy, not one that will cause more problems down the line. For this reason, it is wise to use all fertilizers with caution, and never apply it at a heavier concentration than is suggested on the label; think of the rate which is printed on the package as the *maximum* amount recommended.

If your plants are not growing well, don't automatically assume that a lack of nutrients is the cause; before reaching for the fertilizer, consider that something else may be causing the plants to languish. Perhaps the pH is too high or too low, making the nutrients that *are* there unavailable. Ask yourself if the weather might be affecting plant growth. Too much or too little water, or unusually hot or cold temperatures for instance, can affect the growth of plants.

Those who garden in sandy soils will need to apply fertilizers a little more often than those who plant in silty loam or clay soils. Sand does not retain nutrients well, and sandy soils tend to be acidic as well, which may make the nutrients that are there less available. Although gardeners who have sandy soil might need to fertilize more often than others, it is still important not to overdo it. A sandy soil is best improved by the addition of compost on a regular basis (you can use as much compost as you can get your hands on) and the use of organic fertilizers when needed.

HOW MUCH FERTILIZER TO APPLY

Knowing the importance of following the directions on the fertilizer package is one thing; deciding how the directions relate to your garden is another. Many a gardener has read something like "Use one pound per hundred square feet," and stood in the garden, mystified, wondering how this applies to the shrub border.

Usually the recommended rate will be given for an amount that relates to the amount in the bag or box. A rate for a ten pound amount will only be given if the bag contains at least ten pounds, etc. The challenge is figuring how your garden relates to the mythical hundred-square-foot area in the directions. If you have neat, straight-edged beds, it is easy to measure the sides and calculate the square footage. (And you swore in fourth grade that you would *never* have a reason to use all this math stuff outside of school!) But what if your gardens are not as easy to measure? What if you can't lay your hands on the tape measure when the moment to put down the fertilizer is at hand?

Sometimes it is best to square off the beds in your mind. Knowing that your border is about fifteen feet long, for instance, you can think that if it *were* ten feet wide, it would come out to about here, which would make it 150 square feet. Standing at that ten-foot place, look where the border actually ends, and you will see what proportion of that 150-square-foot size the shrubs really do take up. If you see that it is about a third of the space, you will know that you need to apply the fertilizer for 50 square feet (one third of 150).

If the tape measure is hiding and you have no idea how large your area is, try picturing it in terms of interior rooms. Most people have a good feel for how large a 10' by 12' room is, or perhaps you know the dimensions of another room in your house. If you think, "OK, the kids' room is 10' by 12', and at least three of these garden beds would fit in the kids' room, so this bed must be a third of 120 square feet."

Once you know how the size of your garden matches the area given in the directions, you can then figure how much of the fertilizer to use. "Let's see . . . my garden is about a third of 100 square feet, and the rate is one pound for 100 square feet. There are two pounds in this bag, so that means that I only need a third of *half* of this bag, or a sixth of the entire package." Taking the time to work this out will make your plants happy . . . and your fourth grade teacher proud.

Fertilizers that are mixed with water are also puzzling since there is no standard size watering can. I have spoken to many people at the garden center who have no idea if their watering cans hold a gallon or a gallon and a half . . . or maybe two! This is an easy one to solve. Most people have access to an empty milk container, either a gallon or a half-gallon size. Fill the milk jug or carton with water and pour it into your watering can, repeating this process until the can is full and you will know how much water it holds. You might even want to mark the half and one gallon levels, if the can does not already have such a reference point. You may discover, however, that a ring or indentation around the can that you had always assumed was decorative is really a mark that measures the volume.

ORGANIC OR CHEMICAL?

While I think that both chemical and organic fertilizers have their places, I think the largest place in our garden sheds should be saved for the organics. On the whole, organic fertilizers are slow to release their nutrients and slow availability is how nature works. Gardeners need to take the slow nature of organic fertilizers into account when they use them; organic fertilizers should be applied regularly, so that the nutrients are available to the plants when they need them.

The organisms that break down the organics so that they are usable are generally active in damp, warm soils. If your plants need nutrients in the early spring, when the soil is cool, an application of organic fertilizers will not be useful to those plants right away. But if you have applied your organic fertilizers every year in the late fall or early spring, there should be the steady release of nutrients that the plants need.

Many of the organic fertilizers that are available have high amounts of a single nutrient. Bloodmeal, for example, is all nitrogen. However, more and more complete organic products are coming on the market. These products, either liquid or granular, make it easier for the average gardeners to fertilize their plants without worrying that they are applying too much of one nutrient and not enough of another. Seaweed, a component of many of the products sold, has the added benefit of containing micro-nutrients.

There are times, however, when it is necessary to apply a fertilizer that is more quickly available. Annuals are fairly heavy feeders, since they must produce strong root systems, leaves, flowers and seeds all in a single season. Many people find that feeding their annuals two or three times during the summer produces stronger plants and a better show of flowers. Other plants may need a shot of a liquid fertilizer early in the spring or in mid-summer. Gardeners may choose between a liquid synthetic feed, or an organic mix of fish emulsion and seaweed extract; either of these contains nutrients that are immediately available to the plants.

In general, I believe that gardeners should turn to the organics first; they add organic matter to the soil as they break down, and often contain micro-nutrients in addition to the "big three." By using organic fertilizers we work with the natural processes, which is always wise.

WHEN TO FERTILIZE

Organic fertilizers can be applied in the late fall or early spring. If you are adding compost or other organic matter to your garden, it is wise to spread a granular fertilizer on the surface before the compost is spread on top of it. Mulch can then be placed over the soil amendments and fertilizer at the same time or later in season.

Chemical fertilizers should be used in the spring. Because they are more quickly available to plants, they shouldn't be spread in the fall. Early in the fall they may stimulate new growth that will not be hardened off by the arrival of cold weather. In areas where the ground does not freeze until very late in the winter, if at all, most of the nutrients may wash away with winter rains if the fertilizer is spread in the fall.

Lawns should be fertilized twice, once in the late fall and once in the late spring. Many people tend to forget about their lawns in the fall because it is colder, the season's almost over, and besides, most lawns look pretty good come September. Lawns do thrive in the cool temperatures and regular rains that most areas of the country have in Autumn. But using a slow release fertilizer, or one that is formulated for an autumn application, helps a lawn grow a strong root system and be ready to grow in the spring.

Another common error when it comes to lawn fertilizing is an early application of lawn food. Because a percentage of most lawn fertilizers is a quickly released nitrogen (put there to provide a fast greening of the grass), this is leached out of the soil before the grass can make use of it if it is applied too early. Grass doesn't start growing until the soil is warm, so it won't make good use of a fertilizer—especially a chemical fertilizer—until the night temperatures start staying high enough to raise the soil's warmth.

If you are unsure when the soil temperatures are warm enough to make the application of lawn fertilizers most profitable, call your cooperative extension for a recommended time for the application of lawn food in your area.

FERTILIZING NEW PLANTINGS

Tempting as it may be to give a newly-planted shrub or tree several applications of fertilizer to "get it going," remember that some things are best not rushed. A light application of a fertilizer formulated for new plantings (generally high in phosphorus to stimulate root development) is fine, with an emphasis on *light*. Make sure that the shrub or tree is well-watered first, and refrain from fertilizing it again for the next year. The goal with anything newly-planted should be a strong, healthy plant, not one that instantly looks mature.

Newly planted perennials don't even need one of the starter fertilizers, although a small amount won't hurt. If you are adding compost and perhaps an organic fertilizer to the perennial bed in the fall or early spring, the newly placed plant will benefit from the nutrients already in the soil.

FERTILIZING ANNUALS AND CONTAINER PLANTINGS

Annuals and plants grown in containers are treated a bit differently than shrubs, trees and perennials. Because annuals are grown for their show of flowers all summer long, they tend to be heavier feeders. If you are amending annual beds with compost and organic fertilizers in the fall or early spring, you may want to supplement this in midsummer with a liquid organic feed. There are several fish and seaweed emulsions that make fine supplements for foliage plants but not bloomers.

Any of the many mix-it-in-water-to-make-a-blue-liquid fertilizers are fine for annuals as well, although the directions may tell you to fertilize every time you water. Don't! Keep in mind that the directions on fertilizer packages are a bit like those on the shampoo bottles that urge you to "rinse and repeat." Your annuals will do quite well with one or two of the liquid-blue feedings per month.

Container plants are treated like annuals and can be given a liquid fertilizer once a month, or more often if you are using an organic product on foliage plants. Because organic liquids have a fairly low percentage of nutrients, plants given such a feed are not likely to suffer from fertilizer burn, making a more frequent application less harmful.

Another option for both annuals and container plants is a time release fertilizer. These products are encapsulated so that they are released over a period of about three months. Many commercial growers use these time release products because they can be quickly applied and the plant is fertilized over a long period of time.

These encapsulated fertilizers are equally convenient for the home gardener, but care must be taken to get a time release product that is intended for the type of plants that you are feeding. Some of these products are intended for non-blooming house plants, so they are high in nitrogen. Annuals and container plants should be given a fertilizer with either equal percentages of NPK or more phosphorus and potassium than nitrogen. Time release fertilizers, like any other chemical fertilizers, should be used according to directions.

FERTILIZING VEGETABLE GARDENS

Vegetables are essentially annuals, in that they grow, flower, and set seed in one season. The only difference is that you eat either the vegetable that forms around the seed, leaves, or flowers. Vegetable beds are best amended by lots of organic matter and compost, with an organic fertilizer worked into the soil in the fall or early spring. Once again, a liquid feed of fish and seaweed emulsion in midseason, or an application of another liquid fertilizer may be needed.

COMPOST

As authors continue to write about what great things compost does for the soil, even those with little time to garden get around to thinking about compost. Eventually it occurs to even the busiest person that the kitchen garbage, a prime ingredient of compost, is being thrown out and good money is being spent on other soil amendments.

Making compost has almost become a necessity in some areas, as local landfills refuse to accept yard waste and the composting of kitchen garbage is highly encouraged. Because the places we throw our garbage are filling up so rapidly, it becomes a necessity to reuse as much as we can. Making compost is one of the easiest recycling activities we can do.

Anyone who looks into composting can get the idea that it is anything but easy, however. There are *thick* books written on the subject, and a multitude of gadgets, store bought and homemade, to assist in the process. But having a limited amount of time for gardening and making compost makes the choice of a method and equipment more straightforward; you choose the easiest.

THE ESSENTIALS OF COMPOST

All organic matter eventually breaks down. You could have an open pile on your property where all organic garbage (with a few exceptions—see below) is placed, and *voilà*! It's a compost pile! Perhaps not the most attractive compost pile, or the quickest to create the finished product, but a compost pile none the less. When you think of it, the forest floor is one large composting operation.

Whether you compost in an open pile, an enclosed bin, or a purchased tumbler, the whole endeavor can present some problems. In the interest of promoting composting while keeping the process simple, I offer some basic information that will help.

COMPOST INGREDIENTS

In order to break organic matter down efficiently, the compost pile needs nitrogen-rich wastes, which can be thought of as the fresh, green ingredients. These can include vegetable and fruit garbage from the kitchen and fresh plant material from your yard, including the grass clippings. Dried, brown items such as small sticks, leaves, and even newspapers or paper towels, are high in carbon, also necessary in the compost pile. Other necessities include moisture and microorganisms that are present in the soil.

If you have too much nitrogen, your compost will smell. If you have too much carbon, it will take forever (seemingly) to breakdown. If you don't have any moisture or microorganisms, it will sit and sulk. Although there are many formulas for the percentages of these ingredients and how they are to be layered or mixed, it is really only necessary to know that you need them all and that compost cooks best if there are large, roughly equal quantities of the first two (nitrogen and carbon) and small quantities of the last two (water and soil or another source of the microorganisms such as a purchased compost starter). Making compost then can be as easy as making soup; once you know that you need broth, vegetables, and seasonings, decisions about the proportions of these ingredients can be based on periodic "taste tests" as you go along.

WHAT'S THE RUSH? WE ARE NOT IN A HURRY.

Making compost is even easier than preparing a soup because you don't have to worry about it being ready by supper time. Anyone who does not have much time to garden and wants to get the maximum enjoyment out of the whole process, should take a laid back position on composting.

Fortunately, in a hurry or not, we don't have to taste our compost to decide if it is lacking a crucial ingredient. Once a receptacle is chosen, the brew itself will tell you what is needed. If the primary ingredient in your bin consists of kitchen scraps, you will need to add some carbon-rich materials so your pile doesn't stink. If it ends up smelling, add more carbon. Leaves, shredded newspapers, sawdust, or even paper-towels will do the job.

Add a shovelful of dirt from your garden to supply the micronutrients. If you know that you've placed a great deal of carbon-rich material, such as dried leaves in your bin, and you want to speed the whole thing up, add more nitrogen. Grass clippings are probably the most easily obtainable nitrogen-rich compost material around. Other sources of nitrogen are cottonseed meal, bloodmeal, and fruit and vegetable scraps.

Leave the ingredients open to the rain or squirt them now and then with a garden hose and that's basically it.

Well, not quite it. A good soup needs a dash of salt to make it come alive, and compost needs oxygen. The manufactured compost tumblers speed the process because the tumbling adds oxygen to the mix. Articles and books that advise you turn your compost pile, make it with slotted sides, or place pipes with holes through them in the center of the pile, are all describing ways to get oxygen to the center of the pile. The center of the compost pile is where the action is, and once the available oxygen is used up, it helps to have a way to deliver more to the interior of the pile.

Supplying enough oxygen to the pile helps it to increase the composting process which generates heat. A pile which is "really cooking" is doing just that; active compost piles are hot in the center. Many people have noticed steam coming from a pile of grass clippings on a cool morning. This steam is the result of compost in action. If your compost pile isn't being turned regularly, it will not get as hot because the center of the pile—where the action is—won't have enough oxygen.

Compost piles that are not regularly turned will still produce compost, but they will do it more slowly. Such a "cool" composting method will not burn up seeds that are in the pile nor destroy any pathogens such as a fungus. Gardeners who have such a cool pile shouldn't put weeds with seeds or diseased plant materials in their pile.

Most home composters use the cool pile method because they simply don't have the time or inclination to turn the pile with any frequency. The cool pile method may be slower, but why are we in such a hurry? There is no reason to turn composting into just one more thing to get done; if time is limited, just throw it in a heap and rest assured that compost happens.

CHOOSING A RECEPTACLE

How your compost is contained is largely a matter of budget and style. Whether you choose the open pile method, a plastic bin, a homebuilt enclosure made of wire or wood, or one of the many "tumblers" on the market depends on the size of the area where the compost is to be located and the size of your pocketbook. Every garden magazine advertises many whiz-bang compost bins, some of which are quite expensive. There are reasonably priced models available though, and many towns sell inexpensive bins in order to encourage residents to recycle organic garbage. Check with the public works department in your area to see if such bins are offered for sale.

When deciding on a compost container and its location, it is wise to consider purchasing two. If there is only one, and you keep adding fresh material, there is no chance for the whole pile to decompose. Even if you decide not to turn the pile, leaving one stack to "cook" while you put new things into a second means that over a period of time you will be able to take what was in the first and put it on the garden. If you only have one bin you will have to move the top layer of lemon peels and coffee filters aside in order to reach the bottom layer of compost. There are bins available which allow you to remove finished compost from the bottom while still adding material to the top. This style is good for those who only have room for one compost bin.

Those who are constructing their own containers may want to consider building a long, narrow bin. This compost bin uses the movement of organic matter from left to right to provide both the oxygen to keep things cooking and the mechanism to allow for addition of new materials and removal of the finished product.

This style of compost bin is about four feet in width, and between nine and twelve feet long. Gardeners who don't have room for such a large bin, or those who don't have much material to throw in the pile, can make the rectangle which suits their property or needs. The enclosure can be made of any materials that you desire (wood, wood and wire fencing, or wood and lathe) and should only be about three or four feet high.

The basic idea is that you mentally divide the bin into thirds: all new materials are thrown in on the left; when the left side starts to get full, that pile is tossed into the middle third, and new material is again only put in on the left; when the left side is filled again, begin by tossing the center materials into the right side, then move the newer ingredients from the left into the center. Moving each pile two times provides the oxygen, and the space to allow two piles to be cooking while all new material is added to the third.

The only downside of this method (other than its slow speed, which we have already decided is not a problem) is that animals can get into bin with ease. You may find this objectionable, or you may not, depending on your outlook and which animals you find rooting around in the compost. I myself never minded the skunks and crows that seemed to view my pile as their personal five star restaurant. I was less than accepting, however, the day I saw rats in the bin. That same day I ordered two enclosed tumblers, putting an end to the free lunch my compost had offered to all the neighborhood wildlife.

A homemade bin can be designed to fit the space available. A simple compost bin can be made by taking a length of stiff wire fencing and curling the ends around to join each other. Tie them together with pieces of wire, and stand the resulting round wire bin up on end. The weight of the contents will keep the wire cylinder in place in a short while, but until there is a thick enough layer of ingredients to weight it down, you can stake it into the ground.

When you want to get at the contents to turn them or use the bottom, composted materials, pull the bin away from the heavy pile, which will remain in place on the ground. The wire cage can be moved slightly to the right or left, and the newer layer from the top of the old pile forked into it, leaving the compost that was at the bottom of the pile exposed and ready to use.

WHAT TO PUT IN YOUR COMPOST BIN

The nitrogen-rich, green yard and garden items that can be made into compost include grass clippings, small prunings, weeds, old annuals, and cuttings from the perennial garden. Do not add diseased plant material to the bin, as this can spread pathogens to the rest of the garden when the compost is spread. If your roses had blackspot or if the phlox were covered with mildew, for example, toss that refuse somewhere else when you clear your garden in the fall. Do not add grass clippings from a lawn recently treated with weed killers.

The kitchen is the next best source of organic matter that is high in nitrogen. All vegetable and fruit waste can be put into the compost. Egg shells, tea bags, and coffee grounds (filter and all) are great compost materials, as are human hair and the fur from the family pet . Do not put any meat, fish, or cheese in your compost; they attract a whole range of animals other than the crows and cause the compost to smell.

Dried leaves are good carbon rich-materials, as are small sticks and twigs. Be sure to keep the carbon-based items small, however, because they take the longest to break down. Other common sources of carbon are paper towels and shredded newspaper. The newspaper needs to be shredded so that the sheets don't compact, limiting air and water flow through the pile.

Because most home compost piles do not get hot enough to burn the seeds that may be in the plant refuse, you may want to put self-seeding annuals, perennials, or weeds somewhere else. I have a separate pile for such things as *Lychnis, Phlox,* and *Malva.* This is not to say that my compost is then weed and seed free; I have had times when I weeded hollyhocks, cleome, and cosmos out of my compost enriched gardens, as well as a million small tomato plants. These plants are easily pulled, and there is usually only one crop of them. If I get the mulch put over the compost in time, I don't get much germination of any of these seeds to speak of.

TO SHRED OR NOT TO SHRED

You might hear or read about the advisability of shredding, grinding or chopping the materials that you put into your compost pile. There are some people who go so far as to run the lawnmower over their leaves, and run the kitchen waste through the blender. These are fine practices if you have the time; the smaller the pieces, the faster the composting process. Small pieces also make consistently fine textured compost. I would love to have my compost materials magically shredded, but I don't have the time. Perhaps it's more accurate to say that I don't care to use what gardening time I do have on shredding my garbage. Since you are reading this book, you probably don't either.

Put yard waste and kitchen scraps in your compost bin as is, and let them decompose at whatever rate they will. Larger branches can be dealt with by either hiring someone with a shredder to come chop once every year or two, or putting them into a brush pile in some out-of-the-way corner of your property. A brush pile is an ideal home for wildlife and provides a place for gardeners to leave large branches and seed-filled plants.

WHEN COMPOST IS READY TO USE

Finished compost is dark brown or black. It should be moist and crumbly, looking like good, dark earth. You might be able to see a few pieces of carbon-rich materials, such as twigs or leaf pieces or an occasional avocado pit. This is not a problem because these will continue the composting process in your garden. But if you can identify such things as orange rinds or broccoli stems, the compost isn't ready to use.

Finished compost can be spread on top of established gardens and worked into the soil in new beds or those that are cleared annually. Compost may also be mixed into the soil when planting new perennials and shrubs. Fall is the ideal time to clear out the bin if the ingredients are decomposed enough, especially if you live in an area where the winter is frigid. Activity in a compost pile slows or almost stops in cold weather, particularly if the materials are not finely shredded and regularly turned. In areas where the winters are below freezing, the majority of the materials that will be added to the compost are from the kitchen, with the possible addition of shredded newspaper or paper towels. Clearing the pile out in the Fall leaves room for this material to stack up over the winter.

Q & A: SOIL ESSENTIALS

Q. *I have clay soil with very poor drainage. Some people tell me I should mix organic matter into the soil to help this situation, and others tell me I should put a layer of rocks underneath everything I plant. What is the best way to garden in this type of soil?*

A. One would think that adding a layer of rocks or sand underneath the planting area would allow water to drain quickly away from the clay. In fact, this is not how it works. Drastically changing the soil from one section to another will make the drainage worse, not better!

Water moves through clay slowly for two reasons. All soil particles have an electrical charge which attracts water to them; the moisture flows around these particles through the air spaces which surround them. The space around sand is large, so water drains rather quickly through sandy soils. There are many more spaces in clay soils but they are very tiny. Not only is drainage impeded by the size of these pores, but there are many more soil particles whose electrical charges all attract water to them.

Because the clay particles attract the water to them better than the sand particles do, putting a layer of sand or rocks underneath a layer of clay can actually keep the clay layer wetter for a longer period of time! The clay will only release water to the sand once the soil above the sand is fully saturated. The whole point of putting the drainage area under the clay is to keep it from getting fully saturated, but it has the opposite effect.

Water does not move well from one area to another which is radically different in composition, whether it is sand on top of clay, or clay on top of sand. For this reason it is wise to augment the soil in a *large* area around a plant if amendments are being added. Mixing sand into the clay over a wide area will improve the drainage more then placing a layer of sand or rocks underneath the clay.

Mixing sand into clay is heavy, hard work however, and most gardeners are not willing to go to the trouble and expense. Organic matter is lighter and more easily obtained, with the added benefits of bringing microorganisms to the soil improving the structure.

Gardeners who plant in clay should also be cautious about heavily amending the soil in one area but not in another. Again, creating any layers of soil which are radically different from each other in content and structure will impede water flow.

Peat should be used sparingly in clay soils because it is so efficient at holding water that it can make a clay soil even wetter then it already tends to be! Mixing peat into clay is like placing tiny sponges in the clay; they will absorb the water instead of creating air spaces to allow better drainage. Compost and composted manure are better choices for soil amendment in clay.

A pH test is important for heavy soils. If your soil is acidic, the addition of limestone can help improve soil structure as well as raise the pH. Gardens that are not yet permanently planted can be improved by a "green manure," which is a crop grown for a season and then tilled into the soil. Clover, winter rye and marigolds are commonly grown in clay for this purpose.

The best way to deal with clay is the one which requires the least work. Use soil amendments, adding compost to the surface of the soil on all permanent plantings. Choose plants which will thrive in your soil, or at least will tolerate any wet conditions. The following perennials, shrubs and trees will grow in moist soils.

PERENNIALS FOR MOIST SOILS

Aruncus dioicus (Goatsbeard)
Astilbe spp. (Astilbe)
Astrantia major (Masterwort)
Brunnera macrophylla (Brunnera)
Chelone obliqua (Turtlehead)
Cimicifuga racemosa (Snakeroot)
Eupatorium fistulosum (Joe Pye weed)
Filipendula palmata or *rubra* (Meadowsweet)

Ferns (most species)
Hibiscus coccineus (Scarlet rose mallow)
Hibiscus moscheutos (Swamp mallow)
Incarvillea delavayi (Hardy gloxinia)
Iris ensata (Japanese iris)
Iris pseudacorus (Yellow flag iris)
Lobelia spp. (Cardinal flower and other lobelias)
Lythrum salicaria (Purple loosestrife)
Myosotis scoipioides (Forget-me-nots)
Rudbeckia nitida (Shining coneflower)
Tradescantia virginiana (Spiderwort)
Trollius europaeus (Globeflower)
Viola species (Violet)

SHRUBS AND TREES FOR MOIST SOILS

Acer rubrum (Red maple)
Amelanchier canadensis (Serviceberry)
Baccharis halimifolia (Salt marsh elder)
Betula nigra (River birch)
Chamaecyparis thyoides (Atlantic white cedar)
Clethra spp. (Clethra/Summersweet)
Cornus amomum (Swamp dogwood)
Cornus sericea (Redosier dogwood)
Fothergilla gardenii (Witch alder)
Ilex vomitoria (Yaupon holly)
Itea virginica (Sweetspire)
Lindera benzoin (Spicebush)
Liquidambar styraciflua (American sweetgum)
Magnolia grandiflora (Summer magnolia)
Magnolia virginiana (Sweet bay magnolia)
Myrica pennsylvanica (Bayberry)
Ostrya virginiana (Ironwood)
Pinckneyea bracteata (Poinsettia tree)
Platanus occidentalis (Sycamore)
Quercus nigra (Water oak)
Quercus virginiana (Live oak)
Rhododendron atlanticum (Coast azalea)
Rhododendron arborescens (Smooth azalea)
Rhododendron viscosum (Swamp azalea)
Salix most varieties (Willows)
Sambucus canandensis (Elderberry)

Vaccinium corymbosum (Highbush blueberry)
Viburnum cassinoides (Withrod viburnum)

Q. *I have swarms of tiny fruit flies in my compost bucket in the kitchen,
and the pile outside. What can I do about this problem?*

A. Those tiny black bugs are mostly an annoyance, especially when
they are inside the house. There is no wonderful, non-toxic
control for them outdoors, but you can easily rid the indoors of
these insects. Use a plastic bucket which has a tightly locking
lid to hold the kitchen scraps; food storage containers work well
and are widely available in supermarkets and discount stores.

Some gardeners find that these small insects also come
into the house with the house plants that have spent the warm
season outdoors at "summer camp;" although they do not harm
the plants, their presence can be irritating. The best way to
control these bugs is to purchase a package of yellow sticky
traps, and hang them in the area where you have seen the fruit
flies. Insects are often attracted to the color yellow (the search
for pollen?) and these cards are nothing more than bright yellow cardboard covered with a *very sticky* coating. The tiny
black bugs fly to the color and are trapped on cards. Yellow
sticky traps are available from garden centers, some hardware
stores, and mail order from garden supply catalogs.

Q. *I have heard that compost helps my garden in ways other than
improving soil structure. Is this true?*

A. Compost is filled with microorganisms, and researchers have
begun to study the effect of these beneficial microbes in soils.
Not only do the fungi and bacteria help break down the organic matter, but they fight insects and disease as well.
Sometimes harmful organisms are simply crowded out when
the beneficial microbes use up the available food; other fungi
in compost attack pests directly when they produce antibiotics
or other toxic substances.

In a healthy environment a multitude of complex food
chains are present which help prevent any one insect or disease
from decimating the area. Compost helps to keep soils teem-

ing with such life, one organism feeding on or helping the next. Research continues to show that when compost is added to diseased plants, the plants recover faster than those to which nothing is added. It does not matter if the compost is made from manure, vegetable waste, sewage sludge, or a mixture of ingredients.

Compost helps sandy soils to hold moisture and facilitate good drainage. It helps lighten heavy soils and fosters deep root growth. But in addition to its effect on the soil structure, compost provides an environment for many beneficial micro-organisms which insure the health and vitality of your soil.

The Essentials: Planting, Watering, and Tools

When you grow or purchase a new plant for your garden, it has begun its life either in a pot, or as a field grown plant that has been dug and potted or wrapped in burlap. When the time comes to put it in your yard or garden, all you do is dig a hole and stick it in, right? Well, almost. Planting is another instance when taking time for a few key practices can mean the difference between a healthy plant that won't have to be fussed over or fiddled with and one plagued by time-consuming problems down the line.

PLANTING ANNUALS

Assuming that your soil is already amended, annuals can be planted in the ground with little fuss. Because annuals are often grown in plastic six-packs or other small containers, their roots have often become congested and curled around and around in the space where they are growing. It is important to notice if the plants are "root-bound" in this way, and if so, to gently loosen or pull the roots apart a bit before the plant is put into the soil. Sometimes a gentle squeeze is all that is needed to push the growing tips of the roots out of the tangled root ball.

Releasing some of the roots in this manner speeds the growth of the roots into the garden soil. This is important because the roots can continue to grow in a congested ball since they are wound so tightly together. Until new roots grow out into the surrounding area, this root ball dries out very quickly, even though it has been planted in the soil. A root mass

51

like this allows no room for water or nutrients to stay near the root hairs and thus be taken up into the plant.

Most plants sold today include a tag in the pack or pot that gives a recommended spacing between plants. These recommendations are usually pretty accurate, although typos do occur on such labels, often with hilarious results. (A few years ago I started a collection of labels with amusing mistakes on them, such as the *Eupatorium* tag which advised to "Plant in a missed spot" instead of a moist spot.) If the advice on a label does not sound right to you, discuss it with an employee at the garden center or with another gardener.

When planting large numbers of annuals or vegetables, you can save time by first taking all of the plants out of the package and placing them just to the side of where you are going to dig the hole. Placing all of them to the same side allows you to clearly see how they are placed, and at the same time it eliminates the need to handle them again as you plant. If you are right-handed, place the plants to the left of the hole.

Dig the hole to the depth of the rootball with the trowel in your right hand, and with your left, pick up the plant, stick it in the hole, and move a bit of dirt back around it. Plants grown in six-packs have small rootballs which can be planted the space that is created by pushing the soil aside with the trowel. Those who are left-handed would place the plant to the right of the hole, and proceed with the trowel in the left hand. Placing the rootballs out in the air next to their future location will dry them out, so be sure to water the bed well as soon as you are finished planting.

Remember that a newly planted annual or vegetable bed might need frequent watering at first; those root systems are small for the first two weeks, so they tend to dry out quickly, especially if the weather is hot and sunny. Since mulch helps keep the soil from drying too quickly, it is good to get the newly planted garden mulched as soon as possible.

PLANTING PERENNIALS

Perennials that have been container grown can also be root-bound, and those roots should be gently loosened as described for annual plants. Because these plants tend to grow in the same location for several years it is important to take the time to amend the soil in which the perennial is to be planted. Adding a handful of superphosphate in with the soil amendments will supply phosphorous when the roots grow into that area.

Be sure that the hole where the plant is placed is neither too deep nor too shallow; the surface of the growing medium in the pot should be even with the soil in the garden. If the plant is placed too deeply, the soil which is piled against the stems might rot the plant. If the surface of the dirt that was in the pot is above the garden soil, the plant will dry out even more quickly than otherwise, and any rainwater will flow off that elevated area and away from the plant.

Perennials should also be well-watered after planting and will need more frequent applications of water for the first two months in their new locations. Like annuals, container grown perennials have root systems that are only as large as the pot they were grown in, and will therefore dry out more quickly than established plants.

PERENNIALS USUALLY GROW OUT AS WELL AS UP

One of the most frequent mistakes gardeners make is to plant perennials too close together. I have been guilty of this myself. In our desire to see a full, lush flower border right away, we place the plants 12" to 18" apart, only to see the plants so crowded the following year that they push together in an unattractive way. Plants that are crowded too closely will shade each other quickly, resulting in less full, healthy plants.

Not only are the plants not as vigorous, but the crowding causes more work for the gardener since the plants must be dug and moved much sooner than would otherwise be necessary. When most gardeners plant perennials, they do so partly because the plants will return to their gardens year after year, meaning there is less involvement for the gardener. Or so it is hoped. But if the plants are too closely placed, the gardener may end up digging and moving large plants every year, which is even more work than planting those small annuals.

Perennials not only increase in height as they mature, but most of them spread horizontally as well. Some perennials spread into the surrounding area very quickly (more about invasive plants in Chapter 4) and others rather slowly, but the clump size will definitely grow. Perennials that are tagged usually have a recommendation for spacing on the label; double-checking this with an experienced gardener will be of help as well.

There are gardeners who will tell you that all perennials should be planted at least three feet apart. While this may be true for those that grow tall and bushy, like asters, or those whose leaves flop out to the sides, such as the Siberian iris, such a hard and fast rule would not apply to smaller plants with a more contained growth habit. There are plants such as *Sedum* 'Autumn Joy' which are fairly compact; although room must be left for their expansion, placing them three feet apart from any other plant would make the garden look odd.

Other plants, particularly short ones that don't mind being shaded, or those that bloom in the beginning of the season then go on to die back as the later maturing plants take over, can grow quite nicely in between the taller ones that need room around them. Perennials should always be planted with their neighbors in mind, as well as by following the general guidelines on the labels.

I know that you are wondering if your garden will look like a bare, mulched wasteland if your young perennials are planted two-and-a-half to three feet apart. This problem can be easily dealt with in two ways. During the first year that a new border or bed is established, annuals can be planted in between the new perennials. Be sure to use annuals that are not taller than the perennials, because their vigorous growth will shade the permanent plants, preventing them from growing as they should in their first year. A mass of small annuals will look all right in a bed of taller plants, because the sea of color from the flowers will take the focus away from the younger perennial plants.

The second way to deal with this problem is also a matter of focus. If you have planted a new batch of perennials and don't want to spend the time or money to also put in annuals, decide that your young bed will look like what it is for a year or two. We Americans are so impatient; we tend to treat our gardens like we do food. We want it quickly, and we don't tend to take the time to savor it when we have it. Savor your new garden. Take pictures of it after it is planted, at the end of the first season, and throughout the years to come. You will be amazed when you compare the pictures in the future. As discussed in Chapter 10, a great deal of the pleasure in the garden comes when we can enjoy the process as much as the product.

PLANTING SHRUBS

Soil amendments, watering, and careful placement are just as important with shrubs as with perennials. Loosening pot-bound roots is even more important for container grown woody ornamentals because the roots are larger and often become hard and woody with age. If a shrub has been in the container long enough for the roots to have circled the bottom of the pot or become a hard mass, it is possible for the newer roots to continue to grow round and round within this mass. Some gardeners have had the experience of planting such a plant as is, only to see it die two or three years later; when the dead plant was dug up to make way for a replacement, the roots were seen to be still in the shape of container, just as they had been when they were planted.

Roots of container-bound shrubs may be loosened with your fingers, perhaps with the help of a trowel or claw tool. This is best when done as gently as possible; the advantage of container grown plants is

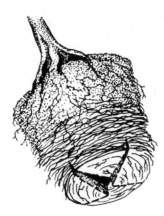

Slitting the bottom of a root-bound plant helps encourage new root
growth to travel away from the congested mass.

that they may be planted without severe disturbance to the root system.
If the roots are not tightly wound around each other they will be easily
pulled away from the dirt ball and spread out in the planting hole once
the plant is in place. The less the roots are damaged in the planting
process, the faster the plant will become established in the new site.

If the roots have grown so tightly together that pulling them gently
away from each other is impossible, the bottom of the root mass can be
cut open. This is best done using a sharp knife, cutting four or five
inches into the bottom of the roots in an X across the bottom of the root
ball. The quarter-sections of the circle of roots are pulled back a bit from
the center, spreading the cut areas open. When the new roots start to
grow, they are more likely to move away from the root ball if it has been
slit in this manner.

DIG A WIDE HOLE, ADD ORGANIC MATTER . . . BUT NOT TOO MUCH

The hole that a shrub is to be planted in should be dug at least three times
the width of the pot that the plant was in. At the garden center I usually
tell people this, but add "Dig it bigger if you can stand it." A wider hole
allows you to amend the soil with compost or composted manure, as
well as with bonemeal or superphosphate, for a greater distance away
from the center of the plant. Face it—you will in all likelihood not dig
this area up to add either organic matter or phosphorus again, so why not
take the opportunity to do so now?

The amount of compost or other organic matter that is added to the
soil when planting a shrub should not be so great that substantial changes

to the native soil cause shock to the plant when it outgrows the amended area and hits the real thing. If the soil in a small area is very rich with organic matter, and the natural dirt very heavy, the amended area can become a bowl that collects too much water, thus rotting the roots.

Studies have shown that the roots of plants do not tend to cross very well from one type of soil into a radically different one. If the area you are amending is small, it can create a growing situation which limits a plant's root growth, similar to being planted in a pot. For these reasons, it is probably wise not only to amend a wide area, but to keep added amendments down to about a fourth of the quantity of the total that is filled back into the hole. (One part organic matter to three parts native soil.)

The hole that a shrub is to be planted in needs to be wider than the pot, but it does not have to be deeper. Amending the soil underneath a new plant can create problems down the line in that the organic matter continues to break down over time. Eventually that area will sink as the material decomposes, and since there is no way to get more soil amendments under the shrub, the plant sinks down as well. Plants growing in a depression are more subject to rot, as the depression can fill with water. This is especially problematic in soil with a high percentage of clay.

After the hole is dug, place the plant in it, checking to be sure that the surface of the soil in the pot will be even with the surface of the soil where it is planted. Once again, you don't want to create a bowl that will hold water, nor do you want to have the root ball stand above the soil surface. If the root ball was split to break up a pot-bound root mass, you may need to pile a small amount of soil in a mound for that root ball to sit on.

At this point, remember to check that the plant is facing in the direction that you want. Most plants have a "good side," as well as a bare spot or two. You might have noticed one and intended to plant the shrub with that spot toward the house, for example, but it is easy to forget this in the heat of hole digging and soil amending. By the time the plant goes into the hole you might be so anxious to get into the house for a glass of iced tea that the orientation of the plant's imperfections is forgotten.

It is a horrible moment when, sometime after the hole has been filled in and the iced tea consumed, you notice that the side of the plant that you intended to face the house is facing the front yard instead. Flagging the good side of the shrub or tree with a piece of colorful cloth or ribbon will serve as a reminder to orient the plant in the proper direction.

Some make it a standard practice to fill the planting hole with water and let it drain before a shrub or tree is planted. This is not really necessary provided the plant is well-watered after it is in place and the soil filled back in, but the hole-filling practice won't hurt anything and may help if the surrounding soil is very dry. The point of filling the hole with water is so that when the newly planted shrub or tree is watered, the water does not travel right through the recently dug area and disappear into the surrounding soil.

If you choose to fill the hole with water, it is most important that you do take the time to let all the water drain away. If the soil is placed back into the area before the water is gone, there will either be airspaces left when it does drain, or the area will sink into the space where the water was pooled as you filled the hole. In heavy soils the water may take some time to trickle away; *now* is a good time to get that glass of iced tea.

As you fill the hole with the amended soil, *don't* stomp on it to pack it down. This was a method people formerly used to get air holes out of the replaced soil, presumably so that the plant wouldn't sink as the soil settles. Unfortunately, it also compacts the soil so much that the new roots have trouble pushing into it. With any new plant, the goal is to help its new root system get strongly established as soon as possible. A strong root system underground means a strong plant above ground. If you haven't disturbed the soil underneath the rootball, the plant won't sink much. The amended soil around the perimeter of the plant might sink as the soil amendments decompose, but you will be adding soil amendments and mulch to the top of the soil every year or so, and this will more than make up for any minor sinking.

After everything is in place, take some dirt and build a small berm (mound or ridge of soil on top of a flat surface) two or three inches high around the drip line of the plant. A plant's drip line is the area where rain would drip off its outermost leaves and fall to the ground. Most plants grow roots at least to their drip lines, although many grow roots beyond that point. The berm holds water in around the plant for the first few months after it is planted.

The berm should not be so high or solid that it lasts forever, or creates a permanent bowl in which the plant sits. Since newly planted shrubs and trees need regular watering for the first year after they are planted, the berm is constructed to hold that water over the area where the roots are growing long enough to trickle down into the soil before it runs off. When watering newly planted shrubs and trees, the area inside the berm will need to be filled with water several times in order to give the area a deep soaking. Soaker hoses, or an attachment that slowly burbles water out of the end of the hose, can be used instead of filling the bermed area with water.

PLANTING TREES

Trees are treated like shrubs, except in most cases the amending of native soils is not recommended for trees. Studies have shown that trees seem to get more quickly established if the soil is not amended or changed. When you plant a shrub it is possible to amend an area large enough so that for the first few years the shrubs roots grow out into the amended soil.

Trees roots travel much farther, however, and unless you are willing to amend the entire yard, it is better not to change the native soil when the tree is planted. The surface of the soil can be regularly amended with compost or composted manure as recommended previously—this is how nature does it, amending her trees from the top down. It is best to get a type of tree that will thrive in your native soil and add your compost to the surface of the area, rather than try to change the soil.

Digging a hole that is wider than the rootball is still desirable, because the soil is loosened by doing this and makes it easier for the new roots to grow through it. A larger hole makes it possible to remove any big rocks that might be in that area. If the hole is too small, it will be difficult to remove the burlap from the rootball when it is in the hole, a task that is best done when the tree is already in place.

BALLED & BURLAPPED PLANTS

Larger trees and shrubs are often sold with their rootballs wrapped in burlap. These are field-grown plants whose roots have been pruned (if they have been grown correctly) so that they are contained in a small area around the plant. When it is time to move the shrub or tree from the field to the nursery, the plant is dug up and the rootball wrapped in burlap which is then held in place with heavy twine or a wire basket. These plants are often grown in heavy soils (sandy soils would fall away from the roots before the burlap could be put on) so many a gardener is left standing next to a hole looking at a burlapped ball that seems to weigh a ton.

The proper way to plant this heavyweight is to first undo the burlap that is wrapped around the trunk of the tree. You want to loosen it enough to check the top of the ball, but not so much that the burlap falls away leaving you with an unmanageable ball of dirt to maneuver into the hole. Luckily, most B&B plants are well-bound, top to bottom, so this is not difficult.

It is necessary to check the height of the ball because you want to determine how deep your hole needs to be *before* you move the plant into it. These plants are often so heavy that you don't want to move

them more than necessary. In the process of wrapping the rootball in burlap, dirt is sometimes pushed up around the tree trunk, making it appear that the soil surface is much higher than it really is. Once the burlap is removed from around the trunk, push down the soil on the top of the ball until you can see the flair of the tree trunk.

All tree trunks slope outward at the point where the trunks enter the soil; this is where the trunk emerges from the largest roots. If you push the soil away a bit, you can see this obvious flare and the beginning of the root system. This is where the soil surface should be, and this is where you should begin measuring to see how deep the root ball is.

Once you have determined how high the root ball is, and have dug the hole to match that size, the ball can be moved into the hole, burlap, binding and all. Position the tree in the hole before you cut off the twine or snip the wire basket. If the ball is rather large, the wire can be snipped all around the bottom, and whatever small portion remains under the soil can be left in place.

The burlap should also be snipped off, leaving a small piece directly under the ball if necessary. Never leave the burlap on the entire ball. Although it is usually made of organic fibers, some burlaps are now made of plastic, which won't break down. Even a natural fiber won't decompose quickly enough to be gone when the roots reach it. Leaving the burlap on might bind the roots for a period long enough to kill the tree.

Burlap that remains in place around a rootball will also act like a wick, carrying the moisture from the ground around the roots up through the fibers and out into the air. Removing as much of the burlap as possible prevents both the binding of roots and the wicking of moisture from the soil.

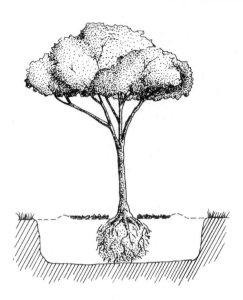

A correctly planted tree. The hole was dug wider than the root ball, but
no deeper, and the flare of the trunk is at the level of the surrounding soil.
Containers, burlap and wires have been removed, and the soil replaced
around the root ball. A small berm captures water so that it drains around
the roots for the first year or two. Mulch helps to hold the moisture in
the soil, but the mulch does not touch the trunk of the tree.

After the wire, twine and burlap are removed as much as possible,
the hole can be filled in with the soil that was dug out initially. The soil
should not be packed down hard by stomping on the ground. Let a thorough watering remove any airspaces from the area. A berm may be
constructed that is about a foot outside of the diameter of the root ball.
Constructed the same way described for planting shrubs, this berm is a
small ridge built on top of a level soil, *not* a concave bowl of soil with the
tree at the bottom of a hole.

STAKING NEWLY PLANTED TREES
It used to be standard procedure to stake a tree after it was planted, and
this practice still goes on, even though it is unnecessary in most cases
and can even be detrimental to the health of the tree. If a tree has a large
crown of leaves on top, you might want to support it loosely for the first
six months. I emphasize *loosely* because it is the action of the tree sway-
ing in the wind that signals the plant to produce a strong root system.

The supporting structure seems to be strengthened according to need, and if the plant is so firmly staked that there is little movement, it is not getting the message to grow roots that will anchor it against the wind. Any staking that you do should allow the tree to sway, but provide enough support to hold it in the event of an unusually strong storm.

Staking can also be detrimental because people forget to take it off. Once we are used to seeing something like a stake and rope in place, it becomes a part of the landscape. The trunk of the tree around which that rope is tied continues to grow, but the rope does not. If the rope remains in place too long, the tree will press against it, then try to grow around it, but the rope will be so tight that eventually it will girdle the trunk. This can kill a tree, or severely weaken it, because it strangles the tree's vascular system and creates a wound where disease can more easily infect the plant.

WATERING THE NEWLY PLANTED SHRUB OR TREE

The main reason people lose newly planted nursery stock in the first year is that they don't water the plant enough, or they don't water it correctly. In average temperatures, new shrubs and trees need a good deep soaking once a week; in hot weather it may be necessary every four days, especially if your soil is sand or sandy loam which dries out quickly. The two most important words are *deep soaking*.

Standing by the plant for five minutes with the garden hose is not enough. Let the hose trickle into the bermed area for quite a while, or set up a soaker hose that curls around any newly planted shrubs and trees, leaving the water on for over an hour. What is your goal for your newly planted nursery stock? Right—you want a strong, deep root system. The roots won't grow deeply if there isn't any water down there to keep them moist. When the surface of the soil is squirted with a hose by hand, the soil is only dampened two or three inches below the surface.

This deep soaking is important once a week, but it shouldn't be done too often. Remember that air is important to the roots as well; if you water any plant too much, especially a new one, it will drown. Don't forget that if it does not rain you need to continue watering the new plant right up to the time the ground freezes if you live in an area where it gets so cold.

If the ground does not freeze in your area but the temperatures get cooler in the winter, remember that all through this season the plant still needs either regular rainfall or watering. Many people forget to water once the air gets cool. Although the plant isn't losing as much water through its leaves when it gets cool, it does lose some moisture daily as long as it has leaves. Even when the leaves have dropped, the roots continue to grow slowly unless the ground is frozen.

After a shrub or tree is established, and it has a strong, deep root system, it can better tolerate periods of drought and irregular rains. But the root system of a container grown or balled-and-burlaped plant is not large enough to go for long periods without water. For this reason it is vitally important that the plant be watered regularly throughout this first year.

It may seem obvious that you don't want a plant to dry out, but time after time people come into garden centers wondering why the trees that they planted the previous year died. Usually, they were quite conscientious about watering for the first month or two after it was planted, but as time went on the tree was left to depend on rainfall for moisture.

Although most people are quick to complain about a two or three week stretch of rain, they do not complain about an equal period of sunshine. We do not tend to make note of long periods without rain because this is considered "good weather," even though it may not be good for our new plants. After a new shrub or tree is placed in the landscape, it might be wise to write a watering reminder on every month of your calendar.

MULCHING RECENTLY PLANTED SHRUBS AND TREES

A layer of mulch can help the soil around new plantings stay moist. You might want to leave the area inside the berm clear of mulch for the first few months, or you can place the permanent layer on the soil surface right away. As previously described in the discussion of mulch, leave a clear space of a few inches so that the mulch is not touching the stems of the shrub or tree.

PLANTING SEEDS OUTDOORS

There are some plants that are best seeded directly in the spot where they are to grow. Some vegetables such as beans, for instance, sprout and grow so readily that it would be foolish to start them in containers. Other plants, like poppies, dislike being transplanted or having their roots disturbed. And plants like lettuce can be purchased in packs, but are so easy to grow and so much less expensive from seed that there is no reason not to throw a handful on the ground in early spring.

Some seeds are easily germinated when sown directly in the ground, but others are a bit more tricky. (See the sidebar list of easily grown plants from seed.) I hear many people complain that their directly seeded plants either didn't come up, or that they disappeared shortly after germination. Growing plants from seed is not the most low-maintenance garden task because you can't (usually) put seeds in the ground and forget them.

The key to successful planting of seeds is to first choose the right seeds, and then to keep them watered as they germinate and grow. Some seeds require chilling for a period of time before they will germinate, some need to sprout in the dark, while others have to have strong light. There are seeds that require scarification, which is a nicking or scratching of the seed coat to foster germination.

Clearly a gardener without much time does not need to fool around with growing those sorts of plants from seed. If eventually you get seriously bitten by the gardening bug, you will find yourself popping some of these seeds in and out of the refrigerator, along with other mad endeavors, but this is another story and another book.

Thankfully, many seeds are not as picky and require a minimum of care. Annuals and vegetables are the easiest plants to grow from seeds sown directly into the garden. Although shrubs, trees and perennials will grow this way as well, they are often slower to germinate or more likely to have special requirements for germination. (See growing perennials from seed, Chapter 6) Annuals are geared to grow from seed, bloom, and produce more seed in one season so they are less likely to spend any time being finicky.

When growing plants from seeds placed directly in the ground, it is most important to keep them watered. This requires some attention, especially for the three weeks or so between the sowing of the seeds and establishment of a strong plant. Seeds must be moist to germinate, but most seeds don't want to be waterlogged. If seeds are planted in a time when it is cool and cloudy, the soil will not dry up quickly, so it won't require daily sprinkling. If the sun is hot and the sky is clear, however, the area may need water at least every morning, and perhaps in the afternoon as well.

If you are not in the position to check the area where seeds have been planted twice a day, perhaps you should forgo direct seeding and buy your plants at the garden center. But if a twenty minute watering with a gentle sprinkler is not out of the question, direct seeding can provide many lovely flowers quite inexpensively.

Given the wide variances in weather, there is no general rule about how often seeds need watering; you will need to monitor them and use your good sense about when to water. A seedbed needs to be moist, but too much water will wash the seeds away. A sprinkler does a good job of watering seeds, and handwatering is possible if a watering wand or nozzle on a mist setting is used. The area needs to be watered long enough so that the water penetrates two inches down into the soil; unlike established plants, seeds and seedlings don't need a good deep soaking because their roots don't go down very far.

Check your seeded area twice a day to see if it looks dry. The goal is to catch it *before* it dries completely; if the plant has just germinated, and the first tiny sprout or root dries up, it won't produce another. Established plants can go for short periods without water and if some of their roots get dry they may not be happy, but they aren't dead either. Baby plants are like baby humans; they are much more fragile than the adults.

Being more delicate, they are also more vulnerable to insects, animals, slugs and drought. Slugs love fresh greens, and the moist soil necessary to keep the seedlings alive makes it easy for them to slither around the garden. Insects love new growth as well, so if your seedlings were there one evening but gone the next morning, suspect a nightfeeding insect or slugs.

Complete decimation of seedlings does happen, but it is not a given; a gardener shouldn't be discouraged from trying direct seeding. Plant more seeds than you really need, spaced a bit more closely than the package recommends. If some are eaten or don't germinate there will still be enough in the garden to make a good show. If all of them germinate and grow, extras can be transplanted elsewhere or (gasp!) pulled out and added to the compost.

DID I PLANT THIS?

One of the main problems with direct seeding into the garden is that as the seedlings emerge from the soil, so do the weeds. This is less problematic when your vegetables or flowers are planted in straight rows, since the tiny seedlings are easier to spot and differentiate from tiny weeds if they are all lined up. If the seeds have been broadcast, as they often are for wildflower meadows for instance, it is harder to spot which small, green sprout is a flower and which is a weed, particularly if you are growing something that is unfamiliar.

Novice gardeners might want to stick two or three seeds (or a representative sample of seeds in the case of flower mixes) into a pot at the same time they are planted directly into the garden. If the pot contains fresh potting soil or a seed starter mix, it is relatively certain that there will be no weed seeds in the starting medium. Keep the pot well-watered so that the young plants do not dry out. Small seedlings in the pot can be compared to the ones sprouting in the garden, making it easier to tell which seedlings are the desired plants and which can be pulled out.

TOP TEN ANNUALS FOR EASY DIRECT-SEEDING

1. *Cleome Hasslerana* (Spider flower)
   This sun-loving annual grows to four or five feet tall and is available with white, pink, or purplish blooms. The spiky seed pods develop along the stem, adding to its charm.

2. *Cosmos bipinnatus* (Cosmos)
   Bright flowers in white, pinks, red or orange cover this plant all summer. White and pink varieties are usually tall (4' to 6') and may need support; red and orange cultivars are shorter. They prefer warm weather, so grow in full sun.

3. *Eschscholzia californica* (California poppy)
   Although this is really a perennial, it is grown as an annual in most locations. Available in pinks, yellows and oranges, this plant prefers cool weather and will not bloom all summer in hot areas. Sow in autumn if your winters are mild, or grow as a winter flower if your temperatures don't go below freezing. California poppies grow to 12" tall and will usually self seed every year.

4. *Helianthus annuus* (Sunflower)
   Always a favorite to rim a vegetable garden, this annual has attracted new interest as a cut flower and is now available in a wide assortment of colors and sizes. The standard tall variety grows to ten feet or more, and is always a favorite with children and birds.

5. *Ipomoea purpurea* (Morning glory)
   Although this vine comes with white, blue or pink flowers, it is the blue that captures most people's hearts. Germination is hastened by

soaking the seeds in a saucer of water overnight before planting. Plant in full sun and provide a trellis, fence, post or shrub for it to climb over.

6. *Lobularia maritima* (Sweet alyssum)
Sweet it is, and easy to grow. Alyssum is another perennial that is grown as an annual. It prefers cool weather, so it may dwindle away in hot summers. Low growing and fragrant, this self-seeder makes a good winter edging in warm areas, and puts on a show in spring or fall where the winters are cold and the summers hot. Sun or part shade.

7. *Mirabilis Jalapa* (Four-o'clocks)
Available in a variety of solid colors and variegated blossoms, these flowers open in the late afternoon shade so they are best planted in an area where you sit or pass by at that time of day. A perennial that is often grown as an annual, four-o'clocks grow two to three feet tall and do well with at least five hours of direct sun.

8. *Nicotiana alata* (Flowering tobacco)
One of the best annuals for season long blossoms, Nicotiana comes in a wide range of colors, and prefers full sun but will grow in part shade. Water it well during dry spells. The white flowered variety is very fragrant at night.

9. *Nigella damascena* (Love-in-a-mist)
The common name alone makes this flower appealing, even though it tends to bloom best in cool weather. The seed pods are as interesting as the flower, and it usually self-seeds. *Nigella* grows well in gardens that get at least five hours of sun per day, is available in blue, white, pinks and purples, and comes in a variety of heights.

10. *Tropaeolum majus* (Nasturtium)
Charming traditional cottage garden flower, nasturtiums prefer cooler weather so should be planted as a winter flower in hot climates. It blooms well all summer in northern areas, and both leaves and flowers make spicy additions to salads and sandwiches. Compact and vining types are available in an assortment of "hot" colors. Although generally an easy flower to grow, nasturtiums are a magnet for aphids and mealybugs.

TOP TEN VEGETABLES TO DIRECT SEED

1. *Beans.*

   All of the beans—pole, bush, Italian, yellow wax, purple podded, and traditional green beans—are equally easy to grow. Plant when the soil is warm in late spring/early summer. Pick the beans daily to encourage a longer period of production, and pick them young for the most tender crop.

2. *Beets.*

   Plant your beet seeds at least four inches apart so that you don't have to spend any time thinning young plants. Look for varieties that will stay sweet even when they grow large so that you can harvest them at your leisure. Use the beet greens along with the beets in soup. Yum.

3. *Carrots.*

   The only thing that is tricky about carrots from seed is the sowing; the seeds are small and the tendency is to sow them too thickly. This makes it necessary to thin out small plants so that those left will have enough space to grow their thick roots. Thinning carrots can be pretty time-consuming, so it is better to go to the extra trouble of spacing the seeds at planting time. Plant the seeds about three inches apart.

4. *Radishes.*

   Children love to grow radishes even if they don't love to eat them. Radishes grow quickly, and it is so satisfying to pull the pink globes out of the ground. Space the seeds about two inches apart so that you do not need to thin them.

5. *Cucumbers.*

   In addition to the standard green cuke, there are long skinny varieties, fat yellow lemon cucumbers, picklers, and many others. Some plants grow in long vines and some in bushes; choose which variety suits the size of your garden and your taste buds.

6. *Lettuce.*

I wish more people would catch on to the value of growing lettuce as an ornamental since the diversity of leaf colors is so great. Lettuce can be sprinkled in rows, groups or large patches. There is no need to thin the plants until they are large enough to eat; then they can be thinned as you pick your salad. Lettuce seeds can be sown on the surface of the garden, or covered with just the bare minimum of soil.

7. *Pumpkins.*

Large Jack-o-Lantern or small pie pumpkin seeds are planted in groups of eight to ten seeds. When the seedlings have their second leaves, thin to the five or six strongest looking plants. Pumpkins are heavy feeders, so plant them in soil that is enriched with manure, water them often, and feed with a liquid fertilizer every month. Pumpkin vines need a great deal of room, so plant them next to crops such as radishes and peas; as the early crops go by, the pumpkins can grow into their territory.

8. *Peas.*

These love cool weather so plant them early. Whether you grow regular peas, snow peas or sugarsnaps, they form quickly once they start to come in and are best picked daily. For this reason, plant them in a spot where it is convenient to pick a bowlful right before dinner. I grow sugar snap peas in large pots on my deck, containing them with bamboo teepees and string. Although the directions usually say otherwise, peas can be planted as close as an inch apart.

9. *Chard.*

Full of vitamins and flavorful in soup, chard is also lovely in the garden. Space seeds to the distance recommended for growing plants so that thinning is avoided, or grow twice as thick as recommended and eat the young plants as you thin them out.

10. *Squash.*

Both summer squash (such as zucchini) and winter squash (acorn squash, for example) are easy to grow from seed. Plant them in groups of about ten seeds, thinning to the six strongest plants once they have their second set of leaves.

WATERING

When regular rains water our gardens we must accept the amount delivered, and its timing, without question. Our hope is that the rain will come at least once a week, and deposit an inch or two of water in a slow, steady sprinkling . . . preferably overnight, and not on a weekend. In many areas the reality is that there are long periods of drought and occasional times when the rain seems not to stop. Even those places where it rains fairly consistently go through stretches of unseasonable heat, downpours or drought. The only thing constant about the weather is that it is always changing.

Although it is obvious that plants must occasionally be watered, it is not as obvious how much water they need, or when and how it should be delivered. Many people come into the garden center asking about a plant that is not doing well. My first question is always "What has the watering been like?" The usual reply is "Oh *that's* not the problem!" and when pressed to tell me about their watering practices, they will go on to say "Oh, you know, regular."

Regular watering for many is either a squirt with the hose every evening, or no watering at all, even in a drought. Knowing the amount of water your plants need and the best time to give it to them can mean the difference between a healthy plant and one that is ailing.

WATERING DEEPLY, LESS OFTEN, IS BETTER THAN A LITTLE EVERY DAY.

That daily squirt of the garden hose may be doing more harm than good. When most people hand water, they don't have the patience to stand there for very long. Once the surface of the soil looks quite wet they move on to another plant. These brief dousings *don't* drench the soil very far down, and this is a problem for anything other than seedlings.

Our goal as gardeners is to have a beautiful, healthy garden, preferably with as little work as possible. Healthy plants have large, deep root systems, because the deeper the roots, the better able the plant is to withstand periods of drought as well as any freezing and thawing of the ground in the winter. If the soil is routinely dampened only a few inches down, the plant will only grow roots near the surface.

Shallow roots will dry up quickly if you go on vacation and are suddenly unable to give the garden its accustomed daily squirt. The freezing and thawing of the surface soil will break off shallow roots more quickly than the gradual temperature changes that occur around roots growing deeper in the ground.

A handheld hose may also be an inadequate way to water because a good deal of the water may run off before it soaks into the ground. This is especially true on heavy or clay soils which are less permeable and drain slowly. Using soaker hoses or sprinklers for a slower, steady application of water is clearly a better way to give your plants the moisture they need.

Because plants also need air around their roots, watering them too often can be just as detrimental as not watering them enough. Although a good, deep soaking will encourage roots to extend down into the soil, thorough watering should only be given when the soil is getting dry. If your garden looks parched, dig down three or four inches with a trowel to see if it is also dry that far below the surface. When dry at that depth, the garden may need water. Gardens that contain drought tolerant plants might not need watering at this point, however, so make the decision to water based on the type of plants that are growing there rather than a strict time schedule.

WATERING SAND, LOAM AND CLAY SOILS

Sandy soils drain more quickly and dry out faster, so those that garden in sand need to water more often. Because the water travels down into the soil quickly and deeply, less water needs to be applied at any one watering. An inch of water penetrates about 12 inches of sandy soils, so to moisten a garden two feet down you would need to apply two inches of water to the surface.

That same inch of water in loam travels about seven inches down, so sprinkling two inches on a silty-loam garden would wet the soil 14 inches deep. A garden planted in loam will need to be watered longer than sand, but it retains that water longer and so will need watering less often.

Clay retains water the best of all, but an inch of rainfall penetrates only four inches. This is not only because the water moves through clay very slowly, but also because the water has a chance to spread laterally as well as sinking down. Water falling on sand drains straight down; on clay it travels both out and down, with loam somewhere in the middle. When watering clay soils you will need to leave the sprinkler or hoses on longer in order to get the moisture down deep.

HOW TO TELL WHEN YOU HAVE APPLIED AN INCH OF WATER
Given the depths that an inch of water soaks into the various soil types, it is easy to calculate how much water needs to be applied to your garden, but many people wonder how it is possible to tell the amount of water that their sprinkler puts out. If you have a rain gauge you can stick it under the sprinkler, but be sure to place it in a central location; some sprinklers pause longer on one side of their cycle than the other, causing more water to fall on one end of the garden.

An alternate way to measure your sprinkling is to set cans out in the area that you are watering. If you have both a rain gauge and cans or cartons, you will feel puzzled from the start. The rain gauge might tell you that there is an inch in the tube, when there is obviously more than that if you held a ruler to it. But in the same amount of time, the cans will fill with liquid that will actually measure an inch.

Some rain gauges may have a narrow opening, so they compensate for this by calculating how much water will fall into the gauge when it has, in fact, rained an inch. For this reason the marks for an inch of water on some rain gauges are often more than an inch in measurement. It seems almost as convoluted and needlessly confusing as the wind chill factor, and it's probably best not to put much thought into it.

Measuring with tin cans or cottage cheese cartons may be a bit less accurate, but it seems more straightforward, and aren't we relieved! Place two or three identical containers in various places under the sprinkler, and wait until they contain the number of inches that you have calculated that you need. The advantage of placing more than one carton out is that you will also be able to tell if your sprinkler is hitting one area with more water than another—not that you necessarily need to do anything with that information.

Once the output from a sprinkler has been measured a couple of times, you will know how long to let the water run; it then becomes unnecessary to race around the yard with tin cans every time you water. The rain gauge is helpful to have out all of the time, however, because it will tell you at a glance how much moisture Mother Nature has put onto the garden, so you will know how much—or how little—you need to augment her efforts.

You might be dismayed at the amount of time it takes to accumulate the water you need, but remember that a deep watering does not have to be done as often because a plant with deep roots won't suffer if it goes short times without watering. A garden that is mulched will be able to go even longer without watering, and if you have chosen drought-tolerant plants you will be able to stretch the times between sprinkling even further.

THE BEST TIME OF DAY TO WATER

I used to have a neighbor who watered his garden and lawn at five o'clock in the afternoon because he had heard that much of a daytime watering evaporates before reaching the ground. While water does evaporate from the leaves of the plants when they are watered during the day, late evening watering encourages the development and spread of fungi which thrive in moist environments.

Whenever possible, watering in the early morning is the best compromise. The sun is not yet strong enough to burn off the moisture immediately, but it will evaporate it quickly enough to discourage pathogens.

Knowing the ideal time to water does not mean that it will necessarily fit into *your* timetable. Many people don't have two hours to monitor sprinklers before they go to work in the morning. Sometimes you have to water at a less than ideal time, and hope for the best. Several products are available which make watering at the ideal time possible, or make watering at the wrong time less harmful.

PLANTING WITH YOUR WATERING IN MIND

It may seem silly, but the time to think about your watering is before you have planted. With some forethought, your gardens can be planted so that plants that are drought-tolerant are all grouped together. It makes sense to plant those areas that are far from a water source with plants that do not require as much moisture. Plants which require more frequent watering can be placed together, preferably near a faucet or in-ground sprinkler.

Such groupings are especially important in areas where long dry spells are the norm. In periods of drought, gardeners that fill many beds with thirsty plants will spend all their time hauling hoses, and are likely to grow weak at the sight of their water bills. Many areas restrict the watering of lawns and gardens when rain is scarce, and this seems to be the way of the future. Even if water is not restricted in your area, it is wise to plan gardens with water conservation in mind.

WATERING EQUIPMENT

In-ground sprinkler systems can save a great deal of time, so anyone with the opportunity (a new house or garden) and the money should consider installing such a system. The sprinkler heads can be set to water only specific areas, or faucets with soaker hoses attached can be installed instead of a sprinkler head. Such systems are usually installed by someone in the sprinkler business, and they need to be drained (or blown out) every fall in areas where the winter temperatures drop below freezing.

In addition to eliminating the need to drag hoses and sprinklers around, in-ground systems also offer the possibility of custom fitting your plantings with various types of drip irrigation. There are many models available, but they all deliver water slowly at reduced water pressure. This method waters the soil, not the foliage, so there is less evaporation; because it is slowly applied there is little runoff.

If installing a permanent system is out of the question, or if your gardens are not extensive enough to warrant it, soaker hoses will save time in the garden and give your plants the occasional deep soaking that they might need.

TIMERS AND SOAKER HOSES

Timers are available that will turn the water on and off at a certain time of day, even for those who don't have an in-ground sprinkler system. Be sure that you set the timer to go on and off as you need the water, not automatically on the same day every week. I have often driven by yards that are being given a good, deep soaking in the middle of a pouring rain.

Those who don't want timers (they can be expensive) and find that they invariably don't get to watering until seven o'clock in the evening, might want to consider purchasing soaker hoses. Just a few years ago these were made of canvas, but inexpensive soaker hoses are now available that are manufactured out of recycled car tires.

Soaker hoses let the water seep out all along their length. Because the water sinks directly into the soil, the leaves of the plant do not get sprinkled on, making evening watering less likely to encourage leaf spots and other fungi. Do not confuse soaker hoses with the models that are made of regular hose material that is perforated; such models *do* get leaves wet since the water usually spurts out of the tiny holes and shoots many feet into the air.

Soaker hoses are laid on the garden soil before mulch is spread. The mulch hides the hose as well as retaining the moisture in the soil. Be sure to cover the end where the garden hose attaches, or have it stick out of the mulch to prevent mulch and dirt from getting into the soaker when it is not attached. If dirt or other particles get into the soaker it will become clogged over time. Most soakers have a removable cap at the other end, so that they can be periodically flushed and cleaned.

A soaker hose can be curled around shrubs and trees, or wound through perennial and annual gardens. If you are watering clay soils the water will spread laterally about a foot to a foot-and-a-half, as well as traveling downward, so the hose can be placed every two to three feet for good coverage. Sandy soils drain straight downwards, so soakers need to be closer, about a foot to 18 inches apart. Gardeners with loam can space soaker hoses in between those two measurements.

Two or three soaker hoses can be attached together to form a hose that is about 75' long, but after that length is laid, another hose, hooked to a different water source, should be begun. Because the water seeps out as it travels along the hose length, at a certain point there won't be any more water left. Even a 75-foot length might be a challenge for a low pressure water supply. String the length of soaker that is needed together and hook it up to running water before it is laid into the garden. If it is apparent that the water is not reaching the end, remove one piece and install two separate sections in the garden.

HOSES

You may not pay much money for inexpensive, lightweight hoses, but you will pay in frustration from the moment you hook them to your faucet. They fold and bend, which stops all water flow. This requires frequent trips back and forth to untangle the kinks. After two or three years in the sun they start to break down, making leaks common. Although the purchase of the top-of-the-line hose may not be necessary, a slightly more expensive one is worth it. The weight of the hose and the distance that it needs to be hauled around your yard will help you decide if you want a really heavy duty model.

Most gardeners end up wanting certain hoses to be constantly available; it is time-consuming and impractical to put the hose in the garden shed or garage after every use, and to haul it out again for the one new plant that needs a drink. But hoses left in heaps are easily kinked or knotted, as well as creating an eyesore. Many devices to hold a coiled hose are available. Some are freestanding and others attach to the outside of the garage or house. There are inexpensive no-frills models as well as decorative front-of-the-house styles available.

One of the nicest hose holders I have seen for the edge of a flower garden was made by placing a 4 x 4 post in the ground, against the pipe that came out of the ground and ended in the faucet. The hose was attached to that faucet. The post was about three or four feet tall, and had a hose holder attached at the top side. On the very top was a simple cut out of a bird, and the whole thing—post, pipe, faucet, and bird—was painted dark green. Because the hose was also dark green, it all functioned as a garden ornament when the hose was curled onto its holder, as well as when the hose was in use and the post with bird stood alone.

My mother, who is an interior designer, has always said that if you have a problem item or difficult area in your house *accentuate* it; such a place or thing can often be "hidden" by making it a focal point. This is a good strategy with garden hoses as well. I'm waiting for one of the garden equipment companies to catch on to this: I can envision a line of garden ornament/hose holders with color-coordinated hoses.

CLICK-ON CONNECTORS

Fitting your hoses, sprinklers and watering wands with click-on connectors saves an enormous amount of time, given the following caveat: you must fit *every* hose, sprinkler and watering wand with them. If just one of those items does not have the connector attached, you will need to take the fitting off the one that *does* before you can join them. Then you will need to return the connector that is not now being used (but will be needed in the future for all of the other watering devices that have connectors) to a place where you will remember where it is when you next need it.

If your household is anything like mine, the connector ends up in a pocket (then through the wash), the kitchen junk drawer, or (our house's equivalent of a black hole) the basement workroom. When this connector is needed again, it has invariably gone into hiding, making it necessary to remove the connector from the device that you wish to attach. After all of this screwing and unscrewing, there are now two connectors that have been removed. These will float around the house, to be found again only when you are looking for something else.

Click-ons are a wonderful product; just be sure to buy one for every hose and watering device that you have, and a spare of each type (male and female) to keep in the garden shed.

SPRINKLERS

The only perfect sprinkler is a rain cloud; unfortunately you can't buy one anywhere. Given a lack of regular rain, we must make do with manufactured sprinklers, none of which give a completely even distribution of water. The oscillating fan sprinklers are probably the most familiar to people, and they offer the best coverage over a large patch of ground. There are many other types available, and the type that you buy will depend on the size and shape of garden you need to water.

In my experience with sprinklers, you get what you pay for. Inexpensive models seem to break, stick or clog quickly, and they are difficult to adjust with precision. Buy a good one if you can.

ESSENTIAL TOOLS

Sometimes I think that nothing wastes as much time as trying to make do with the wrong tool, be it in the garden or in the workshop. I speak from experience since I have, on many occasions, tried to unscrew something using a kitchen knife as a screwdriver (because I was too lazy to go down to the basement to get one) or cut a large limb with a small pair of pruners instead of a saw (ditto for the trip to the garden shed). Ridiculous, because it takes more time trying to work with the wrong tool, and the job is never done as well!

If there isn't much time to spend in the garden, there isn't time to mess around with the wrong tool. Planting a perennial that is in a one gallon pot takes forever if you are digging the hole and amending the soil with a trowel; a shovel accomplishes both jobs in a quarter of the time. Spend the time and money on the proper tools, and then make the effort to use the proper tool for the job.

There are generic types of most tools, and fancy made-to-last-a-lifetime models as well. Some of the more expensive tools are worth the money, especially if you end up using them frequently. But you don't have to buy the highend tools at first, or all at once. A spade from the local hardware store (or garage sale) will divide your perennials as well as a stainless steel model with a finely finished oak handle.

If I were to sink big bucks into any tool, it would be a pair of bypass pruners . . . in fact, I *did* sink big bucks into a pair of Felco® pruners and have never regretted it. I use those pruners every day at the garden center, and often at home. I overuse them (and sometimes abuse them) but they are still in great shape after three years of such treatment.

When you make time for garden work, you want your tools to be working when you need them. A broken tool, or one that doesn't work well, makes the task at hand more frustrating and time-consuming.

THE GARDEN SHED

I often refer to the garden shed, but I understand full well that not everyone has such a single-use building on their property. I am using it as a term for the area where the garden supplies are kept, be that a space in the garage, basement, back porch or a free-standing small building. Whenever possible, keep all of your tools and garden products in this area, making sure that any fertilizers, pesticides and other garden chemicals are put away out of a child's reach and sight.

Some garden chemicals should not be kept in places that get too hot or below freezing; check the label on any products that you do not immediately use for the manufacturers' recommendations. If there is any question, most companies print a telephone number on their packaging which a consumer can call for advice about the product. If all your garden products are stored in the original containers, you will have these numbers available if you need them. Original cartons are also saved so that the printed instructions may be consulted repeatedly, and the list of ingredients is handy in the event of an accident involving the product.

In addition to tools and chemical products, every garden storage area should have a large container to hold plant labels. If you are super organized (as I am *not*) you can start a separate container annually, labeled with the year. Whether this is an empty oatmeal box or a plastic flower pot is not important; it just needs to be a container that holds the label that comes attached to most plants when they are purchased.

Most plant labels contain information about that particular plant and what it needs to thrive. You might need to refer to that information a year or two down the road. Even tags containing only the name of the plant are worth keeping, since most people don't remember which color impatiens they bought the year before, even though they swore that they would.

If three identical shrubs are purchased, and one of them dies, you may want to replace it with an identical variety. I assure you that the employees of your local nursery will respond quite differently if you have the exact name of the plant that you need, instead of asking them to play twenty questions while trying to figure it out. Many people don't want to take the time to record all of this information in a garden journal, but it takes no time at all to toss the tags in a container. If this container is in the garden shed, it is easy to file the label when returning the tools that were used for planting.

THE TOP TEN TOOL LIST

I've cheated a bit on the ten essential tools list, in that on occasion I've combine two different, but related, tools together because they are so similar. There are many garden tools and gadgets available which can be loosely classified as being essential, helpful, or silly. Of the tools listed on the top ten list, there are only two that I think are nice to have, but I could do without them; they are the bulb auger and the loppers.

There are no lawn maintenance tools on the list. I know that caring for a lawn *is* gardening, but it is almost a subject in itself. (John Greenlee, author of the *Encyclopedia of Ornamental Grasses*, calls the lawn "America's favorite form of topiary.") Because "low-maintenance lawn" is almost a contradiction in terms, many gardeners hire a lawn care company to do the mowing, fertilizing, and other lawn chores, so that their garden time can be spent on the shrubs, trees and flower beds. If you care for your lawn yourself, a mower, fertilizer spreader and leaf rake are the basic tools that are needed.

TOP TEN ESSENTIAL TOOLS

1. *Bypass pruners.*

Pruners come in two styles, bypass and anvil. The blades of bypass pruners pass by each other, cutting the stem as they do so. Anvil pruners have a sharp blade that cuts the stem against a flat shelf; this style tends to mash the stem if they aren't super sharp. Most people who use pruners frequently get a good pair of the bypass style.

2. *Trowel.*

Available in several sizes, trowels are used for planting small plants, turning over small amounts of soil and amendments, transplanting tiny plants, and any other minor digging job. It is always nice to have a variety available. If you are the type of person who takes very good care of your tools and never misplaces them, then one of the expensive models will last you a lifetime. If you are apt to forget a tool in the garden now and then, or if you like to have a trowel stuck into the ground near every flower bed, get inexpensive ones and replace them every couple of years. If you have kids who help themselves to your tools, buy the cheapest ones on sale at the end of the season.

3. *Shovel and Spade.*

A shovel is the preferred tool for digging in the United States; in Britain they often use a garden spade. A shovel has a scooped blade, either squared-off or pointed. If I were to pick just one of these tools I would choose a pointed shovel with a straight shank (the part that holds the blade onto the handle) since it is the most versatile. A spade has a flat blade with a square, flat end. It is fine for digging straight-sided holes, edging, and chopping caked or packed earth. Buy a good quality shovel so that it won't break when you lift heavy loads with it, and choose a spade with a handle that suits your height.

4. *Folding pruning saw.*

These small saws are for use when pruning or trimming any branch or small tree trunk that is too big for your pruners. Because it folds, you can keep it in your pocket or belt-pouch when you garden, and it will be handy when it is needed.

5. *Leaf rake.*

Sometimes called a fan rake, the leaf rake is the one needed if you have any trees. It is also useful for clearing the area under shrubs, and for raking excess grass clippings off the lawn.

6. *Garden fork and hay fork.*

These are two separate tools, but both have a place in your garden shed. The garden fork has flat, sturdy tines and is made for digging up clumps of plants, loosening packed soil, and dividing perennials. The hay fork has round tines (sometimes many of them) and is used for sticking into and lifting piles of fibrous organic matter. Even if you live miles from the nearest haystack, the hay fork is the tool of choice for moving mulch and compost.

7. *Wheelbarrow or cart.*

Anyone who gardens on a small property will want a wheelbarrow, while those who tend large gardens will want a wheelbarrow *and* a garden cart. The barrow will go in small spaces (such as between plants) and will carry your fertilizer to the beds and the plant waste from the bed to the compost. The cart hauls larger, heavier loads, but needs a wider path and is not as maneuverable.

8. *Loppers.*

These are simply a larger pair of pruners with longer handles. They are necessary for anyone pruning fruit trees, or for those who want some extra reach when trimming shrubs. Like pruners, they are available in anvil and by pass styles, with the latter being preferable. If your budget is tight, buy the pruners and the folding saw, and leave the loppers for a time when you are feeling more flush.

9. *Bulb auger.*

This is a giant screw-device that fits into any electric drill. It makes such quick work of planting bulbs, that putting in a hundred daffodils on a Saturday afternoon is a pleasure. The auger itself is not expensive, but you do need the drill and a very long extension cord.

10. *Tank sprayer.*

Sooner or later, every gardener or home landscaper has to spray something on their property. Even those who have decided to stay away from heavy-duty pesticides and fungicides may need to use horticultural oil on a particularly severe insect infestation. Organic gardeners often want to give their vegetables a mid-summer foliar feeding with one of the fish and seaweed emulsion fertilizers.

Any concentrated garden product can be applied with a pump sprayer. Do not confuse a tank sprayer, which has a hand-pump to build up the pressure in the tank, with the hose sprayers that are sold for fertilizers. Hose sprayers are much too inaccurate to use with concentrated garden chemicals. Invest in a pressure pump sprayer; there are many small, lightweight models available for the home gardener.

GARDEN GLOVES

Maybe they aren't really tools, but I consider gloves as necessary as a trowel. They allow you to get your hands in the dirt to pull out weeds, push soil over newly planted seedlings, and handle rough plants and pots without cutting your skin. If gardening work hurts your skin it isn't possible to work as quickly or as well as it is with your hands protected.

Leather gloves are needed if garden work routinely involves work with thorny plants, but use fabric gloves for all other jobs. Fabric can be easily washed (buy them a bit large—most cotton gloves shrink) and most discount stores sell gloves for less than two dollars. I buy a bunch at the end of the season when they are on sale, so that when I lose one, or the thumb gets a hole in it, I still have a mate for the other glove.

LITTLE THINGS THAT HELP

When I started working at the garden center, I bought a pouch to hold my pruners, scissors, and sales book. Such pouches either slip onto your belt, or come with a waiststrap attached. I now put mine on whenever I work in the garden, and although it doesn't quite qualify as an essential item, I personally would never be without it.

I used to put my pruners, etc. in a basket that I took to the garden with me. But as I worked around the yard and garden I would either forget to move the basket with me, or my hands would be too full of plants, shovels, and garden products to hold the basket as well. Invariably I would need the pruners, only to realize that the pruners were in the basket, at the other end of the garden.

Now I slip on my pouch before I go into the garden. If, as I am working, I want to mark a particular perennial clump to remind me to divide it in the spring, I have the plastic labels and marker on me. When what seems like an especially good idea pops into my head as I'm working, I write it on a pad of paper. If I stumble on a self-seeded plant that I want to dig up and move elsewhere, I have a trowel right there in the pouch. And the tool that I use the most, my pruners, is never out of my reach.

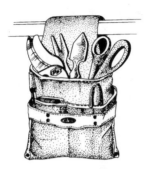

THE BELT POUCH AND WHAT TO PUT IN IT

Keep the following items in your belt pouch at all times, and put it on any time you go into the garden.

1. Pruners. Put your good pair in the pouch and keep the cheap pair in the junk drawer in the kitchen. There are holsters sold that hold pruners, but they don't hold all the other items that a pouch will.

2. Scissors. A sharp pair of scissors is handy for odd jobs such as shearing a heather plant, cutting twine, or removing a tag from a newly planted shrub.

3. A small trowel. Hunt for one that is small enough to go in your pouch, yet big enough to dig up a small plant. I also use a tiny, stainless steel trowel that is made for use in house plants. While not as handy as a small full-sized trowel, it is still quite useful.

4. Pen and paper. You never know when inspiration will strike, and I find that good ideas are most plentiful while working in the garden. A pad of paper and a pen allow me to capture these ideas before they float away. Writing down future

garden chores is helpful as well; while working in the garden I often see that a plant needs relocating or dividing, or realize that I need to grow several more of one plant or another in a particular spot. Making a note of these tasks helps them not to be forgotten.

5. Plastic plant labels and a permanent marker. In addition to writing myself a note about the clump that needs to be moved, I always mark the plant itself with a stiff plastic label. In the early spring, which is a great time to transplant and divide, many plants look the same. If I have marked the particular clump that needs some work, I won't have to spend time standing in the garden thinking "Is this the tall aster or the short one?" and wondering which plant to dig up.

6. Lip balm. You might prefer other personal items in your pouch, such as gum or a small container of sunscreen, but since nothing dries the lips like the sun and wind, the essential item for me is a tube of lip balm.

7. Twine or tie-up tape. It's not necessary to carry the whole roll or ball of twine, just a couple of yards. If you notice a plant that needs tying as you work, it isn't necessary to walk into the house or garage to get the twine.

8. Larger items. Some pouches are large enough to hold a cellular phone, portable tape player, or other large items. If you are expecting a call, having the phone on your hip beats plunging through the shrubbery looking for your basket!

The belt pouch is also convenient to put things in as you work—labels from packs and pots of plants that are being put into the garden, a flower from a plant that you want to identify, or some seedpods for another gardener. These pouches (available at garden centers) are washable, so every once in a while the whole thing can be cleaned before the seeds that you've saved start to sprout in the dirt and mulch that has fallen in!

STANDARD TOOLS YOU MAY OR MAY NOT NEED
There are two garden tools that used to be in everyone's shed or barn, but are not necessarily needed for the small property. Both are made for use

on bare soil. The hoe has been the king of weeding for centuries, probably, and is still useful if you have a vegetable garden that is planted in the traditional rows with bare soil in the walkways. No hand tool cleans these paths between rows as well as a hoe. Hoes are also handy for digging shallow trenches when planting rows of corn, gladiola corms or onion sets.

Many gardeners today plant smaller vegetable gardens, often in raised beds where the space is used more intensively. The close planting of plants eliminates the need for weeding paths, and even where there are spaces to walk, these are often heavily mulched.

Hand cultivators are also used for weeding, and many work well because their curved tines reach down into the soil and pull up the whole plant, roots and all. Like the hoe, this tool is most useful when weeding or turning the soil in bare beds, that is, gardens that are not mulched.

Using a hoe or cultivator on a mulched area will turn the mulch into the soil, which ruins the light-blocking, weed-smothering reasons you've placed the mulch on the garden in the first place. If a garden has a layer of mulch on it, there will be fewer weeds to deal with, and those that do appear are more easily pulled out because the mulch keeps the soil moist, which results in weeds with shallow root systems.

TOP TEN ESSENTIAL GARDEN TIPS TO SUCCESS

1. Add at least two inches of compost or composted manure to your garden and around permanent plantings every year.

2. Be careful not to over-fertilize, and never fertilize a thirsty plant. Water a wilted plant and let it recover before giving it any fertilizer.

3. Follow the directions on all garden products; read the directions and use the recommended concentrations when mixing fertilizers, fungicides and pesticides.

4. Buy disease-resistant plants whenever possible.

5. Give all plants the growing conditions that they will thrive in. Match plants with the required amounts of light, the right type of soil, and the necessary quantity of moisture.

6. Don't buy plants on impulse; find out how a plant will behave, and whether you have the right growing conditions for that plant *before* you bring it home.

7. Give all new plantings regular, good deep soakings for the first year after planting them; if you live in an area where the ground freezes, be sure to keep them watered right up until the time the ground is frozen.

8. Examine the site carefully before planting any plant, making sure there is room for it to grow. Do not plant shrubs or trees too close to a house, power lines, driveways, or each other. Imagine how it will fit that site when the plant is at its mature size; be sure that the plant won't be in the way or block a view.

9. Remember that the purpose of pruning is to improve a plant's appearance, not to control its size. Whenever possible, place plants in spots where they can grow to their full height. Prune to remove dead wood and crossed or misshapen branches, not to keep plants small.

10. Don't apply mulch too thickly or push it right up to the stems or trunk of the plant.

Q & A: PLANTING AND WATERING

Q. *When I asked an employee at a garden center why my neighbor's* Impatiens *were always taller than mine, he said that it was because they were spaced differently than mine when planted. What on earth was he talking about?*

A. Although there are varieties of *Impatiens* which grow taller than others, such as *I. balfouri* and *I. glandulifera*, the common varieties sold grow to 8 to 18 inches tall. *Impatiens* can be made to grow higher by placing them closer together. Most plants grow taller as they stretch toward the light. You might have noticed that a plant placed in part shade grows taller than the same plant in full sun. When *Impatiens* are planted far apart from each other (and other plants) they receive more light on all parts of the plant so they tend to grow shorter and fuller. Plants placed very close together shade each other, so they grow taller as they each reach for the light. Those desiring short, round mounds of *Impatiens* should place plants at least twelve inches apart. If you want these plants to grow tall, plant them in part shade, about six inches apart.

Q. *How often should I water my garden?*

A. It would be much more convenient for both of us if there were a hard and fast rule, but such is not the case. Knowing how often your garden needs water is a matter of experience, observation and common sense. Some plants, such as most herbs and the "Mediterranean group" (like lavender and rosemary), prefer a dryer soil, which is why it is better to group such plants in beds where they can all be allowed to get dry. As discussed in the section on watering, an inch of rain penetrates sandy soils differently than loam or clay soils, and weather conditions influence how long a soil remains damp.

Once you know the amount of water the plants in your garden require, you can determine how frequently the garden needs a supplemental sprinkling by observing the soil. If the soil is dry three or four inches below the surface, watering is probably in order. Gardens require less water in cooler seasons because less moisture is lost through evaporation. In hot weather, water is lost as it evaporates from the soil, and plants are taking more out of the earth to replace that lost through the foliage. Transpiration increases in hot weather, so the plant loses more moisture through the pores (called stomata) in the leaves.

As you tend your gardens over time you will become more familiar with how long it takes for your soil to dry out, and which plants in your garden tend to have a bigger thirst than others. Some herbaceous plants will routinely have wilted leaves on a very hot day, since moisture is lost through the leaves faster than the plant can bring it up from the roots. This does not necessarily mean that the soil is dry; always check the dirt before watering.

There are other plants which will generally be fine in hot weather although they will wilt more quickly if the soil starts to get too dry. If you notice which plants are the first in your locale to wilt in a period of drought, those plants will tell you when it is time to water.

In my area many people grow *Hydrangea macrophylla*, which is a very thirsty plant. When the bigleaf hydrangeas in the neighborhood start to wilt, I know that we haven't had enough rainfall and all the gardens should be watered even though the other plants don't show signs of water-stress yet. Notice which plant is the first to wilt in your area, and use it like the canary in the coal mine.

LOW MAINTENANCE PLANTING

These three words, low maintenance planting, seem destined to become *the* gardening buzz words at the turn of the century. People are busier than ever before, yet gardening continues to grow in popularity. Instead of becoming one more thing that people have less time to do (like cooking), gardening is something that people have decided to include in an already packed schedule.

I believe that this is because the gardening process, and the exposure to plants, is nourishing to those who do it. When we tend gardens, we gain more than beautifully landscaped yards. But although people on some level recognize that gardening offers renewal along with beautiful gardens, they are still interested in doing it as efficiently as possible.

LOW MAINTENANCE DOES NOT MEAN NO-WORK.
The only way to have a landscape that requires no work at all is to let Mother Nature do all your gardening for you, accepting whatever she wants to plant (or not plant) as well as the changes over time. There is nothing wrong with this approach, and perhaps more people should try it. But most of us want at least some say in how our property looks; once we begin to make these choices, some initial work and upkeep is *always* involved.

There are ways to cut down on the maintenance that our gardens require. The previous chapters have detailed how our cultural practices affect the amount of maintenance the garden needs. We have discussed how proper planting, watering and soil preparation can reduce garden work in the future.

Even if we amend soil, plant and mulch in an ideal fashion, our selection of plants will ultimately determine whether the garden requires a little maintenance, or constant involvement.

LOW MAINTENANCE IS NOT "ONE SIZE FITS ALL"

Before any plants are chosen, it is important to decide what low maintenance means to you. This will be partly determined for you by the head gardener herself, Mother Nature. If you live in zone 5, planting a plant that is hardy to zone 6 will not be low maintenance. (See the glossary for an explanation of planting zones.) In order to get the zone 6 plant to make it through the winter it would need to be surrounded with extra protection such as a wire bin filled with hay. You might choose to dig the plant up every fall and move it to a pot in the garage or into a cold frame. Any of this is fine, and people who love plants and are interested in pushing the limits or growing a favorite flower may choose to do it every year. But it is *not* low-maintenance planting. Low-maintenance gardening starts with a knowledge of the limits given to us by the natural world.

Aside from the average temperature range, every gardener also works with other conditions that can't be changed. The soil that is native in your area, the normal rainfall and the distribution of that rain throughout the year, as well as other factors such as wind and wildlife have an effect on your gardens. Because it is always less trouble to work with nature, the first step in determining what low maintenance means to you is to look carefully at what conditions can not be changed.

Knowing what nature has provided, you need next to consider your own temperament. One person might hate lawn mowing while another finds it to be good exercise. Some people hate to weed, while others dislike staking floppy plants. Decide which chores are your least favorites, and choose plants that do not need such care.

If you are uncertain which garden work you like or dislike, choose plants that need a minimum of involvement and start small. You might plant six annuals the first year, only to discover that they do better if the spent flowers are removed. (This is called dead-heading, a term that reminds anyone of my generation of donning tie-dye and following The Grateful Dead around the country.) If you decide that you hate dead-heading, the small number of annuals that you planted will be easy to ignore, and other plants can be chosen in the future.

In addition to considering your likes and dislikes, focus too on your physical abilities. If you have little upper body strength, for example, digging up large clumps of perennials might be difficult, so it would be wise to choose plants that don't need frequent digging and dividing. Those with arthritis might find the operation of a pair of pruning shears to be painful, so they should choose shrubs that require a minimum of yearly pruning.

CHOOSING A PLANT

You know what realtors say about buying a business; there are three things to consider and they are location, location, and location. This applies to plants as well. Where a plant is placed can determine if it is truly a low-maintenance plant or not. If a single person buys a white carpet for his or her living room it might not be a high maintenance floor covering; that same carpet put in a household containing five children and two dogs would be a completely different story.

And so it is with plants; in one location a plant might be trouble-free, but the same plant might require a great deal of maintenance in another spot. A tall oriental lily, for example, will support itself in a protected spot in the garden but would need staking if planted in a windy area.

Notice the particular conditions on your property before you even go to look at plants. Consider the following checklist:

1. Sun or shade. Notice *over an entire day* if the area is in full sun, filtered sun, or shade.
2. Wet or dry soil. Is the earth continually wet or dry, or does it change throughout the season? Are there any other special characteristics of the soil that might determine how a plant will grow? (This would include soil texture, depth, and pH.)
3. Exposure. Decide if the area is sheltered by the house or other plants, or exposed to normally prevailing winds and weather.
4. Other plantings. What else is planted in the area, and how will all the plants grow and mesh over time? Will other plants grow up and shade the area in the next three years, for example, or are you planning to remove that dying pine tree next season?

MICROCLIMATES

Every property has spots that are warmer, cooler, or better drained than the rest of the area. Knowing that the snow always melts away from a particular side of the house first tells you that it is a bit warmer there than other spots in your yard. If the sun hits one area longer than another, plants that love a good deal of heat and sunshine will do well in that location.

Growing conditions can vary over a very small distance, even two or three feet. When I lived in New York's Hudson Valley I had a row of peonies, all divisions of a plant which was given to me by a friend. These five plants were placed in a row on the east side of my house, and every year the plant on the corner grew bigger and bloomed a full two weeks earlier than the others. Once I decided to pay attention to what conditions might be different for this plant, (but not the one three feet away from it) I noticed that the house shaded the other four plants from about one o'clock on. Because the larger peony was on the corner of the house, it received sunshine for two hours longer in the afternoon, and this made all the difference.

Microclimates are created by the placement of houses and trees in relation to the sun and prevailing winds. The topography of your property—whether it is flat or has hills and valleys—will create special conditions for both drainage and moisture, and spring and fall temperatures. If a plant is chosen that suits that particular microclimate it will be a healthier plant, and therefore less work for the gardener.

READ THE LABELS ON A PLANT, OR ASK IF IT WILL GROW WELL IN YOUR LOCATION.

Once you are familiar with the growing conditions on your property, plants can be chosen that match those conditions. Look at the labels on plants and compare the listed growing requirements to the location on your property. Although "full sun" usually means sunshine from early morning until sundown, most plants that require full sun will grow well if they receive 6 to 8 hours of sunlight which includes the strongest period in mid-day. Part sun is at least four hours of sunshine; this can be all at one time of day, or periodic sunshine throughout the day. Plants that receive no direct sunlight at all are growing in full shade.

WHY SOME PLANTS ARE MORE WORK

After evaluating your site, you will know if you are looking for plants that are drought-tolerant or moisture-loving, and if they will need to grow in sun or shade. This is the time to consider the attributes of the plants themselves, and believe me, not all plants are created equal. Many plants need continuing involvement from the gardener in order to look their best. This is not to say that they are bad plants; they just take more work to keep them beautiful.

As the merits of a particular plant are being considered, remember that what might be a low-maintenance plant for one person is another's nightmare. Someone with a small garden would find that an invasive plant takes a great deal of time and effort to control; in a garden where it can fill the entire space allowed, however, the same plant would be another gardener's dream.

Some of the characteristics that qualify a plant to be called "low-maintenance" are disease resistance, drought tolerance, insect or wildlife resistance, and an attractive appearance through at least three seasons. Plants that do not need frequent tending, such as those that don't need to be divided, staked, or deadheaded every year, can also be considered to be work-saving plants.

HIGH VS. LOW-MAINTENANCE GARDENS

A comparison of two fictional gardens will illustrate the difference between high-maintenance and low. The first gardener plants a narrow bed with delphiniums and roses, a *lovely* combination of blues and pinks in early summer, and again in the fall. But in order to keep this garden looking its best, a great deal of attention must be paid to the plants.

Both delphiniums and roses are prone to insect and fungal attacks, so the leaves and new shoots are frequently inspected to see if treatment is needed. Delphinium blossoms are heavy, so they must be staked for support. It is important to stake the plants just as the flower stalks bud up, since at this point the stalks have grown long enough to be approaching their mature height, but they haven't yet gotten heavy enough to bend or break the stem. Once they are in full bloom, it is almost guaranteed that a stem-breaking wind or rain will arrive between the time you noticed that they are heavy, and when you make it out to the garden with the stakes and tie-ups.

Since both plants like their roots moist, they must be watered frequently, but because they are also prone to fungal attacks, care must be taken to water without getting much water on the leaves. Too much water around the stems will rot the delphiniums, so the soil should be well-drained and care should be taken not to water them *too* much.

The roses must be sprayed with a horticultural oil and baking soda spray to retard mildew and blackspot. Because this spray works prophylactically, it must be applied to the plant before it shows any sign of disease, and application must continue every two weeks throughout the summer. In order to encourage a repeat bloom in the fall, both plants need to be deadheaded when the first flowering begins to drop off.

In addition to the standard perennial garden maintenance, new delphiniums will need to be purchased and planted frequently, because they tend to be short-lived plants.

If this same gardener planted this bed with *Euphorbia polychroma* (Cushion spurge) and *Sedum* 'Autumn Joy,' however, the situation would be completely different. Both of these plants are sturdy and do not need staking, and each of them has foliage that is attractive from spring through late fall. The *Euphorbia* blooms over a long period in the spring and early summer, often repeating the bloom if dead-headed. The sedum blooms from late summer into fall, and it is also lovely over an extended bloom time. Sedum's seedheads look appealing through early winter.

Neither the sedum or the cushion spurge are prone to insect attacks or diseases, and each are praised for drought tolerance. Although the size of the clumps increases, these plants do not spread throughout the garden; they only need to be divided every five years or so to maintain vigorous plants.

In addition to the standard perennial garden maintenance, the only attention required through the summer is the dead-heading of the cushion spurge after it is through blooming.

Although these two fictional gardens give a simplified example (it is possible to plant a garden using just two plants, but most people choose to use more), they illustrate the importance of plant selection, and how it influences the time that is spent on garden chores.

INVASIVE PLANTS

Plants that spread very quickly are a problem unless they are used as a ground cover. The ground cover that fills in a spot quickly can be a problem plant if placed in the wrong location. Most people think of very low-growing plants as ground covers, but any plant that covers an area rapidly can be used in this way. Planting a fast-growing perennial is a good low-maintenance way to fill a bed, especially if that plant is attractive at least three seasons of the year. Such beds should be contained in some way. Once the plants grow into their allotted space, they will continue on into your shrub border, vegetable patch, and the neighbor's yard. Invasive plants must be sited with care.

Gardeners should go to great lengths to keep these plants out of a perennial bed; anything that quickly crowds out adjacent plant moves from being a low-maintenance ground cover to a pest. Often referred to in the catalogs as a "vigorous grower," an invasive plant grown in a perennial bed will need to be dug and divided every two years. Some plants that spread quickly, such as *Monarda* (Bee balm), have shallow roots, which make it easier to remove the growth that gets out of bounds. Others, *Lysimachia clethroides* (Gooseneck loosestrife) for example, not only spread rapidly but have dense roots that are difficult to dig and divide.

Occasionally gardeners will feel overrun by a plant that is not, perhaps, considered a pest, but because it grows so enthusiastically in their garden they feel as if they are under siege. I know a man who is currently battling comfrey in this manner. It is easy for me to sympathize with him; I was given a shoot of a comfrey plant once. It was an especially hectic time for me, so I placed the root, still in its plastic bag, in the fern bed where it could remain in the shade until I got around to planting it. Two weeks went by before I looked at the comfrey again. I feared that it might have died during that time, which shows how little I knew about this plant. Not only was it alive, it had taken root (through the plastic bag) in the fern bed. "Oh . . . a hardy plant" I thought, "let me move you to your permanent home." Foolish me. That comfrey had rooted in the fern bed and in the fern bed it was determined to stay.

I took a trowel to that shoot and transplanted it, only to watch in amazement as a new plant sprang to life in the fern bed. I dug it out with a shovel. It came back, healthier than ever. It spread its huge leaves, looking completely out of place, and covering the ferns next to it so thoroughly that even they—shade lovers that they are—got too little light, turned yellow, and died.

I continued to dig up the roots and snip off new shoots, to no avail; I was still battling that comfrey three years later when our waterline broke and needed to be replaced. The line came into the house under the fern bed, so that entire area had to be excavated with a backhoe. Fearful of saving the comfrey with the ferns, I had the backhoe operator move the top two feet of soil—ferns, comfrey, and all—to a pile on the edge of the woods.

Most people grieve when a thriving garden has to be removed for household repairs. All I thought was "Good! At last I will be rid of that comfrey!" When the pipe was repaired and the four foot deep hole was filled in, I planted new ferns in the bed and watched them get established with great satisfaction . . . until three months later when, yes, the comfrey poked up in more or less the same spot.

If you see a plant that has completely taken over someone's garden, be aware that if you plant it on your own property it will, in all likelihood, be just as enthusiastic. Be cautious of any plant that is said to be vigorous. Ask a knowledgeable garden center employee, or another gardener, if a plant which you are considering is invasive.

PLANTS THAT CAN BE INVASIVE:
APPROACH WITH CAUTION!

Aegopodium podagraria (Goutweed/Bishop's weed)
Ajuga reptans (Bugleweed)
Achillea—most varieties (Yarrow)
Anemone tomentosa (Grape-leaf anemone)
Artemisia ludoviciana (Silver King artemisia)
Ceratositigma plumbaginoides (Leadwort/Plumbago)
Coreopsis verticillata (Threadleaf coreopsis)
Eupatorium coelestinum (Hardy ageratum)
Filipendula rubra (Meadowsweet)
Fragaria x frel "Pink Panda" (Pink Panda strawberry)
Galium odoratum (Sweet woodruff)
Helianthus—most varieties (Perennial sunflower)
Houttuynia cordata (Chameleon plant)
Hypericum calycinum (St. John's wort)
Lamium maculatum (Spotted dead nettle)
Leonurus cardiaca (Motherwort)
Lysimachia clethroides (Gooseneck loosestrife)
Lysimachia nummularia (Creeping Jenny)
Lysimachia punctata (Circle flower)
Macleaya cordata (Plume poppy)
Mazus reptans (Mazus)
Mentha—most varieties (Mint)
Monarda didyma (Bee balm)
Oenothera speciosa (Evening primrose)
Parthenocissus quinquefolia (Virginia creeper)
Physalis alkekengi (Chinese lantern)
Physotegia virginiana (Obedient plant)
Polygonum cuspidatum (Mexican bamboo)
Thermopsis montana (Mountain thermopsis)
Tradescantia x andersoniana (Spiderwort)
Valeriana officinalis (Garden heliotrope)
Viola labradorica (Labrador violet)

Invasive plants can often be spotted while still in the pot. If you see a perennial in the garden center that is growing out of the drainage holes in the bottom of the container, know that the plant will be just as vigorous, and more so, in your garden.

DROUGHT-TOLERANT PLANTS

In many areas of the country, low maintenance means drought tolerant. Watering the plants takes time and money; even if there is an automatic sprinkler system, it must be monitored and maintained, and the cost of municipal water is on the rise. Even if your water supply is plentiful and cheap, planting drought-tolerant plants allows you to skip frequent watering, so you are able to turn your attention elsewhere.

Drought-tolerant plants are often tough in other ways as well; these plants are survivors. Group them together to simplify watering. Place drought-tolerant plants in the especially dry areas of your yard, or grow them in sections that are inconvenient to water. Land that is next to a concrete or asphalt street is often hot and dry, so these plants are particularly appropriate in such a location.

Plants that can stand being dry often have tap roots which grow deeply into the soil. Drought tolerant does *not* mean that they can live completely without water, and some take longer dry spells than others. Until their roots are developed, new plants in the garden should receive regular watering whether they are drought tolerant or not.

DROUGHT-TOLERANT PLANTS

Annuals
Brachycome iberidifolia (Swan River daisy)
Cleome pungens (Cleome or Spiderflower)
Cosmos bipinnatus (Cosmos)
Gaillardia pulchella (Blanket flower)
Gazania rigens (Treasure flower)
Gomphrena globosa (Globe amaranth)
Helianthus annuus (Sunflower)
Pelargonium hybrids (Geraniums)
Perilla frutescens "crispa" (Beefsteak Plant)
Portulaca grandiflora (Portulaca)
Portulaca oleracea (Purslane)
Rudbeckia hirta (Black-eyed Susan)

Perennials
Achillea hybrids (Yarrow) zones 3-10
Agave spp. (Century plant) zones 9-10, some species 8-10
Ajuga reptans (Bugleweed) zones 3-10

Ameria maritima (Sea thrift) zones 4–8
Arabis procurrens (Rockcress) zones 3–9
Artemisia spp. (Artemisia) zones 5–10
Asclepias tuberosa (Butterfly weed) zones 3–10
Aster divaricatus (White wood aster) zones3–9
Aster novi-angliae (New England aster) zones 4–9
Aster tataricus (Tartarian aster) zones 5–9
Aurinia saxatilis (Basket of gold) zones 4–10
Baptisia australis (False Blue indigo) zones 3–10
Bletilla striata (Bletilla) zones 5–10
Cassia marilandica (Wild Senna) zone 3–10
Chrysanthemum nipponicum (Nippon Daisy) zones 5–10
Convallaria majalis (Lily-of-the-Valley) zones 3–9
Coreopsis grandiflora (Tickseed) zones 5–10
Coreopsis verticillata (Threadleaf coreopsis) zones 3–10
Echinacea purpurea (Purple coneflower) zones 3–10
Echinops spp. (Globe thistle) zones 3–10
Eringium hybrids (Sea holly) zones 5–10
Euphorbia spp. (Spurge) zones 3–10 depending on variety
Gaillardia grandifloria (Blanket flower) zones 3–10
Geranium macrorrhizum (Bigroot cranesbill) zones 3–10
Helianthus spp. (Sunflower) zones 3–10 depending on variety
Hemerocallis hybrids (Daylily) zones 3–10
Hieracium lanatum (Hawkweed) zones 3–10
Kniphofia uvaria (Red-Hot poker) zones 6–10
Lamium maculatum (Dead nettle) zones 3–10
Lavandula angustifolia (Lavender) zones 5–8
Liatris spp. (Blazing Star) zones 3–10
Liriope muscari (Lilyturf) zones 5–10
Lychnis chalcedonica (Maltese cross) zones 3–10
Lychnis coronaria (Rose campion) zones 3–10
Malva moschata (Musk mallow) zones 3–10
Oenothera missourensis (Missouri primrose) zones 4–10
Perovskia atriplicifolia (Russian sage) zones 5–10
Phlox subulata (Moss phlox) zones 4–9
Potentilla sp. (Cinquefoil) zones 5–10
Rudbeckia spp. (Black-eyed Susan) zones 3–10 depending on variety
Salvia officinalis and varieties (Sage) zones 5-10
Santolina spp. (Santolina) zones 6–8
Saponaria ocymoides (Soapwort) zones 2–10
Sedum spp. (Stonecrop/Sedum) zones 4–10

Solidago hybrida (Goldenrod) zones 3–10
Thymus spp. (Thyme) zones 4–10
Verbascum spp. (Mullein) zones 5–10
Yucca filamentosa (Adam's needle) zones 4–10
Most ornamental grasses (zones vary according to variety)

DROUGHT-TOLERANT SHRUBS AND TREES

Berberis spp. (Barberry) zones 3 or 4–8, depending on variety
Buddleia alternifolia (Fountain buddleia) zones 5–9
Cedrus deodara (Deodar cedar) zones 7–9
Cotinus coggygria (Smokebush) zones 5–8
Cupressus spp. (Cypress) zones 7–9, Leyland zones 6–10
Ceanothus americanus (New Jersey tea) zones 8–10
Ficus microcarpa (Indian laurel fig) zones 9–10
Geijera parviflora (Geijera) zones 9–10
Ginko biloba (Ginko) zones 3–9
Ilex cornuta 'Burfordi' (Burford holly) zones 7–9
Juniperus spp. (Junipers) zones 3–9 depending on variety
Koelreuteria paniculata (Golden-rain Tree) zones 5–9
Lavendula spp. (Lavender) zones 5–8
Ligustrum spp. (Privet Amur) zones 3–7, other evergreen 7–10
Myrica pennsylvanica (Bayberry) zones 3–8
Nerium oleander (Oleander) zones 8–10
Pinus ponderosa (Ponderosa pine) zones 3–6
Pinus sylvestris (Scotch pine) zones 2–8
Pinus thunbergiana (Japanese Black pine) zones 5–8
Pittosporum tobira (Pittosporum) zones 8–10
Rhodotypos scandens (Jetbead) zones 4–8
Rosa rugosa (Beach rose) zones 2–7
Teucrium spp. (Germander) zones 5–8
Tilia tomentosa (Silver linden) zones 4–7
Viburnum lantana (Wayfaring tree viburnum) zones 3–7

INSECT AND DISEASE RESISTANCE

Some plants are more prone to disease than others, and some seem to be on every insect's "top ten most delicious meals" list. Naturally, these are not low-maintenance plants. If your area is filled with slugs, it would be foolish to plant something like *Hostas*, which are particularly attractive to slugs. If you don't want to be bothered with spraying a plant to control fungi, don't plant tea roses. If a plant catches your eye, in the garden center or in another gardener's yard, ask what kind of care the plant needs, or if it is prone to any particular problems.

There are plants that are for the most part care-free that will occasionally be attacked by bugs or some type of fungus. This is especially true in years when the weather is abnormal in one way or another. The previous summer was cool where I live, and the sky was often cloudy. Although we did not get much rain over most of the summer, the clouds did sprinkle a smattering of water every few days, which kept the plants' leaves damp. As a result, it was a fungus festival on Cape Cod, with more fungi on the plants then there were tourists on the beach. A landscaper I know shook his head muttering, "There's mildew on the cosmos! We *never* see mildew on cosmos!"

I report this not because I think you are so interested in keeping track of eastern Massachusetts weather, but because it illustrates that in certain years even the most disease-free plants can have problems. Other plants are routinely prone to insects or fungi, which does not necessarily make them undesirable, as long as the gardener is willing to do what it takes to deal with those problems. See Chapter 5 for a list of plants that are basically trouble-free.

PROPPING THEM UP
Gardeners who love perennials can spend all kinds of time and money on keeping the plants in their gardens upright. Some plants cascade in a "vase shape," ultimately sending their tops (and often their flowers) in a graceful arc that ends right in the mud. Others have tall but fragile stems, prone to breaking off in a strong breeze. Some perennials have been bred to have such large flowers that they become impossibly heavy in good weather, and downright weighty when soaked with rain.

For the low-maintenance gardener there are three ways to deal with plants you do not want to support. The first is to not put them in your garden. Don't plant top heavy or floppy plants if you are not interested in spending the time to prop them up. If a plant that is already growing on your property needs staking, dig it up and give it to someone else. Always ask if a plant might need staking before you buy it. This is especially important for those who garden in windy areas.

The second way of quickly dealing with floppy or fragile plants is to plant them in a location that accepts their natural ways. If a floppy plant is placed at the edge of a wall, for example, that tendency to flop becomes a cascade which softens the wall's edges. That same wall can also be used to prop up any plant that is growing by its base. Plants that need support can be put next to others that have very stiff stems (see companion plants in Chapter 6) or placed next to a fence that they can lean against as they grow.

When I lived near Gloucester, Massachusetts I would often drive by a house that planted a long row of cosmos every summer. Cosmos are famous for needing support, and often the support that seems more than adequate in June proves to be far too flimsy when the plants are at their peak in September. At this North Shore location the gardener planted these plants right next to a white picket fence, however, so that as the cosmos got taller their stems and branches grew next to, and into, the slats. The gardener may have tucked a stem under the cross piece or around one of the pickets now and then, but it was basically a low-maintenance way to grow cosmos.

The third way to deal with floppy plants is to learn to love them just as they are. When a plant flops over, it flops over. If it covers or shades the plant next to it, well . . . so it covers and shades the plant next to it. This is the Alfred E. Newman school of gardening: "What . . . me worry?"

If a plant falls over when it is in full bloom, pick the flower and enjoy it indoors. I take this approach with peonies. When the peonies are in full bloom, and there is rain in the forecast, I don't worry that the water-soaked flowers will soon be in the mud. Instead, I head outdoors and pick every single blossom that is open. The remaining buds don't fall down when it rains, and the peonies perfume my house for days afterwards.

Occasionally, of course, we see a plant that is so beautiful that we must have it in our gardens, "low maintenance" be damned. This is the reason so many people fuss with *Delphiniums* . . . we extend ourselves for some plants just because we love them. If you find yourself with a plant that needs staking against your best intentions, try to make the staking as attractive or unobtrusive as possible.

I saw my favorite example of artistic staking in Joe Eck and Whyne Winterrowd's garden in Vermont. They had built stick cages for some of their plants that were beautiful garden ornaments in themselves. Five long straight sticks had been placed in the ground around the plant and tied together at the top. Some smaller and pliable twigs were twined around and around basket style, creating a woven section about two inches wide near the bottom and another around the top. The rustic result was both elegant and functional.

If you find that you have succumbed to a flop-around plant, consider making the support an ornament in your garden. The staking can suit the style of your plantings, thus adding to the garden instead of screaming "support."

One of these ways of dealing with floppy plants will best suit your own personality; if you know that the site of a fallen plant will bother you every time you see it, don't put the plant in your garden. Most gardeners use all three approaches depending on the plant and the location. Some flopping might be acceptable in the cottage garden, for example, but not in the border along the driveway. Decide which approach sounds most comfortable for you, and then just say no to staking!

PLANTS THAT ARE HIGH MAINTENANCE OR PRONE TO PROBLEMS

Anthemis tinctoria (Golden marguerite). Short lived, requires frequent dividing, may need staking, and may be prone to mildew

Chrysanthemum x supurbum (Shasta daisy). Needs dividing every 3 years, may need support or pinching to control height

Cosmos Usually requires staking

Dahlia Prone to fungal, bacterial, & insect problems; require staking

Delphiniums Usually requires staking, short lived

Iris hybrids (Bearded iris). Prone to iris borer or rot of the rhizomes

Lupinus hybrids (Lupine). Short lived plants

Lychnis coronaria (Rose campion). Short lived, prolific self-seeder

Monarda (Bee balm). Prone to mildew

Phlox. Prone to mildew and other fungi

Rosa (Roses, especially hybrid teas). Mildew, rust, blackspot

Teadescantia x andersoniana (Spiderwort) Spreads rapidly so needs frequent division, foliage flops after blooming

Zinnias. Prone to mildew and leaf spot

DEAD-HEADING AND DIVIDING PERENNIALS

Perennials are often seen as a way to have flowers in the garden without the work of planting annuals every year. While it is true that perennials do not have to be planted in the spring, they are *not* necessarily a low-maintenance alternative. Some perennials, such as Shasta daisies, need to be divided every third year in order to keep them looking their best. Others need to be dead-headed when they are finished blooming, either to stimulate production of flowers, prevent their seeds from forming or sowing, or to remove the top of a plant that looks unkempt after blossoming.

Although most perennials will require some dividing, dead-heading, or other mid-season touchups, there are perennials that do not require such attention on a frequent basis. A list of such plants follows.

PERENNIALS THAT DO NOT NEED FREQUENT DIVIDING

Aconitum spp. (Monkshoood) Zones 2–9

Adenophora spp. (Ladybells) Zones 3–9

Alchemilla mollis (Lady's mantle) Zones 3–9

Amsonia tabernaemontana (Willow amsonia) Zones 3–9

Aruncus dioicus (Goatsbeard) Zones 3–9

Asclepias tuberosa (Butterfly weed) Zones 3–10

Astilbe spp. (Astilbe) Zones 4–8

Baptisia australis (Blue false indigo) Zones 3–10

Brunnera macrophylla (Siberian bugloss) Zones 3–10

Centranthus ruber (Red Valerian) Zones 4–10

Chelone spp. (Turtlehead) Zones 3–9

Cimicifuga racemosa (Black Snakeroot) Zones 3–10

Dicentra spectablis (Bleeding heart) Zones 3–10

Epimedium spp. (Bishop's hat) Zones 4–9

Euphorbia polychroma (Cushion spurge) Zones 3–9

Geranium spp. (Cranesbill geranium) Zones 3–10 according to variety

Hemerocallis spp. (Daylily) Zones 3–10

Hosta spp. and hybrids (Hostas) Zones 3–9

Limonium latifolium (Sea lavender) Zones 3–10

Paeonia spp. (Peony) Zones 3–10

Platycodon grandiflorus (Balloon flower) Zones 3–10

Rudbeckia fulgida 'Goldstrum' (Black-eyed Susan) Zones 3–10

Sedum spectabile and 'Autumn Joy' (Showy stonecrop) Zones 4–10

Thermopsis spp. (False lupine) Zones 3–10

Yucca filamentosa (Adam's needle) Zones 4–10

Some perennials do not need dead-heading because the flowers dry up and fall off in such a way that the involvement of the gardener is just not needed. Others form attractive seedheads that are desirable on their own merit because they keep the garden interesting into the fall or winter. Plants that bloom late in the season usually look attractive as they grow all summer, and do not require dead-heading because by the time the flowers go by, it is well into autumn.

Perennial gardeners should be aware that deadheading is *always* their choice. Many plants like lady's mantle, will bloom a second time if promptly deadheaded, have attractive seeds on the spent flower stalks which do not have to be removed.

PERENNIALS THAT DO NOT NEED DEADHEADING
attractive seeds and stalks

Achillea millefolium (Yarrow) Zones 3–8
Aconitum spp. (Monkshood) Zones 2–9
Belamcanda chinensis (Blackberry lily) Zones 5–10 *
Centranthus ruber (Red Valerian) Zones 4–8
Coreopsis verticillata 'Moonbeam' (Threadleaf Coreopsis)
    Zones 3–9
Dicentra eximia (Fringed Bleeding heart) Zones 3–9
Dicentra spectablis (Bleeding heart) Zones 3–10
Echinacea purpurea (Purple coneflower) Zones 3–8 *
Filipendula rubra (Meadowsweet) Zones 3–9 *
Gaura lindheimeri (Gaura) Zones 5–9
Heuchera hybrids (Coral bells) Zones 3–10 *
Iris sibirica (Siberian Iris) Zones 4–10 *
Knautia macedonica (Knautia) Zones 5–10
Liatris spp. (Blazing star) Zones 3–10 *
Linum perenne (Blue flax) Zones 5–10
Perovskia atriplicifolia (Russian sage) Zones 5–10
Rudbeckia fulgida 'Goldstrum' (Black-eyed Susan) Zones 3–
    10 *
Sedum spectabile and 'Autumn Joy' (Showy stonecrop) Zones
    4–10 *

LOW-MAINTENANCE PRUNING
Most shrubs require some touch-up pruning, even if it is only the removal of the dead wood in the spring. (See the section on pruning in

Chapter 6) There are plants that require more cleanup than others, however, so anyone who does not especially love the pruning of shrubs should be sure to plant things that do not require much of this type of maintenance.

Much of the pruning home landscapers end up doing is done to control the size of a plant. Ideally, the only pruning required of most shrubs should be the removal of deadwood and awkwardly placed branches. If the ultimate mature size of a shrub is considered when it is planted, the gardener will avoid having to spend time pruning a plant in order to keep it from covering the living room windows.

A NATURAL-SHAPED SHRUB TAKES LESS TIME
If a plant is allowed to grow to its natural shape, the gardener will not have to spend as much time on pruning. Planting shrubs that are then sheared into balls and cubes is high-maintenance landscaping. Some people start shearing their shrubs out of desperation to control the size of the plants, others do so simply because they haven't learned any other way to prune, and some simply like the way sheared bushes look.

Home landscapers may have started clipping their bushes back or shearing them into shapes simply because they assumed that the shrubs *needed* to be trimmed in that manner. Some pruning can revitalize growth or improve appearance, but both plant and gardener will be happier if the shrub is permitted to grow to its natural size and shape.

SHRUBS THAT KEEP A NATURAL SHAPE
WITHOUT MUCH PRUNING

Abelia x Grandiflora (Glossy abelia) Zones 6–9
Acuba japonica (Japanese acuba) Zones 7–10
Berberis julianae (Wintergreen barberry) Zones 5–8
Callicarpa dichotoma (Beauty berry) Zones 5–8
Calycanthus floridus (Sweet shrub) Zones 4–9
Camellia japonica (Camelia) Zones 7–10
Enkianthus campanulatus (Redvein enkianthus) Zones 5–7
Euonymus alata 'Compacta' (Burning bush) Zones 4–8
Hydrangea quercifolia (Oakleaf Hydrangea) Zones 5–9
Ilex crenata 'Compacta" (Japanese holly) Zones 5–7
Juniperus conferta 'Blue Pacific' (Juniper) Zones 5–9
Kolkwitzia amabilis (Beauty bush) Zones 4–8
Lonicera morrowii (Morrow honeysuckle) Zones 4–8

Mahonia aquifloium (Oregon hollygrape) Zones 5–8

Myrica pennsylvanica (Bayberry) Zones 2–7

Rhododendron 'P.J.M." (PJM Rhody) Zones 6–8

Rhododendron Yakushimanum hybrids (Yak Rhodys) Zones 6–8

Rhododendrons (many varieties of Azaleas) generally Zones 5–8

Skimmia japonica (Japanese Skimmia) Zones 6–8

Spirea spp. (Spirea, many varieties) Zones 3–8

FOUNDATION PLANTS: THE CHALLENGE OF KEEPING THEM SMALL

Every home landscaper can save endless hours of garden maintenance simply by choosing foundation plants with care. Next time you are out driving, make it a point to notice how many foundation plants have outgrown their space. There are many homeowners who shear their shrubs to keep them contained, but still the plants bulge under windows and against each other. Scores more have given up the fight and are living in darkened rooms, because the bushes have grown over the windows. Every day people squeeze down their front steps because these plants have grown over half of the front porch.

Finally, long past the time when these problems should have been dealt with, the homeowner has to remove this large plant and its huge root system. If the plant is too large to transplant, a mature shrub must be sacrificed simply because it was mistakenly put in that location years ago.

When choosing plants for foundation plantings, remember that the mature height given on most plant tags is an estimate. Plants seldom reach a given height and just stop growing; you can count on your plants getting larger than the height given on a tag, so plan accordingly.

Although plants can be pruned or sheared to control their size, it isn't a good idea, and for anyone who does not have much time to garden, this practice is out and out folly. Pruning a plant to keep it small usually ruins its shape. Even those who are committed to seeing their shrubs retain their natural shape often end up with green meatballs when the plant has been repeatedly pruned to control the size.

Keeping plants small through pruning leads to more and more work, since most plants respond to pruning by putting on a spurt of new growth. If the plant loses leaves to pruning, it naturally figures that it needs to grow *more* in order to have the leaves needed for photosynthesis. Pruning stimulates new growth, which means more pruning.

A FOUNDATION PLANTING IS NOT A POLICE LINE UP

Many years ago most houses were built with full basements, and these basements were usually made of concrete which was left bare for a foot or more above the ground level. Shrubs were planted to hide the space between the ground and the siding on the house. Today, many houses do not have that gap of bare foundation, but it still seems to be the custom to plant a row of bushes all along the outside of a house.

When choosing foundation plantings consider that there doesn't need to be a row of shrubs one after another. A small grouping at the corner of the house, and something next to the walk or the door might be more effective than the traditional line up of the usual suspects. Don't be quick to overplant; more can always be added later, but too many shrubs soon crowd each other and need to be pruned for size-control.

Those who feel uncertain how small groupings would look might want to try taking a color picture of the side of the house that is to be landscaped. Have some 8 1/2" x 11" enlargements of the photo made on a black and white copy machine. These can be used to sketch on, or tracing paper can be placed on to of them to draw different ideas. You could also cut out shrub shapes from construction paper and place them on your picture to see how they might best be arranged. (This is the poor person's version of computer-aided landscape design.) Be sure to use small shapes to see how they will look when planted, as well as large ones that represent how they will look in eight to ten years. It is important to keep in mind that even though you may plan for a tree or shrub growing bigger over the nex ten years, that plant will not stop growing at the end of that time. Most mature plants slow their rate of growth as they get older, but never stop growing completely.

LOW-GROWING SHRUBS FOR FOUNDATION PLANTINGS

Abelia x grandiflora 'Edward Goucher' (Glossy Abelia). 5' x 5' Zones 6–9

Berberis x chenaultii (Chenault barberry). 4' x 4' Zones 5–8

Berberis thunbergii (Japanese barberry). 'Crimson Pygmy'– 2' x 5'; 'Globe,' 'Nana,' or 'Compacta' 2' x 3'; 'Minor'–4' x 5' Zones 4–8

Chamaecyparis obtusa 'Nana' (Hinoki false cypress). 3' x 3' Zones 4–8

Cotoneaster apiculatus (Cranberry cotoneaster). 3' x 4' Zones 4–7

Deutzia gracilis (Slender Deutzia). 2' to 4' x 4' Zones 4-8

Euonymus alatus 'Rudy Haag' (Burning bush). 4' x 4' Zones 4–8

Fothergilla x gardenii (Dwarf Fothergilla). 3' x 4' Zones 5–8

Ilex glabra 'Nordic' (Dwarf inkberry). 4' x 4' Zones 4–9

Itea virginica 'Henry's Garnet' (Virginia sweetspire). 4' x 6' Zones 4–9

Juniperus conferta 'Blue Pacific' (Shore juniper). 1 1/2' x 5' Zones 6–9

Juniperus procumbens 'Nana' (Japanese garden juniper). 2' x 5' Zones 4–9

Juniperus scopulorum 'Lakewood Globe' (Rocky Mountain juniper). 5' x 6' Zones 3–7

Mahonia aquifolium 'Compactum' (Oregon grapeholly). 3' x 5' Zones 5–8

Myrica gale (Sweetgale). 4' x 5' Zones 1–6

Nandina domestica 'Harbor Dwarf' (Heavenly Bamboo). 3' x 4' Zones 6–9

Pinus mugho 'Mops' and 'Slavinii' (Mugho pine). 3' x 3-5' Zones 2–7

Rhododendron many including low-growing azaleas and R. kiusianum, R. P.J.M. 'Victor', R. 'Purple Gem', and R. yakusimanum. Hardiness varies according to variety.

Sarcococca hookerana (Sweetbox) 4' x 6' Zones 6–8

Skimmia japonica (Japanese skimmia). 4' x 4' Zones 6–8

Spiraea x bumalda 'Goldflame.' 3' x 4' Zones 3–8

Spiraea japonica several dwarf varieties. Size according to variety Zones 3–8

Taxus cuspidata 'Densa' (Japanese yew). 4' x 8' Zones 4–7

Taxus x media (Anglo-japanese yew). Several small varieties Zones 4–7

Thuja occidentalis 'Little Gem' and 'Little Giant' (Globe arborvitae). 3' x 5' Zones 2–8

Yucca filamentosa and *glauca* (Yucca). 3' x 3' Zones 4–9

Having considered the location and the desired plant habits and characteristics, you can last, but never least, consider what you love. Since anything that you plant will require *some* maintenance, it will seem like less work if you love the plant. Practicality demands that you choose plants that will do well in your area as well as those which suit your temperament and physical abilities; but once the choices have been narrowed by these criteria, choose plants that make your heart sing.

Q & A: LOW MAINTENANCE PLANTING

Q. *Once I get the plants in the ground I often forget their names. How can I label my plants without cluttering my garden with tags and nameplates?*

A. It is a problem. I have been known to draw a blank on the names of the most common plants, so rest assured that you are not alone. It is nice to be able to give the name of a particular plant when asked, or to have a record of what is planted in case you want to get more. But short of having every plant wear a "Hello, My Name Is . . ." tag, there are ways to keep track of what is planted in our gardens.

I keep a book in which I write the names of plants that are new to my garden. I usually take the tag from a plant and stick it in a basket reserved for this purpose. Once a few labels accumulate I write the information, along with the location of the plant, in a notebook. Hopefully I get around to this before the plant dies. It is a less than perfect system, and I admit that the labels will occasionally float around on a kitchen counter, bathroom sink, or telephone table before making their way to the basket. Last spring my husband picked up a plant label and said, "These things are all over the house!"

Keeping names written in a book works for me, but I have a small property and a fairly good memory for the locations of plants I am growing. Many people would rather have the plant itself labeled, because they are most often in the garden when they need the information. Others have such a wide variety of plants, or several cultivars of one type of plant, that the notebook system would never keep track of which plant is where.

The best in-garden labeling method I know of is to get

some fairly stiff plastic labels and a permanent marker. Write the name on the label and stick it to one side of the plant, sliding it into the ground until just an inch or so sticks above the surface into the mulch. The mulch hides the label but it is easy to find when you move the mulch away. Using a stiff plastic is better than using the thin printed tags that often come in a plant you have purchased; these tags are so flimsy that they degrade and break quickly.

Sticking the label into the ground not only hides it from your view, but it keeps it from fading in the sun. It is frustrating to label plants, only to take up the label the following year and find it so faded that it is indecipherable.

If the labels are consistently placed in the same location in relation to the plant, they are more easily located when you want to read them. Those with little or no mulch on their gardens may want to routinely place the labels behind the plants, so the small end that sticks out of the ground will be hidden by the foliage.

Anodized aluminum labels can be used instead of plastic, and a soft pencil writes well on this surface. These can be buried next to the plants just like plastic. Pencils produce writing that is remarkably legible for years, although those will poor eyesight may find that labels filled in with black marker are easier to read.

I think it is comforting to know that all gardeners occasionally struggle with names slipping from memory; when someone asks the name of a particular plant, there is nothing wrong with responding "I have *no* idea." In his column in the October '96 issue of *BBC Gardeners' World*, Alan Titchmarsh tells of a longtime gardener who perhaps had the best way of dealing with a lapse in memory. If he drew a blank when asked the name of a plant he would cough and say "Ah, that's *Avantaclewia*. Yes. *Avantaclewia damdifino*. Tricky blighter."

Q.   *I have a broadleaf evergreen shrub growing under some oak trees that ends up looking brown and ratty by spring. If I wrap it in burlap it stays nice, but I hate to go to all of that trouble every year. Is there anything else I can do?*

A.   Shade-loving broadleaf evergreens can get sunscald in the winter when the nearby deciduous trees have shed their leaves. In icy regions, the reflection of the sun off the snow can be particularly damaging. Most plants recover nicely by early summer, but they look like hell until the new growth covers the old.

Wrapping the shrub will prevent sunscald as well as providing some protection from drying winter winds, but as you state, such tasks are time-consuming and the wrapped shrubs are less than attractive. The more low-maintenance alternative would be to move this shrub to a place where it would be shaded in the winter as well as in the summer. A needled evergreen tree, a fence, or the shady side of the house would all keep the winter sun away from the sensitive leaves.

5

STARTING FROM SCRATCH

The beginning of any new venture is both exhilarating and overwhelming. Anyone new to gardening can feel swamped by the incredible wealth of information, plants and products available. Those who are facing the process of landscaping newly built homes, or creating gardens where none have previously grown, might feel daunted by the enormous task ahead, even if they have gardened in the past. It is helpful to remember that just as any journey is taken step by step, a garden is created plant by plant.

Before any plants are considered, however, considering the basics of location and design will start you off in a positive direction. Even those who are starting with an empty lot are not starting with a completely blank slate; all gardens are partially planned by the location from the very beginning. If a property is small and surrounded by large trees, for example, it is unlikely that there will be enough direct sun for a cottage style garden filled with sun-loving annuals and perennials. Before making any decision about a new garden, look closely at what is already there.

TOP TEN CONSIDERATIONS WHEN LOCATING NEW GARDEN BEDS

1. Where is the sun? How much light does the area get in the morning,

afternoon, and early evening? Remember that the sun hits an area differently in the early spring than it does in midsummer.

2. Where is the water? Even if the garden you plant will eventually be drought-tolerant, it will need regular watering when it is getting established, or perhaps in periods of long drought. If there isn't a convenient source of water nearby, consider installing a built-in system before the garden is in place.

3. What is the soil like? Find out if it is sand, loam, or clay. Is the location wet or dry? How much organic matter does the soil need? All gardens need some organic amendments, but some need it more than others.

4. Are the areas you want to plant accessible to the equipment that is needed to maintain it? Can you get a wheelbarrow, garden cart, and lawnmower where they are needed, or are rocks, steps or tree roots in the way?

5. Where are the trees now? Where do trees need to be planted, and how large will they grow? Will this area be shaded by trees in the next ten years? Where do you need to plant trees or shrubs to provide privacy?

6. Which areas of the yard do the windows look out to? Be sure that all your plantings are not placed against the house, where they will not be visible from indoors.

7. What is happening on my neighbors' property? If the neighbors have trees that will shade your yard over time, or if they have planted perennial or shrubs that will spread into your property, this could affect where you place a garden.

8. How does the change in seasons affect each area? If snow or rain falls off of the roof, for example, it might mash small or delicate plants into the ground. The sun might be fine against the house in the winter, but the same area might be very hot in the summer. It is common for people to look at property in the spring, when they are interested in planting their gardens, and conclude that the area is sunny. As deciduous trees develop, however, the area becomes shaded. Consider what happens to your property over time.

9. Is it important to open up or preserve a view? Trees might be thinned to reveal a view, and new trees may be needed to frame, but not block, a vista or other beautiful scenery.

10. What are your concerns about safety? Shrubs that are near the end of a driveway might need to stay small so that they won't obstruct the driver's vision when backing out. Tall shrubs and trees may provide privacy, but those who leave a house unoccupied for long periods of time may want the neighbors to be able to see what is happening while they are gone. Be sure that the growing landscape will not block walkways, trip visitors, or whack the UPS driver in the head!

WHERE DO YOU SPEND YOUR TIME?

Gardens should be placed in areas where you are going to get the most enjoyment out of them. People lead busy lives, and not everyone can spend an hour sitting on a garden bench with a cup of tea. So although it is a fine idea to place a seat in your garden for that one Sunday a month when (weather permitting) you *do* sit there, plan to make the garden available for your enjoyment on a daily basis.

If there is a window that you look out of every day, consider siting the garden so that you will view it from this window. If there is a deck or porch where you tend to sit in the morning or evening, plan to place a garden in sight of this area. If you walk up a particular walkway every day on your way to and from your car, it makes sense to place a garden where you can enjoy it from this path. Gardens should be planted for the maximum enjoyment of the gardener, not the neighbors.

ANNUALS, PERENNIALS, SHRUBS OR TREES ?

After studying your location, the next decision is what type of plants to put in your garden. Annuals must be planted every year in the late spring, but they usually bloom all summer and many require little care other than occasional watering. When annuals are planted, the gardener is free to plant a different choice of flowers every year. Annuals are cleared from beds when they finish their bloom period, or die from cold temperatures; periodic clearing of a bed makes it easier to amend soil.

Perennial plants grow each year from the same root systems. Because of this, they don't have to knock themselves out to produce great quantities of seed, so most perennials don't bloom all summer. They do provide a changing kaleidoscope of colors and patterns, however, as one flowering plant finishes its bloom period only to be replaced by another.

Although there are perennials that require quite a bit of attention to keep them blooming well, some perennials require little maintenance except the addition of organic matter and watering in times of severe drought. Watching a perennial plant poke out of the soil, grow tall, and come into bloom each year is a deeply satisfying way to celebrate the return and passing of a season.

The majority of shrubs require even less maintenance than perennials, yet they too return every year. Blooming shrubs provide flowers and greenery, without some of the chores (dead-heading and dividing) associated with perennial plants. Many shrubs provide visual interest in the garden throughout the year, either because they are evergreen, or because their stems are interesting in color or texture.

Trees provide privacy, cooling shade, graceful forms and often, flowers and fruits. Like shrubs, most trees require little maintenance while lending their beauty to yards and gardens year-round.

Most home landscapers choose to place a selection of all of these plants in their yards and gardens, thus taking advantage of all that the plant world has to offer. Gardens are more visually pleasing when they are planted with a variety of sizes, shapes, colors and textures.

Even those who decide that they don't want to bother with any perennial bed chores will often plant a clump of *Hosta* and *Epimedium* in the shade, or a group of daylilies near the driveway. Perennials may supply colorful blossoms or groundcovering greenery, filling spots that surround shrubs or covering places where taller plants would prove inconvenient.

How all these plants work together is partly determined by the location and partly by some basics of garden design. Whether you choose to plant mostly annuals, perennials or shrubs and trees, the results will be more visually pleasing if you take the following top ten into consideration.

TOP TEN GARDEN DESIGN ESSENTIALS

1. *Informal plantings require less maintenance.* Staggering plants instead of planting in straight rows, planting in drifts and curves, and

leaving plants to grow into their natural shapes result in less time spent keeping things neat.

2. *Place your plants in groups and plant odd numbers.* A group of three or five is more pleasing to the eye than a group of two or four.

3. *Take your garden maintenance into account.* Leave room for the lawnmower, garden cart or wheelbarrow to easily reach all areas. If the size of your property allows it, plan a space where a truck can enter to dump a load of mulch or compost and a work area to temporarily hold such piles.

4. *Plant a variety of foliage colors, but don't get carried away.* A perennial or shrub that has variegated leaves is lovely when planted among others with green foliage. A garden filled with many variegated plants looks too busy, however. The same principle applies to plants with purple or reddish foliage.

5. *Avoid a mix of garden styles, especially if you have a small yard.* It looks confusing to see an oriental style pond near an English-type cottage garden. Decide on a style that suits you then use several types of plants for variety within that basic scheme.

6. *Repeating certain plants or colors throughout your property will tie things together.* This does not mean that all of the beds should have a single plant used as groundcover around them, say, but planting a few patches of that groundcover in different parts of your property can visually unite several separate areas. Space these clumps of plants irregularly, unless your garden is formal in style. Placing two groups of the same perennial near each other, for example, and then using a third cluster of the same plant some distance away will look better than if the plants are spaced equidistant from each other.

7. *Don't fill a garden with single plants of many varieties.* A larger stand of three different perennials is more effective than a garden filled with twenty different plants, no matter how lovely. Bigger groups make more of an impact. An assortment of heights, shapes, colors and textures will provide the needed contrast. Although some shrubs in a mixed shrub border can be one of a kind, planting others in groups of three will showcase the singles and unite the border.

8. *Be sure that every area contains something which looks good in all seasons.* Evergreens and deciduous plants with interesting bark provide winter interest in areas where the winter is cold; warmer parts of the country can plant "winter flowers" for color at this time. Blooming bulbs give color in the early spring, and many shrubs, trees and even perennials have bright, colorful foliage in the fall. Plant perennials that bloom in different months, and include a few annuals for continual summer color.

9. *Breaking a small area into two or three separate sections can make a modest property seem bigger.* Dividing the yard into separate "rooms," and creating paths and entries that afford a glimpse of the space beyond, create the illusion of greater space. Using fences, arbors, shrub borders, terraces or stone walls to divide a small space creates a structure which looks appealing in all seasons.

10. *Allow for about 40% non-landscaped area.* This percentage can be planted in lawn, or it could be a manmade, flat space such as a patio, decking, or stone and brick paths. Such places are not only desirable areas for walking, sitting, and children's games, but they serve to "frame" the gardens and provide some visual contrast.

THE WISDOM OF STARTING SMALL

Novice gardeners, or those starting out on a new property, are prone to catching a severe case of garden-greed. We want the long, sweeping borders that are pictured in the magazines, and as long as we are gardening, why not some raised beds for vegetables, some fruit trees, an herb garden and an annual cutting bed? A grape arbor is a must, along with a rose garden, a water garden and some topiary shaped like the grandchildren!

I exaggerate, of course, but it *is* very easy to get carried away when gardens are being planned. Remember that new beds and plants can always be added later, but taking them away isn't as easy—or exciting—as putting them in place. Worse even then scaling down is the daily sight of gardens and landscaping that need attention. Gardens are supposed to bring beauty and pleasure to peoples' lives, not large doses of guilt and regret.

By starting small, the home landscaper is able to grow into the role of gardener gracefully. Once he/she has gone through a year with a small flower bed and a shrub border, there will be a realistic, base of knowledge about the amount time gardening takes, and which tasks are most pleasurable to the individual. Gardeners are then better able to plan for expansion because they know what they have time to maintain and what type of chores they prefer to do.

DEVELOP A LONG-RANGE PLAN

Another reason for starting small is to give yourself the time to dream. In the rush to get every area of your property planted, it is possible to find yourself locked into plants and arrangements that will later seem boring, unmanageable, or unsuitable. But starting small does not mean that you can't have a grand plan in your mind or on paper. Allow time to let the garden grow in your mind for awhile before it is planted in the ground.

Planning a garden begins with a camera and a pad of paper. The camera is for taking before and after shots, as well as providing pictures of how your property looks in all seasons. As you look at the lovely catalogs and garden magazines in January, it is very helpful, for instance, to have a picture of how your yard looks in June. Gardens, like puppies, have a way of growing more quickly than we realize so it is nice to have a record of how different they looked a mere three years ago.

Once the entire area has been photographed, you can measure the places that are scheduled for planting or possible change. Use these photos and measurements to draw plans on paper. Sketch in the plants that are already in place. Those who struggle with perspective and in-scale drawings might want to use the technique suggested in the discussion of foundation plants (Chapter 4).

When drawing top-view plans or side-view sketches, always draw shrubs and trees at or near their mature size. The finished garden will not look like your drawings when the plants are first installed, but you will be saving yourself a great deal of work down the road.

START ON A SHORT-RANGE PLAN

Once you are happy with a plan, identify those items that should be installed first. Large, permanent fixtures such as patios, decks, fences and in-ground sprinklers need to be in place before plants are placed in the ground. If the plan calls for the planting of many shrubs or trees, it makes sense to get some of these started the first year. Decide which are the most important and which ones can wait.

When there are aspects of the plan that you are not convinced about, wait to begin work on that area. If you are new to gardening, it is probably wise to delay any large installation of plants, be it a perennial border or backyard pond garden. Look at your plan and see if there is a way to gain experience with the type of plants you want to grow before you commit to a large planting. Many a gardener (myself included) has *thought* that a large area planted with a particular perennial would be lovely, only to discover a year or two later that the plant didn't measure up to the description in the plant catalog.

If a long shrub border is desired, for example, you might want to start by planting three sections of that border, leaving the rest to be filled in once you know which plants grow well and look best in that area. The same approach can be used for perennial beds as well. If the property contains three areas that will be planted with mixed groups of shade lovers, you might start by planting either the smallest space, or the area that will be seen most frequently.

Planting parts of a garden over a two or three year period allows you to spread out both the time and money spent, and makes it possible to gain experience with the plants before committing the entire garden space to them. If the choices that were planted in one bed prove to be less then wonderful, the plan for remaining areas can be altered the following year, keeping in mind, of course, that first year plantings *never* look the same as mature plants.

GETTING THERE IS HALF THE FUN

As those who love to travel know, planning the journey is half of the fun. The trip itself may need to be confined to a two-week vacation period, but the research and decision-making can bring pleasure for three months in advance. So it is with gardening. View your garden plans as an opportunity to dream, not as an item on the "things to get done" list.

Just as established gardens provide the satisfying beauty of mature plants and lush landscapes, new gardens bring gifts as well. An unplanted garden is a feast of possibilities! When you look at your three small shrubs, freshly planted and surrounded by mulch, take some of the same pleasure in their newness as you do in the newness of a baby.

CANVAS YOUR LOCAL NEIGHBORHOOD

Anyone new to gardening has two excellent local places for research. Libraries often have a good collection of gardening books and magazines, and these are especially helpful for novice gardeners who want to "test-drive" a publication before laying down money for one of their own.

Aside from the library, however, a great deal of information can be had simply by opening your eyes and ears in the neighborhood. Take a walk around the area where you live, and notice what people have planted.

Walking is better than driving for this activity, since a slow-moving car with a driver who is intently scrutinizing the area may be mistaken for a burglar canvassing the neighborhood . . . "Officer, I swear I was only looking at the *shrubbery!*"

Notice which plants grow well in your area, and take note of those you find attractive. If you are friendly with your neighbors, ask them if there are any special problems for gardeners in that locale. Ask if the gardens in the neighborhood are often visited by rabbits, deer or other wildlife, for example, or if there are invasive weeds that you should be aware of. Most avid gardeners are happy to share their experiences with plants that do well for them; be sure to tap into this source of information in your area.

TEMPORARY PARKING

Asking an avid gardener about plants often leads to generous offers. "Would you like some?" is often the response when a new gardener asks about a particular plant. Most perennials increase the size of their clumps, making it possible to divide an admired plant and give a piece away. Many plants scatter seeds around the garden, and a fair number of these germinate; gardeners hate to waste such self-seeded plants, so they often leave the seedlings, waiting for an opportunity to transplant them or give them away.

The new gardener is in a bind when someone is willing to be generous with their plants. The bed may not be ready to receive this plant, or the gardener may not be sure that this is really the plant that should go in that location. We have all heard not to look a gift horse in the mouth, however, so what should the novice gardener do? This is one of the many times a nursery area comes in handy, and any gardener who has enough space should include such a place on their property.

The nursery area is a small piece of land where the soil has been turned, amended, and mulched for direct planting, or made suitable to hold a collection of plants in pots. It is a place where clumps donated by other gardeners can be temporarily parked until planting. Placing plants in this area also gives the gardener time to evaluate both plant and garden; if it seems that this may not be the best plant for the job, so to speak, then it can be given to someone else.

PARKING PLANTS IN THE GROUND VS. PARKING THEM IN POTS

Placing plants directly in the ground has some advantages over putting them into pots. Plants in containers need to be checked on a daily basis, but plants that are temporarily planted can be ignored to some degree. This could even become your "Charles Darwin Memorial Nursery" in that you will be able to test which plants will do well with the care that they are apt to receive in the future. Survival of the fittest.

The natural world did not anticipate container gardens when gene pools were developed however. Few plants are bred to be hardy when they are potted and ignored. Because containers dry out quickly, those who put plants into pots will need to check them daily, and perhaps water them at that time. In very hot, sunny climates potted plants may need watering twice in one day.

The nursery area can also be used to grow small plants to mature size. If plants are started from seeds or cuttings, they need an area to grow where larger plants won't overwhelm them. The nursery bed is ideal for this purpose.

Gardeners may find that they need to remove a plant from one area of the garden, but have no place to move it to at that time. Other plants may not be growing well, yet the gardener is unwilling to immediately banish them from the property. The nursery bed is the ideal spot to temporarily park these plants.

Nursery plots are most convenient if they are located near a utility area; having it near the piles of compost and mulch, garden shed, and a water source is handy. Ideally, the nursery bed should be half in the sun, and half in part shade, so plants can be placed in the light they will grow best in. Realistically though, few of us have properties where everything—even the utility area—is ideally located and set up. We speak of the ideals for the sake of those who do, and so the rest of us can dream.

SHOPPING FOR PLANTS

Once you have decided which plants should go in your gardens, it is time to shop. If possible, buy your plants locally, so that you can lay actual eyes on them before they are purchased. Plants purchased by mail tend to be small, and it is impossible to choose the healthiest one. Mail order plants are important to gardeners, however, because many more varieties are available from catalogs than are sold in local garden centers. If a plant is not available from growers in your area, then by all means order it from one of the many fine catalogs.

When the plant you have decided to purchase is available locally, look for the healthiest one available. It should be well-rooted in its pot, and have compact, healthy growth. Always choose the healthiest plant, not necessarily the one that is in bloom.

Look for plants that are not wilted. When plants wilt they are *be-*

yond thirsty, and this is stressful to a plant. Just living in a pot is stressful because there is no room to spread roots, and the soil dries quickly. Buy plants from a store that recognizes the value of keeping the stock watered regularly.

If the plant that you want to purchase has a few holes or spots on the leaves, should you buy it anyway? The answer to this partly depends on the type of plant, and the extent of the damage. Shrubs and perennials in nurseries are often watered at night using overhead sprinkler systems. It is difficult to water hundreds of pots when the customers are around them during the day. But having their leaves constantly doused in the night may cause leaf spot fungi on some plants. If the growing tips of these plants look healthy, and the plant is otherwise in good shape, the plant will probably recover with no ill effects.

Damaged leaves may be removed if they are few in number. When most of the leaves are spotted, removing them would be harmful to the plant, since its leaves are important as it gets established in its new home. It is better to remove such leaves from the garden after they have dropped from the plant in the fall. Cleaning leaves with leaf spot out of the garden helps prevent the spread of the same fungus the following year.

Any perennial or shrub with severe case of fungus should be avoided unless you are certain that the plant will recover. You will need to use your judgment with annuals as well; sometimes even the healthiest plant will have a leaf with a spot or two. I once got some *Nicotiana* which had been in the six-pack too long; they all looked stunted and spotted. I was sure they would recover because the growing tips looked good, and sure enough, in two weeks they were two feet tall and blooming. Part of this assuredness depends on experience with plants, and part of it is instinct I suppose. The oft mentioned green thumb. Those who are uncertain of the color of their thumbs should avoid all but the healthiest looking plants.

BASICALLY TROUBLE-FREE PLANTS
TO PLEASE ALL GARDENERS

Annuals
Ageratum spp. (Floss flower) Plant in full sun; blooms all
summer. Get the tall variety (if you can find it) because it is
pretty in the garden and as a cut flower.
Begonia semperflorens cultorum (Wax begonia) Nice in sun
or part shade; attractive foliage in green or bronze. Flowers
all season with no need to dead-head.

Impatiens spp. (Impatiens) Another name for this queen of the shade is 'busy lizzie,' but I have *never* heard it called that. Best in part sun or filtered shade.

Portulaca spp. (Moss rose) Plant these bright-flowering annuals close together for the best effect. They like bright sun and well-drained soil, and are nice when massed in a wide, low container.

Salvia spp. (Salvia) This annual prefers full sun and will reward you with blossoms all summer. Dead-head if you get around to it, otherwise just enjoy.

Tagetes spp. (Marigold) They are drought-tolerant, like full sun, and will grow in the worst of soils, bless them. All this and a choice of colors of blossoms and size of plants . . . how can it be summer without just a few? A favorite for Cub Scouts and Brownies to start in paper cups and then plant into the garden.

Perennials

Alchemilla mollis (Lady's mantle). This long-blooming perennial flowers in the spring and grows well in sun or shade. When dead-headed it often blooms a second time, but even without added blossoms the attractive foliage makes it a necessity in my garden. Lady's mantle likes a good, rich soil and is a knockout when planted with *Heuchera* 'Ruby Veil.' Zones 3-9.

Coreopsis verticillata (Threadleaf Coreopsis 'Moonbeam'). I admit that I had to remove the pink variety of this coreopsis from my garden because it was just too enthusiastic (invasive), but 'Moonbeam' and 'Zagreb' are not quite so rambunctious. They bloom for a long time in midsummer and are drought-tolerant. Rabbits have a fondness for the foliage, so don't plant these if Thumper lives nearby. Zones 3–10.

Dicentra spectabilis (Bleeding heart). The old-fashioned spring bloomer no garden should be without, even if the foliage does disappear in midsummer. Plant it in sun or part shade where later blooming plants such as asters or *Chelone* (turtlehead) will cover the dormant bleeding heart. Zones 3-10.

Euphorbia polychroma (Spurge). This plant has so much to recommend it I hardly know where to start! Drought-tolerant, tidy and long-lived, it is covered with bright greenish-yellow flowers in the spring. It combines nicely with Siberian iris and purple tulips. The only disadvantage of Euphorbias is that their sap can sometimes irritate the skin. (Wear gloves and grow it anyway!) Zones 3–9.

Echinacea purpurea (Purple coneflower). A care-free flower which blooms in mid to late summer. Coneflowers like full sun, and make nice cut flowers. The seedheads look attractive in the fall and will self-seed around the garden although not in a pesky way. Zones 3–10.

Hemerocallis 'Stella d'Oro' (Stella d'Oro daylily). All daylilies are long-lived and easy to grow in sun or part shade. 'Stella d'Oro' is especially popular because it will bloom repeatedly until fall, although this is best accomplished if the spent flowers are promptly removed. Stella's golden-yellow flowers are only 18–24" high, making it a good plant for the front of the border or for small gardens. Zones 3–10.

Heuchera species and hybrids (Coral bells). Coral bells are an old favorite, but many new hybrids with colored foliage are introduced every year. My current favorite is 'Ruby Veil,' which has burgundy/red leaves which combine well with the greens of other foliage. All coral bells make good cut flowers (they bloom in late spring) and the dried flower stalks look good on the plant or in bouquets; a plus for those who don't have the time or inclination to deadhead. Plant *Heuchera* in sun or part shade. Zones 3–10.

Liatris spp. (Gayfeather). A native American plant that prefers well-drained soil and a sunny location. It will not do well in soil that is wet over the winter months. Gayfeathers make good cut flowers, and the stalks of dried flowers are attractive to both gardeners and birds, so don't be too quick to dead-head them. Blooms midsummer. Zones 3–10.

Perovskia atriplicifolia (Russian sage). Plant Russian sage in a group, or among other fall bloomers such as the white-flowering *Boltonia*, because it makes an airy, blue cloud when in bloom. Cut the old stalks down to three or four inches in late fall or early spring before new foliage buds out. *Perovskia* likes good drainage, is drought-tolerant, and blooms over an extended period from midsummer into fall. Zones 5-10.

Platycodon grandiflorus (Balloon flower). Balloon flowers come in purples, blues, pinks and white, and grow well in sun or part shade. They bloom in mid- to late summer, and the flowers in bud delight children and adults alike. A nice plant. Zones 3-10.

Pulmonaria saccharata (Lungwort). *Pulmonarias* bloom in the spring, often with flowers that start as one color and turn to another as they age. The real reason to grow this shade-loving plant is the foliage, however, which is usually a dark, rich green, often with assorted white spots or other variegations. Many cultivars available with a variety of foliage types. Nice with ferns, *Epimediums* and impatiens in the shade. Zones 3-9.

Rudbeckia fulgida "Goldsturm" (Black-eyed Susan). This cultivar of the black-eyed Susan is deservedly the most popular of the *Rudbeckias*. It is attractive all season, coming into flower in late summer. The flower stalks are stiff enough to hold themselves up and provide flowers for cutting. The central cones are attractive even when covered with the first frost. This plant does spread (although not aggressively) so it might not be the first choice for a small garden with other plants. Zones 3-10

Salvia x supurba (Hybrid Sage). These hybrid sages make lovely companions with yellow flowers such as *Coreopsis* 'Moonbeam.' The flower bracts are purple so the plant appears to be in bloom long after the blue flowers are gone. Dead-heading, or cutting the plant back by a third, will usually stimulate a second blossoming. Zones 5-10.

Scabiosa caucasica (Pincushion flower). A good choice for the front or mid-border, and create the best show when planted in a large group. The hybrids 'Butterfly Blue' and 'Butterfly Pink' are shorter varieties, known for their extended blooming. Yes, they do attract butterflies. Zones 3–10.

Sedum "Autumn Joy" (Autumn Joy Sedum). If you only have room for one plant, this is it. A.J. sedum looks classy from the moment it pops its shoots out of the soil in the spring until the snow covers the seed heads in winter. The foliage is a pale green which looks good with other perennials or shrubs, and the flower heads change from pale green to whitish to pink over the season. After the deep pink passes in the fall, the seedheads turn a dark rust color. Sedum Autumn Joy looks great with ornamental grasses such as the *Penstemon alopecuroides* (Fountain Grass); combine these two with some spring-blooming bulbs such as narcissus, and a low-growing plant with attractive foliage such as Ajuga reptans atropurpurea, and you have a handsome, low-maintenance flower bed. Zones 4–10.

Shrubs

Abelia x Grandiflora (Glossy abelia). Abelias bloom all season on new growth; the flowers are dainty and pale pink, so the shrub is never covered with knock-your-socks-off color such as an azalea would be, but is charming nonetheless. This shrub can be evergreen in warmer zones and is pretty much pest-free. It should only be planted by those who can keep their hands off the shears because it becomes a twiggy, ugly mass if pruned into unnatural shapes. Zones 6–9.

Calycanthus floridus (Carolina allspice). A very adaptable plant which is not fussy about soil; it will grow in sun or shade. This shrub will grow to 6'-9' with an equal width, and the flowers smell sweet and fruity. Worth seeking out. Zones 5-9.

Hydrangea quercifolia (Oakleaf hydrangea). My favorite shrub for shade and part shade, the oakleaf hydrangea is handsome in foliage all through the growing season. White flowers brighten shady spots in midsummer, and the burgundy/rust foliage is beautiful in the fall. The species grows 5' to 6' in height, and just as wide, but smaller cultivars are available. Zones 5-9.

Ilex crenata 'Compacta' (Japanese holly). Although the name is 'Compacta,' this Japanese holly can grow to six feet tall. Unless you love topiary, resist the urge to shear it into a cube, and enjoy its natural shape and fine, evergreen foliage. Zones 5–7.

Ilex x meserveae (Meserve hybrid hollies). These hollies need acid soil, and you must plant a male and female in order to have berries on the female. (Hide the male near the back of the property since they tend to be scrawny at best.) 'Blue Princess' and 'Blue Girl' are lovely and hardy to around -10°F, and will be pollinated by 'Blue Prince.' A related variety, 'Nellie Stevens,' is equally hardy and nice, and said by Michael Dirr to be one of the best for growing in the south. Prune before the winter holidays to provide greens for the indoors. Zones 6–9.

Juniperus conferta 'Blue Pacific' (Juniper). The foliage of this juniper is a particularly dense, bluish green. Like all junipers, it is drought-tolerant and makes a nice evergreen groundcover. 'Blue Pacific' is low growing, to about 12". Zones 5–9.

Rhododendron 'P.J.M.' (PJM Rhody). Although it is almost sacrilegious to say this if you live on Cape Cod, I am not a big fan of most broadleaf Rhododendrons, probably because I see to many of them misused as foundation plants. I am fond of the P.J.M. hybrids, however, because the plant fits in small properties, is very hardy, and the small, evergreen leaves have such a pleasant odor. This is one of the earliest rhodys to bloom. Zones 6–8.

Rhododendron Yakushimanum hybrids (Yak Rhodys). If you must use them as foundation plants, by all means get one of the 'Yaks' which will stay small over time! This variety is also appealing because of the felted look of the underside of the leaves. Zones 6-8.

Rhodotypos scandens (Jetbead). I don't know why this plant isn't more popular. It thrives in sun or shade and a variety of soil types, and is basically insect and disease-free. One of the first shrubs to leaf out, jetbead retains its seeds all winter and into the spring, so that the plant has its new leaves, white flowers, and 'jetbeads' all at the same time. Lovely golden fall color; nice planted with Clethera and oakleaf hydrangeas in a shady border. Zones 4–8.

Spirea x bumalda 'Goldflame' (Spirea). New spring foliage on this spirea is a bright golden-pinkish green color which looks great with evergreen shrubs. The flowers are pink and bloom in summer and then sporadically into the fall. A tough plant for sun or part shade (five hours of sun required) and well sized for small properties. A related variety called 'Limemound' (you can imagine the foliage color) is worth seeking out. Zones 3-8.

Trees

Acer ginnala (Amur maple). A nice small maple which grows to around 20' in height. Adaptable to a wide range of soil types, it does best in moist but well drained soil and in sun or light shade. Zones 2–8.

Acer griseum (Paperbark maple). The peeling bark makes this tree desirable for year-round interest. Although slow growing, it will reach 30' or more over time and is basically trouble free. Zones 4–8.

Acer triflorum (Three flower maple). Although not as dramatic as the paperbark maple, Acer triflorum also has exfoliating bark and is a fine small maple which has good foliage color in the fall. Zones 5–7.

Betula nigra 'Heritage' (Heritage river birch). The river birch does well in moist soils and will grow to 40'–70' or beyond. Young trunks have exfoliating bark. Zones 4–9.

Carpinus betulus (European hornbeam). Tolerant of a wide range of soils, hornbeam grows in sun or light shade to around 50' in height. Zones 4-7.

Cercidiphyllum japonicum (Katsura tree). A lovely tree which grows quickly once established, but requires regular watering in its youth. It can grow 40'-60' with a 20'-30' spread. The leaves turn a beautiful yellow or apricot color in the fall. Zones 4–8.

Chamaecyparis pisifera (Sawara false cypress). The cultivars of this false cypress prefer acidic soils which are moist and well-drained. 'Plumosa' and 'Squarrosa' have soft, feathery foliage and grow to around 35' tall. Zones 4–8.

Chionanthus virginicus (Fringe tree). A fringe tree in flower takes your breath away. If you have a sunny spot which will hold a tree which is 12' to 20' tall with an equal spread, and your soil is anything close to being deep, fertile, and somewhat acidic, plant this tree! When I saw one in bloom at the Heritage Plantation in Sandwich, Massachusetts, I could hardly tear myself away. I don't have room on my property for another tree but there is lots of space in my neighbor's yard . . . Zones 3–9.

Cornus kousa (Kousa dogwood). This tree is hardy, and isn't prone to the anthracnose which is killing the spring flowering dogwoods (*Cornus flordia*) all over the country. Not only is it fairly pest-free, but it blooms in mid-summer when other trees are finished flowering. The fruit is edible but I must say that I would rather leave it for the birds . . . I ate one at the nursery and am in no way tempted to make it a habit. Kousa dogwoods like an acid soil with organic matter mixed in it, but they cope with the sand here on Cape Cod, so although they like good drainage they don't seem to be too picky about soil structure. This tree grows to 20' or 30', and has lovely horizontal branching which works well in the average yard and garden. Zones 5–8.

Evodia daniellii (Korean evodia). This small tree grows to 30' fairly quickly and is not prone to any insects or diseases of note. Evodias are pH adaptable, asking only for good drainage, full sun and regular water. Midsummer flowers and attractive fruits make this a tree worth planting. Zones 4–8.

Ginko biloba (Ginko). Grows in most soils when planted in full sun. The ginko is slow-growing but will get to be 50' to 80' and up to 30' wide over time. An impressive, trouble-free tree for those who have the room to plant one. Great fall color. Zones 3–9.

Halesia carolina (Carolina silverbell). A lovely small tree which flowers in the spring and has attractive fruits in autumn. The silverbell grows to around 35' in height and prefers rich, moist, acidic soils that are high in organic matter. This unusual tree looks good with evergreens, and grows well in sun or part shade. Zones 4–8.

Ilex pedunculosa (Longstalk holly). A large shrub or small tree, this evergreen holly has red berries that the birds love. Zones 5–7.

Juniperus chinensis (Chinese juniper). There are so many cultivars of Chinese junipers that you could find one for most sunny spots in the yard; there are horizontal varieties that make good groundcovers and tall, narrow types which combine well with other evergreens to create a living fence or screening. Check your local garden center to see which cultivars are available in your area. Zones 3–9.

Koelreuteria paniculata (Golden rain tree). The golden rain tree is a medium to fast growing tree which eventually reaches 30' to 40' in height. It blooms in early to midsummer, and the clusters of yellow flowers are quite showy. This tree adapts to many soil types and prefers to grow in full sun. Zones 5–9.

Magnolia grandiflora (Southern magnolia). A lovely, large tree in flower late spring. Plant in full sun or part shade in rich acid soil, and water regularly in order to encourage the most rapid growth. Zones 7–9.

Magnolia stellata (Star magnolia). Smaller than the Southern magnolia, this tree grows to around 18' in height and blooms in the spring. Plant in sun or light shade in an acidic soil that is rich in organic matter. A nice specimen tree in the yard or near the corner of buildings. Zones 4–8.

Magnolia virginiana (Sweetbay magnolia). This magnolia requires acid soil and will tolerate a wet area as well. It grows to 15' to 20' high and a similar width. Flowers appear in the late spring/early summer, and are pleasingly fragrant. Plant in a protected spot in the coldest zones. Zones 5-9.

Oxydendron arboreum (Sourwood). A beautiful flowering tree which is covered in flowers in early summer, and is famous for its fall color as well. The sourwood grows to 30' in peaty, acid soil. Although it prefers a moist environment it is fairly drought-tolerant and will thrive in full sun or some light shade. Zones 5–9.

Punica granatum (Pomegranate). A large shrub or small tree, the pomegranate grows best in fertile, well-drained but moist soils. It flowers best in full sun. A long, warm growing season is required to ripen the fruit. Zones 8–10.

Quercus myrsinifolia (Chinese evergreen oak). The hardiest evergreen oak, this tree will grow to 25' to 30' tall with a similar spread. Adaptable to a wide range of soils, *Quercus myrsinifolia* is a fairly slow grower that is untroubled by most pests and diseases. Zones 7-9.

Sciadopitys verticillata (Umbrella pine). This evergreen is good as a specimen tree planted in full sun. It grows in rich, moist, acidic soils, and will reach a height of 30' or more although it grows very slowly. Nice texture and dark green color. Zones 4–8.

Stewartia pseudocamellia (Japanese stewartia). One of the many lovely Stewartia species, this tree grows to around 30' or more. Nicely shaped, a stewartia should be planted in the open where its shape and beautiful bark can be appreciated year-round. It prefers full sun (although not in an excessively hot spot) and moist, peaty (acidic) soil. Lots of organic matter in the soil pleases the stewartias. Zones 5–7.

Styrax japonicus (Japanese snowbell). The snowbell blooms in late spring and grows to around 30' at a medium rate. Because it has a lovely, horizontal branching habit, it would make a fine substitute for the spring flowering dogwood that is dying from anthracnose. Trouble-free, snowbell likes acid soils rich in organic matter. Zones 5–9.

Q & A: GETTING STARTED

Q. *If I buy smaller plants and plant them according to their future size, won't my garden look bare for two or three years?*

A. It is true that small plants placed in a sea of bare, mulched earth look like survivors of a clear-cut forest, not a garden. This look is not only disheartening for the gardener, but for the garden as well. Nature does not love bare earth, so she rushes to fill it—with weeds. The solution to this problem is to replenish the area with temporary plants, which gardeners call "fillers." Fillers are often annual plants put in the garden each spring until the permanent plants grow up. Choose annuals whose height, shape and color will compliment the other plants in that garden.

Perennials can also be used as fillers, although they should be carefully chosen. Groundcover perennials look nice when planted around shrubbery, and these will not compete with small shrubs or become a problem later. Other perennials that stay fairly contained, and that look good even as young plants, might be planted in young shrub or perennial beds and moved when the other plants in that area grow larger. *Sedum* 'Autumn Joy' is one plant that fits this description. Any plant that is at all invasive, or has a tough root system, would not make a good filler.

One of my favorite fillers is lettuce. Yes, leaf lettuce! It is inexpensive to fill large areas with lettuce seed, which is sown fairly thickly in areas that are to be filled. If they grow too thickly, the plants can be eaten as they are thinned. Leaf lettuces are available in a variety of textures and colors, so they add contrast to the garden. Although it can be pulled in midsummer and replanted, most lettuce is also interesting as it flowers and goes to seed.

Lettuce combines well with annuals, especially the tall *Ageratum Houstonianum* 'Blue Mist." Tall *Ageratum* comes into its own in mid to late summer and is spectacular in the fall. The blue flowers and dark green foliage combines beautifully with lime-green or red-leaf lettuce.

Q. *I want to build a reference library, but I'm unsure which books I should invest in.*

A. This is a very good question; gardening books can be very expensive, and while some will become so worn from use that you may need to replace them, there are others whose glossy photos might be gorgeous and appealing, but after a look or two will remain untouched on your shelves.

Once you have looked through a book, reading, perhaps, sections that are of immediate interest, think about how often you might refer to it in the future. If it is a book of pretty pictures, or one that contains such specialized information that you might have need to consult it only occasionally, then it makes the most sense to borrow such books from library when you need them.

After becoming familiar with what the library has to offer, begin searching local bookstores, focusing on books which target the type of gardening you do. Books that address your specific location should be of interest and value, in that every region has its particular pleasures and challenges. I think that books which focus on the plants which are native to the area where a gardener lives are especially useful, but such books do not exist for every part of the country.

Although I am constantly adding to my reference library, the following are books that I continually refer to often and recommend for every gardener's bookshelf.

TEN RECOMMENDED GARDEN BOOKS

1. *Common-Sense Pest Control* by W. Olkowski, S. Daar and H. Olkowski. The subtitle to this book is "Least-toxic solutions for your home, garden, pets, and community. A tall order you might think, but this book fills it admirably. The authors never shortchange the reader by resorting to cookbook solutions (This bug is eating your plants? Spray with such-and-such pesticide.) but give, instead, hard information and choices. A book for people who like to think.

2. *Dictionary of Plant Names* by Allen J. Coombes. Those of you who, like me, never took Latin in school will find this small dictionary an invaluable help when trying to decide how a Latin name is pronounced. Because it describes the plant in addition to its pronunciation, this book is an excellent source to turn to when coming upon the name of a plant that is unfamiliar to you.

3. *Gardening by Mail* by Barbara J. Barton. When you can't locate the plant, ornament, or other garden accoutrements you desire at a local store, this is the book to turn to. In addition to a large list of retail suppliers of everything from seeds to garden videos, this book also contains information about horticultural societies, garden magazines, and libraries with horticultural collections.

4. *Gardening With Perennials Month by Month* by Joseph Hudak. I wish there was a single, definitive perennial book, but perhaps the subject is just too large for that to be feasible. Joseph Hudak's book is one of the three or four perennial books I refer to often, and it contains information on plants that are not listed in other sources. Because climate influences the rate of a plant's development, be aware that the month given as a plant's bloom period may vary in the region you live.

5. *Landscape Design, Renovation, and Maintenance* by Cass Turnbull. This is my favorite book about pruning, written by a landscape professional who clearly loves plants. It is especially useful for those

who are dealing with shrubs and trees that have outgrown their sites. A "must have" book for the home landscaper.

6. *Manual of Woody Landscape Plants* by Michael A. Dirr. Without a doubt, this is the most used book in my library. For home landscapers it would probably be most helpful to those who plan on future plantings of shrubs and trees. It is also useful in sorting out why a plant is sulking ("Oh! This shrub wants to be growing in a damp location!"), how large your current plantings will ultimately grow ("We better move this Rhododendron *now*, Fred! It will get three times this size in the next fifteen years!"), and which shrub or tree is the best choice to replace old or diseased plants. Those who think they would consult this treasure only occasionally should do the entire community a favor and donate one to the local library.

7. *Perennials for American Gardens* by Ruth Rogers Clausen and Nicolas H. Ekstrom. Another good reference for the perennial gardener which contains a great deal of information about a large number of plants. I am perhaps being picky when I say that if it had more photographs, and twice as many plants listed, it would be the perfect perennial book.

8. *The Taylor Guides.* A series of books for almost every gardening subject from annuals to shrubs and trees. All of the Taylor guides are good, basic garden reference books which are useful for gardeners of all levels of experience. Because they publish separate volumes that address a variety of plants and gardening situations, you can buy the books which will be the most appropriate and useful.

9. *Sunset Western Garden Book* and *Sunset National Garden Book.* It is easy to understand why I purchased the *Western Garden Book* 25 years ago when I gardened in Southern California, but you might be surprised to learn that I recently bought the revised edition, now that I am gardening in Cape Cod, Massachusetts. Sunset has recently published the National Garden Book for those living in the rest of the country. Good basic information and plant lists.

10. A general encyclopedia of gardening. There are several on the market, each with a slightly different focus, so the one you choose should depend on the information you are most likely to use. I am told that the one that I use is now out of print. If this is so, gardeners may want

to search for it in secondhand bookstores or those that deal in close-outs. It is *The Wise Garden Encyclopedia* published by Harper Collins. Originally published in 1970, the book was revised and updated in 1990, and it contains an alphabetical listing of hundreds of plants, garden terms, techniques and tools. I appreciate that pronunciations are given for all Latin names.

The Garden Primer by Barbara Damrosch. Although it contains some listing of plants, it is primarily a comprehensive source of other garden information. My friend Donna, also a Master Gardener, says this is the book she turned to again and again when she was a novice in the garden. It is a reasonably priced paperback, which is not over-whelming to new gardeners.

Horticulture Gardener's Desk Reference by Anne Halpin. This is a good source of basic plant and garden information. Anyone searching for plants that will grow well in specific areas or cultural conditions will find that this book contains a plant list for just about every situation.

America's Garden Book by Louise and James Bush-Brown has been recently updated and improved by Howard S. Irwin and the Brooklyn Botanic Garden. This large, comprehensive book contains specific information about numerous plants, general gardening information, and many color pictures.

Both the *Gardener's Desk Reference* and *America's Garden Book* are large, expensive books; they would be especially valuable for public libraries to have on their shelves.

Q. *Books are fine, but they sometimes they don't answer my questions; where can I take gardening classes?*

A. Many adult education programs offer classes in gardening, as do some community colleges. Garden clubs are good places for beginners to hear a variety of people speak about gardening, and some cooperative extensions offer classes as well. If you live near a city which has a botanical garden, contact the education or outreach departments; most public gardens offer classes and symposiums.

KEEPING IT GOING

I hope that every gardener has the experience of watching a garden grow and mature. It is truly a delight to plant a stick which is as tall as an average twelve year old boy, and see it grow into an apple tree large enough for that boy to climb. Great satisfaction comes from watching the young plants that were planted around the house develop into beautifully shaped, nicely colored shrubbery. And perennials become old friends as they increase in size and mark the seasons with the growth of their foliage, opening of their flowers, and the development of their seedheads.

When your gardens are established, the almost overwhelming job of choosing the right plants and preparing new beds is done. But mature plantings have problems of their own; there are always chores to be done, unexpected problems to solve, and information to learn. (One of the things I love about gardening is that it keeps both my body *and* brain working.) Once some of the big decisions have been made, we can take delight in the continuing process, as well as the new information and plants which come our way.

It is the realization that gardening is an ongoing process that relieves a great deal of stress we may feel about our gardens. Those who have tended gardens for even a short amount of time soon see that a garden is never finished. Learning how to care for an established garden brings problems and pleasures that new gardeners don't experience. There are different jobs to be done, things to be learned (more grist for the mill), and lovely flowers to put into bouquets.

The standard calendar of garden maintenance described in Chapter

8 applies to new and maturing gardens alike. But aside from basic chores, there are other tasks to be done including dividing the perennials, pruning older shrubbery, and raking the leaves from larger trees. Just as our choices in plants and how they are initially planted contributes to a low-maintenance garden, so too does our *care* of older gardens.

MAINTENANCE OF SHRUBS AND TREES : PRUNING

Indoors, the programming of the VCR causes otherwise intelligent people to become so paralyzed that they live with the clock-light flashing for *years*. Outdoors, it is pruning that leaves many smart people completely flummoxed. This is mostly due to some common misunderstandings about pruning. Most people think that all shrubs need to be pruned to control their size. Although a plant that is inappropriately sited may need to be trimmed to keep it in bounds, most shrubs only need a bit of cleanup pruning to keep them growing well and looking good. *When at all possible, pruning should be done simply to keep a plant attractive, not to keep it small.*

There is also great confusion about what pruning actually is. Many think that pruning and shearing are one in the same, and they trim all the shrubs on their property with hedge shears. Clipping all the growing tips off of a shrub so that the plant becomes a smooth, green (hopefully) ball or cube is called shearing. This is the appropriate treatment for maintaining topiary, hedges, or some evergreen shrubs in a formal setting. Shearing is inappropriate for any shrub that blooms, and it is a make-work project for the home gardener. Unless you are already saddled with topiary balls and blocks, leave the hedge shears in the hardware store and invest in a good pair of pruners instead.

When plants have outgrown their sites, or are in danger of soon doing so, consider transplanting them instead of pruning to keep them small. If a group of shrubs was initially planted too close, look to see if moving a central plant to another spot might open the area so that the others can grow without crowding. Overgrown foundation plants that block windows should be moved, and shrubs that frame windows and corners should be thinned so that light and air can reach the building even though the plant stays in place.

Transplanting or removing large plants might seem like a great deal of work, but it is a job that will only need to be done once. Shrubs that are being pruned to control their size will need attention every year, especially since pruning a plant actually stimulates new growth.

TOP 10 STEPS FOR SENSIBLE PRUNING

1. Whenever possible, prune to improve appearance, not to control size.

2. Remove deadwood first.

3. Remove crossed branches, weak or diseased growth, and excess suckers; suckers are young, straight shoots that grow from around the base of some mound-form or tree-like shrubs.

4. Prune according to the type of plant. Cane-like shrubs should have some of the oldest wood pruned to the ground. Mounded shrubs and tree-like shrubs should be trimmed only to improve shape. When in doubt, ask at your extension office or a local garden center about a specific plant.

5. In general, prune spring-flowering shrubs immediately after they stop blooming, and summer-flowering shrubs in early spring.

6. Don't prune needled evergreens back to bare wood; they don't usually sprout leaves from older growth.

7. Prune back to about an inch above an *outward* facing bud. When this bud becomes a branch it will grow away from the center, which gives the plant a pleasing shape.

8. Cane growers can have up to a third of the oldest growth cut off to the ground (details below). Plants that grow quickly and bloom on new wood, such as roses, *Caryopteris* (Blue-mist shrub) and *Buddliea* (Butterfly bush) can be pruned to 12"-18" from the ground in the early spring.

9. Don't overprune—it stimulates growth. Stop when the plant looks neater and cleaner but before it looks "pruned."

10. Keep shearing to a minimum. (Hint: if you never buy a shearing tool you won't be tempted.) Don't shear deciduous flowering shrubs, *Rhododendrons, Pieris,* Mountain Laurel, Burning Bush, *Euonymus, Aucuba, Camellias* and *Magnolias.*

THE KINDEST CUT

Let's assume that all of your shrubs are growing in areas where they are free to reach their natural size and shape. Is any pruning necessary for these plants at all? In theory, you could leave the plants alone, as nature does all the time. (Some might argue that the deer are Mother Nature's pruners, but that is a topic for Chapter 9!) Plants benefit from having any dead wood removed, however, and this results in a cleaner, neater-looking landscape. *When pruning any plant, the first step is to remove all dead wood.* Cut off dead twigs and branches just above where they meet living tissue.

Once the dead branches have been removed, how a shrub gets pruned depends on what type of plant it is. The following are some general guidelines.

1. Before you begin to prune, look at the natural shape of the plant. Remember that the goal is to leave a plant that does not look as if it had been pruned.
2. Some shrubs, such as *Kerria japonica, Forsythia, Hydrangea macrophylla, Leucothoe fontanesiana,* and the red-twigged dogwoods grow many straight stems from the base of the plant. Cass Turnbull, a landscape gardener refers to these as "cane-growers."

   Begin pruning these plants by removing a quarter to a third of the oldest stems every year. These are cut right to the ground, which helps stimulate new canes to grow from the base of the plant. Blueberries, raspberries, and shrub roses are treated the same way. Be sure to cut only up to a third of the oldest canes, not the total number of stems, since the removal of a third of all of the canes might leave the plant looking as if it had been pruned by Slash and Trash Landscaping!
3. Many deciduous shrubs have three or more woody stems coming from the ground, but they do not produce new shoots coming from the ground. The exceptions are plants such as *Syringas* (Lilacs) and *Clethera* (Summersweet) which routinely grow suckers from the ground around the main stem.

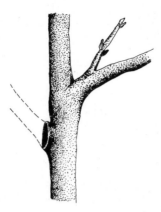

Cut large limbs off at the branch-collar area, usually an inch or two away from the trunk of the tree. Small stems and twigs should be cut at an angle about an inch above an outward-facing bud.

These suckers are clipped off at the ground. If you would like to encourage a new stem or two, leave the strongest or best-placed sucker to grow.

These stemmed, deciduous plants are usually mounded or vase-shaped, and require little pruning when well-sited. After removing dead wood and crossed branches, remove any branches that look out of place or awkward by cutting them back inside the shrub so that the cut does not show. Proceed slowly, pausing to visualize how the shrub will look before you make the cut. Most mound-type shrubs only require a minimum of this type of pruning to keep them tidy.

4. Shrubs that grow into a tree-like size and shape don't need much cleanup either, and are best left to grow to their natural size and shape. Remove dead or diseased growth, and lightly prune for shape only if needed, removing a branch that is crooked or grows in a manner different from the rest of the plant. If a large tree-like shrub must be opened up to allow light into a building, for example, cut a few of the lateral (side) branches back to the main stem, taking care to remove them in a balanced way. (Don't take them all from one side or section of the plant.) Keep such trimming to the bare minimum.

5. Trees shouldn't need much pruning other than the removal of dead or diseased growth. Never cut off the top of a tree

to control its size; this is called "topping or heading" a tree, and it is not only ugly, but produces new, weak growth and exposes the tree to disease. Lower limbs of a tree may need to be cut back to the trunk, but this should always be done with restraint. Removing more than an eighth of the total foliage (moving from the ground up) will result in a poorly-proportioned tree. When the removal of limbs is absolutely necessary, be sure to make the cut just outside the swollen area where the limb meets the trunk. This area is called the branch-collar. Limbs cut too far from this branch-collar are ugly, and those cut right next to the trunk won't heal well and may kill the tree over time. Don't paint a pruned area with sealant, as it can trap pathogens under the paint and do more harm then good. (People may need bandages, but trees do not.)

MAINTAINING PERENNIALS

Every perennial bed will need some maintenance, even if you have filled it with plants that don't need frequent dividing, dead-heading or water-ing. The secret to maintaining a perennial garden with less fuss and bother is to do such work just *before* it needs to be done.

Dig a dying plant out of the garden before it has died and remained in place for the season. If you know that it does not have something contagious, but has suffered from something such as a lack of water or too much fertilizer, you might want to try reviving the plant first. But in the long run, it is easier to remove a sick or diseased plant right away before any pathogens spread to other parts of the garden.

Even healthy perennials must sometimes be dug and divided. Any plant that doubles or triples its size every year needs regular dividing, and this should be done every two to four years. Plants that stay in a tightly contained clump that increases in size but does not *double* in size, can be left for longer periods, unless the clump begins to die out in the center or grow with less vigor.

A mature clump of perennials is more readily split than one which has been allowed to grow two years or more *past* the time when it needed reviving. Digging up a root ball that measures two feet in diameter is easier than trying to lift one that is four feet across.

HOW TO DIVIDE PERENNIALS

Early spring is the best time to divide perennials although it can be done after the plant has bloomed or in the fall if necessary. Perennials that have been divided in warm or hot weather should be watered well for two months after replanting since they will require extra moisture for the renewed growth of roots and leaves.

Less time will be spent on cleanup if you get something to temporarily place the plant on once it is removed from the garden. Put a plastic tarp or a layer of newspapers as close to the plant as possible so that when the clump is divided you won't leave a mound of dirt, mulch and old perennial roots on your walk or lawn.

Using a shovel and perhaps a garden fork, dig straight down into the soil all around the circumference of the plant, a few inches away from the outermost stems if possible. After this area has been cut, dig the shovel under the plant to lift it from its spot. If the clump isn't too large it can be dug out in one piece, but if it is larger than 18"–24" across you might need to cut the clump through the middle before lifting.

Once the plant has been placed on the tarp, use your gloved fingers to move some of the dirt away from the roots in order to better see how to take smaller clumps away from the whole. With some perennials it is easy to pull groups of the newest shoots—and their roots—away from the main clump. Other plants have root systems and stems that grow so tightly that only a cut through the clump with the blade of a shovel or spade will separate them.

I have seen illustrations in books about dividing perennials that show clumps being divided using two garden forks. Each of these forks are placed in the same area, back to back, and the clump is then pried apart using the forks working against each other. I am not surprised that this method is shown in drawings and not photographs, since every time I've tried it I find it more trouble than it's worth . . . but perhaps I haven't yet mastered the proper technique. In any case, roots that separate easily using this method come apart just as easily using your fingers or one fork pushing away. Roots that are difficult are most easily divided by cutting the clump, even though you sacrifice some of the roots in the severed area.

When separating perennials, I usually divide my clumps so that I am left with a new chunk about the size of a dinner plate. Pieces of this size re-establish quickly, and they are large enough to look like something in the garden, but not *so* large that they will need dividing again the next year. Be sure to take the new group from the edge of the older plant, since this is where the vital, young growth is. Throw the inner core away.

Before placing your divisions in the garden again, take this opportunity to amend the area with organic matter and bonemeal or superphosphate, making sure to mix these well where the roots are to grow in the future. Use excess small clumps elsewhere in the garden, or plant them in the same area in triangles or an S-curved line. Since their roots have been injured, it is important to keep all newly divided plants watered well while they get re-established.

RENEWING AN ENTIRE PERENNIAL BED

When perennials are divided just before each clump needs it, the task can be spread over two work sessions in the early spring and perhaps a day in the fall. Not every clump of perennials will need dividing every year, so it is a job that can be done on a plant-by-plant basis.

Sometimes, however, we let such chores go by the wayside for a bit longer than we should. When perennials are not divided in a timely fashion they grow into each other, and the more aggressive plant often will crowd out the others. Other plants, such as shasta daisies, will become less and less vigorous, and the centers of their clumps will be bare soil or dying stems. While this process is appropriate for a meadow or some cottage-style gardens most people want their perennials to look tidier and more tightly packed than the average wildflower patch.

Once the perennial bed has gotten overgrown, it is time to dig all of the plants, place them on a tarp to be divided as described, and replace them in newly amended soil. As you might imagine, this is a job that may take two days or more, depending on the size of the bed. My best suggestion for those of you who find your perennial garden in need of such rejuvenation is to get help.

Assistance does not have to be a hired helper. Find people who are starting new gardens and offer the excess of your divisions in exchange for their help for a day. You might try connecting with such folks by contacting a local garden club, "newcomers" organization, or by posting a note on the library bulletin board.

Three to five people can make short work of a garden revival if the necessary tools and soil amendments are in place when they start the job. Have your helpers bring plastic bags, used flats, or newspapers to put the divisions in, and plant labels and a marker for labeling each clump. Even if they only assist with digging and dividing the plants, leaving you to replace them as desired, this is an enormous help which will speed the entire project along.

ADDING NEW PLANTS TO AN ESTABLISHED PERENNIAL GARDEN

As gardens mature, every gardener finds that there are times when new plants need to be added to an established bed. Perhaps a particular plant didn't make it through an especially harsh winter, or maybe it was food for the wildlife or succumbed to disease. And even when we make the effort to choose our plants with care, there are usually one or two that are more invasive then we ever imagined, or have other habits that make them undesirable in the garden.

A plant may not be living up to its reputation and may never have grown well for you. Experienced gardeners learn that this is one of the mysteries of the universe . . . there are plants that grow well for everyone else, but either sulk or die when planted in *their* gardens. Tastes change over time as well, and the plant that we were crazy about five years ago may not look as good to us any more. In such instances it is best to dig these perennials up and give them to someone who will treasure them.

Once a space has been cleared in the perennial bed, a new plant must be put in that location. If an older, large plant of the variety desired is available from a garden center or another person's garden then it can be put into place right away. Often however, the perennial we want may only be available, or affordable, by purchasing a younger, smaller plant.

If a first year perennial is placed in an established garden, in all likelihood it won't get the light it needs because the mature plants will be towering over it. First year plants do not grow as large as they will in their second year, and most perennials don't reach their mature size until the third growing season. If you have a nursery area on your property you can grow the plant there for the first year, transplanting it to its permanent home the following spring.

Those without such an area can either let the plant mature in another garden were there is more space, or place it in a two or three gallon pot for that first growing season. (Be sure the pot is large because the maximum growth and health of the plant depends on enough room to stretch it's roots.) A plant that has been in a pot all summer can be put into the established bed in the early fall since the roots will not be disturbed in transplanting. It will have all autumn to grow roots in its new home, and the following spring it will be large enough to hold its own with the mature plants around it.

Plants that are grown in pots should be checked daily to see if they need watering. If your schedule does not allow for this, it is better to put young perennials in the ground, perhaps in the vegetable garden, for that first season.

While the younger plants are getting "bulked up," their future home can be filled with annuals, vegetables, or a series of potted plants. These areas make good places to play with temporary garden ornaments such as large rocks, gazing balls or cement figurines.

ADDING TO THE GARDEN BUT KEEPING THINGS SIMPLE

Here is the dilemma: you don't have much time to garden, but you love plants. Or you have had a garden for a few years, and you want to try something new . . . add to it in some manner, without increasing the size of your beds and thus the workload. The following suggestions are for you.

CREATIVE ADDITIONS

1. *Posts and Vines.* Place a decorative post in the garden and grow a vine or two around it. Such posts can be as fancy or as plain as you desire, and they function as vertical elements that gives height to the garden, as well as objects that give structure and interest to the garden in all seasons. Posts can be made from a plain piece of 8" x 8" lumber, or it could be an older, porch turning salvaged from a junk store or garage sale. The top can be left bare or filled with a finial, ornament or birdhouse. Match the post to the style of your garden.

   Depending on its size, a perennial vine might be grown with an annual vine, creating more visual interest and a longer period of bloom. Be sure to match the height of the vine to the post. A plant such as the climbing hydrangea, beautiful as it might be, would be far too large for a post planting.

   Perennial vines that bloom on the current season's growth are most suitable for post plantings because they can be pruned back in the early spring, keeping their size suitable to the post but allowing

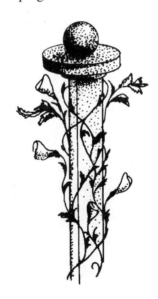

them to flower as well. A wide variety of annual vines are available in seed form. Most vines (annual and perennial) whose size is suitable for a post have twining stems or tendrils and will need to have wires strung next to the post for support.

An alternative to wires might be a wire cage placed over the post by bending a length of wire fencing around it. (Run the fencing lengthwise from the top of the post to the bottom, using the width to wrap around.) Wire fencing can be left as is, or painted the same color as the post in order to make it less noticeable. By painting the fencing a contrasting color the entire post becomes an ornament in addition to a support for the vines.

Some vines (English ivy, Virginia creeper and trumpet vine, for example) will cling to any surface with "holdfasts," but most of these grow far too large to be planted by a post unless the gardener is willing to continually prune the plant back each year. Check with your garden center if you have questions about the most suitable plants for post plantings.

2. *Plants grown on plants.* Go for a walk in the woods sometime soon, and look at all the plants with the eyes of a gardener. Imagine that the woodland you see is a garden planted by the most experienced, innovative garden designer in the land. You will notice plants growing on top of plants; there is one group that grows on the forest floor, another section of "understory" bushes and small trees, and a third "canopy" layer above it all. And scrambling throughout these layers might be an assortment of vines.

As gardeners, we sometimes keep our plantings too simple. A tree here, shrub border there, and annuals or perennials in neat clumps in assorted separate areas. One way to enjoy a few more plants in the garden is to take a tip from Mother Nature's Landscaping Co. and plant layers of plants together. Choose plants that are not prone to problems, and that will grow well in the setting you have chosen for them.

Low-growing annuals and perennials can be grown under shrubs and trees, be these an assortment of traditional ground covers, native wildflowers or other choices. Small vines can be planted under shrubbery for added flowers, foliage colors and textural interest. Clematis vines are often grown up into shrub roses, but they can be interplanted with other plants as well.

There are smaller, vining annuals that can also be grown among shrubs or large perennials. The old-fashioned vining petunia makes a lightweight companion to shrubby perennials such as lavender and santolina, and the vining nasturtium works well when grown with perennials, shrubs or small trees.

The secret for a good combination of plant-on-plant is to choose two that are different enough in foliage and/or flowering period so that they are each noticeable, and the season of interest is extended. The plant that provides the support should be strong enough to hold the second plant, and that plant should not be one that will grow so large that it will overwhelm its host. If the vine you have chosen is a small sun-lover, it would be wise to grow it in a pot in bright sunshine until it large enough so that its companion does not shade it completely.

3. *Fill a large container.* Clusters of many smaller pots filled with plants make lovely additions to the deck and patio, but frequent attention is required. Pots dry out quickly, so in hot weather they need to be checked and watered daily. Because there isn't much soil for the roots to draw nutrients from, container plantings need to be fertilized more often, and the plants may need trimming and dead-heading to keep them looking their finest.

Larger boxes or containers are not as prone to rapid water loss, however, and can be an excellent way of adding some beautiful, low maintenance plants to your landscape. Large planters are particularly nice for containing plants that would otherwise be too invasive for small properties. I have two 28" cubes in which I have planted golden bamboo. The high boxes combined with the tall stand of bamboo create a screen for an area that would otherwise be open to the street, and they allow me to grow this lovely plant even though I don't have the space on my property to let it spread.

Ornamental grasses are good choices for large containers as well, and most of them are drought-tolerant, making them even more suitable for growing in tubs and pots. Whether the containers are filled with annuals or perennials, choosing plants that do not need to be kept moist will allow you more latitude in watering schedules.

Gardeners who buy whiskey barrels and other large containers often place upside-down plastic flower pots in the bottoms of these planters so that less potting soil is needed to fill them. If the container is to be filled with annuals, this technique does save money and because the annuals have fairly short roots, no harm is really done. But those who want to be able to go a day or two without watering their planters should fill the entire container with soil, preferably mixed with some organic matter such as composted manure. A deeper layer of soil and compost will retain more water, and plants that grow deeper root systems are less vulnerable to drought.

Container plantings are easy to maintain because they seldom need weeding. A light layer of cocoa or buckwheat hulls is an attractive mulch that will help keep moisture in the soil and block the seed-germinating light from any weed seeds that may blow in.

If large containers are to be filled with perennials, choose especially winter-hardy varieties if you live in a climate where the winters drop below freezing. Because the containers are exposed on all but one side, they get twenty degrees colder than the earth, and are subject to more frequent freezing and thawing. Pull containers into an unheated garage or shed for protection.

Fertilize container-planted annuals with a liquid feed, or for added convenience, mix a time-release product into the soil before planting. Most pelletized fertilizers release nutrients to the plants over a three-month period. As with all fertilizing, remember to go easy and never put fertilizer in the water if the container plants are wilted. Water the planter first, and fertilize when the plants have revived.

4. *Garden ornaments.* Whether your taste turns toward shiny, bright gazing balls or simple cement orbs, garden ornaments are a nice way to add interest to an established garden. They can be large and permanent, or small and temporary. An ornament can stand in bold view or be almost hidden beneath plant growth; it remains attractive throughout all seasons, doesn't need watering, and isn't prone to fungi attacks.

Most garden centers sell a variety of outdoor sculptures, and garden magazines have ornaments advertised in every issue. But such decorations for the garden need not be bought. Junkyards are great sources of garden ornaments, as are garage sales or even your own garage. Found objects can be lovely in the garden, and large pots or architectural pieces are always at home there.

I recently hung my son's first bicycle on the side of the garden shed as ornamentation. A secondhand bike to begin with, it has had several colors of paint applied in its lifetime (by not so steady six year-old hands) and the paint is dull and flaking from years spent in foul weather. The chain has long ago rusted, and the tires are flat—in other words, it was perfect for the garden!

I attached a length of chicken wire to the side of the shed, running it from under the bicycle down to the ground, and planted the lovely *Dicentra scandens* next to it. This vine is hardy in zone 7 but is a worthwhile annual in colder areas. It grows quickly in dappled shade, and is covered all summer with yellow bleeding-heart type flowers. The vine fastened its tendrils onto the chicken wire, and within a month it had entwined itself all over the bicycle. The colors of the flowers and the bicycle brighten a gray shingled building; it is a playful adornment for a shady spot.

Don't overlook the use of natural objects as garden ornaments either. A well-placed boulder, seashell or tree stump can be beautiful, especially as it weathers or becomes covered with moss. To encourage moss and algae to grow on your ornaments, paint them with milk or beer. This is most effective on porous materials such as wood, rock or terra cotta. Such areas can be "seeded" with moss by taking a small piece of moss from another location and placing it in a blender with a couple of cups of water. Blend briefly to create a moss slurry, and pour this on your ornament.

NEW PLANTS FROM SEEDS

Raising perennials from seed is an inexpensive way to acquire many plants of a single type. A packet of seeds costs less than five dollars, so it is possible to grow a dozen or more plants for what one would cost in the nursery. Some perennials are very easy to grow from seed, while others are difficult to germinate or slow to get going.

I feel conflicted about telling any gardener *not* to try raising perennials from seed because I get such pleasure out of starting a few new plants every spring. In the early spring it is too cool or wet to go outside with my tea first thing in the morning, but I love going into the sunporch every day to check on the flats of germinating seedlings that I have under lights. I cannot, however, deceive you; growing plants from seed is definitely *not* low-maintenance.

The following information is given for those who, like myself, are so hopelessly addicted to trying new plants that they cannot restrain themselves from buying a few seed packets. Anyone else can regard the following ten tips for success as their own personal ten step program. After reading what is involved in starting perennials from seed you may realize that it is something that you have *no* interest in trying.

TEN STEPS FOR SUCCESS WHEN GROWING
PERENNIALS FROM SEED

1. *Start with store-bought seed starter mix.* Yes, you can make your own with compost and vermiculite, but it takes time and the compost should be sterilized in the oven or microwave, a process which really stinks up the house. If you are going to the trouble of starting plants from seed, it is important to have a sterile starting medium. New seedlings are prone to a fungus called "damping off," but this can be prevented by the use of sterile planting mix and pots. Compost and soil from the garden will also contain an assortment of seeds, making it difficult to determine if the seeds you want to start have germinated, or if the seedling is an interloper from outside.

2. *Select your seeds with care.* If you are purchasing the seed in the garden center, be sure to read the instructions on the label. Information about any special treatment required for germination will be given on the packet. Many seed catalogs will also classify their seeds as easy or difficult to start; stick with the easy ones if you are not yet experienced with starting plants from seeds. Be sure to note the germination time as well as other requirements (such as a period of chilling) for successful starting; knowing how long it will take a seed to germinate will help you know when to start it. If the seed commonly takes more than 30 days to sprout, you will need to start it earlier in the spring than you would seeds for plants such as tomato or cosmos, which germinate so quickly that they almost leap out of the soil. Perennials commonly take longer to germinate, but there is still a great difference between a plant which takes 20 days to sprout and one which can take up to 12 months! If you are inexperienced in starting seeds, stick with those that have a shorter germination time.

3. *Follow the time table given on the packet.* If the directions recommend starting the seed six weeks before the planting time, wait until that time to start them. This is most important when starting annuals,

since they often grow so quickly that they outgrow their pots and indoor locations long before the weather warms enough to place them outdoors. Perennials too, however, can be problematic when grown indoors for too long. Plants are not as strong or insect-resistant when grown inside, so the goal is to get them large enough to survive, then move them outside as soon as possible.

4. *Plant one or two seeds per pot or cell in the plastic six-pack.* Yes, you can start more and then divide them into separate containers, but this is time-consuming. If you are anything like me, you will notice that the seedlings are ready to separate (when they have their second set of leaves), but by the time you get to it they have their sixth set of leaves, are practically *blooming*, and their roots are so hopelessly intermeshed that separating them is out of the question. Start a maximum of two plants per cell and be hard-hearted: snap the weakest one off when the plants have their second leaves. (If you pull it out it will likely damage the roots of the remaining plant, so it is better to cut it off at the base) Those who will find it impossible to sacrifice the weaker plant should only place one seed per container.

5. *Wet your growing medium before the seeds are planted.* It is amazing how much moisture these seed-starting mixes can absorb, and it often takes a bit of time for them to become saturated. If seeds are fine, and are placed on top of the soil, they may wash away as you continue to sprinkle. Fill the containers with dry mix and water it well, allowing plenty of time for the moisture to soak the entire area thoroughly.

6. *Follow the directions about the depth of planting.* Some seeds need light to germinate, so if you cover them with starting medium the light will be blocked. If the information on the packet says "barely cover" then that is what you should do. Usually, very fine seed is not covered at all but is sprinkled on the soil's surface.

    Be sure to label your pots or six-packs. I have found that labels stuck into the cells are a nuisance; they fall out or get switched by the gremlins in the night. Plastic strips with the plant name embossed on them work well; the hand-held gizmo that makes such labels is available at discount stores and is not expensive. Gold or silver metallic markers work on dark pots and six-packs as well, and the names won't wash off the plastic.

7. *Cover the newly-planted seeds* with clear plastic, such as a cut-open

dry cleaning bag or a plastic foodwrap. This plastic should remain on only until the seeds germinate; check daily for signs of green sprouts, and take the cover off as soon as you spy something. If only one seed has germinated, it is helpful to cut away the plastic over that little plant but leave it over the others. (I told you this wasn't low maintenance!) Usually, most seeds germinate within a few days of each other.

8. *Place the flats of seeds under a bank of flourescent lights.* Unless they are in a greenhouse, there will not be enough sun coming through the windows to grow good, strong seedlings. The lights used can be either the "gro-lights" made for plants, or regular flourescent bulbs, or a mixture of the two. Gro-lights are full spectrum lights, but the distance the bulbs are placed from the plants is more important than the type of lights used.

The easiest and most economical way of setting up a group of lights is to purchase "shop lights." These are standard fixtures which hold two flourescent bulbs each; they are already wired and ready to plug in. Two shop lights hung side by side provide good light for four standard trays of seedlings.

The good news about shop lights is that they are available at most hardware or building supply stores and are not expensive. The bad news is that they are often very poorly made. I commonly have to tape the light bulbs into these fixtures with electrical tape because they are just slightly too large to hold the tube in securely. There have also been occasions when I needed to exchange a set of shop lights because it was slightly too small, and the bulbs wouldn't be forced into the opening allowed. You get what you pay for I guess, so be forewarned.

Lights should be hung two or three inches above the plants. Naturally, as the seedlings grow you will need to either raise the lights or lower the seed-trays. If you are starting several types of seeds, the young plants will most likely grow at different rates, making several banks of lights necessary. Taller plants can be placed under one bank of bulbs, while shorter, slow-growing seedlings are two inches from another set. If the lights are too far away from the young plants, the seedlings will grow weak and spindly.

I have a tower of shelves in my sunroom which has four shelves and four banks of lights on it. I shuffle flats around all spring in order to keep the plants as close to the lights as possible. All the light fixtures are hung with hooks and chains, which makes the raising and lowering easier. The mass of timers (lights need to be on twelve hours a day) and extension cords is formidable; the addition of a couple of fans (to provide good air circulation) makes the entire set up resemble a Rube Goldberg cartoon.

9. *Keep the seedlings moist but not wet.* Check the flats daily to see if water is needed. Seed-starting mixes hold quite a bit of water, so when the seeds are first germinating you won't need to add any more moisture. Small sprouts don't use much water, so although they should be checked every day they may not need additional watering. As the young plants grow larger, however, they will be using the moisture in the soil more quickly. It is important that the plants not be allowed to wilt. Feel the soil before adding water, however, since root rot might develop if the plant is kept too wet.

10. *As soon as day time temperatures reach 60°F, you may begin the process of "hardening off."* Plants that have been raised indoors are artificially tender; a sudden exposure to the breezes and direct sun in the out-of-doors will kill them. Many a gardener has placed carefully grown tomato seedlings out on a balmy, spring day, only to find them with white, sunburned leaves three hours later.

　　The process of hardening off seedlings is almost the definition of high-maintenance. Flats of tender plants should be put outside for only twenty minutes for their first outing, and this first exposure should never be to the strong, noonday sun. The period of time spent outdoors can be increased by twenty minutes a day for the first two weeks, but again, the plants should only be out in the open if the day is cloudy and not too windy. Just as the leaves need to gradually toughen in order to stand the harsh sun, the stems need to strengthen in order to withstand the wind. If the day is sunny or windy, plants should be sheltered in some way until they are stronger.

　　Once the sheltered plants are outside for the entire day, they must still be brought in if the temperatures fall below 50°F at night. After warmer weather arrives and the seedlings are accustomed to being in their sheltered location all day and night, they can be moved, again gradually, into a place where the direct sun hits them, and they are exposed to more wind. *Gradual exposure* in all stages of hardening off is essential.

　　Perennials grow at different rates. Some can be left in six-pack cells for three months as they grow, and others develop so rapidly that the plant will need larger pots by the end of the first month. Young plants grow better if they have a larger pot to stretch their roots in, however, so don't leave a seedling in the small starting cell for too long.

It is unnecessary to fertilize new seedlings while they are still in the six-pack, but once they are transplanted to a larger pot they can be given some supplemental nutrients. Whether you are feeding with an organic fish emulsion/seaweed product, or a chemical fertilizer, be sure to mix it on the mild side and only fertilize the plant after it has been watered well. Time-release fertilizers are a convenient way to feed new plants over time, but again, caution must be taken not to overapply this type of nutrient as well; chemical burn is just as possible with the overuse of time-release products as with other types of fertilizers.

Pop a growing perennial plant out of its six-pack once in awhile to look at the roots; if the root system is beginning to circle the bottom of the container, transplant the seedling to larger pot right away. This will usually need to be done at least once before the plant can be put out into the sun, so plan the space under the lights to hold larger-sized pots of plants as well as small six-packs.

After a plant is moved outside, growing it in a larger pot will not only give it room to spread its roots, but will provide an area that won't dry as quickly as a small pot. Transplant young perennials into one or two gallon pots, or to a nursery area to grow over the first summer. First year plants can be placed in the garden the following fall. If they are to be left in their pots until the next spring, the pots will need to be placed in a protective coldframe or another similar, sheltered location.

A house with old-fashioned window wells has cold-frames in the making; just cover the wells with a sheet of Plexiglas to create an instant, in-ground winter location for your new perennials. No matter what protection is used, do not place the plants in such an area too early in the fall, since the artificially warm environment might stimulate new growth.

DO YOU STILL WANT TO GROW PLANTS FROM SEED?

Growing plants from seed is a very satisfying process, even if it is an endeavor that should be entered into with your eyes open. Often, more seeds germinate then we could possibly plant in our gardens, making it possible to share the wealth with other gardeners. Besides making it feasible to grow many plants economically, it is sometimes easier to find the seed for a particular plant than it is to find the plant itself at a local nursery. Some lovely varieties of annuals or perennials are often not carried at garden centers, not because they don't deserve a spot in our gardens, but they may not be popular enough for large growers to bother with them.

Q & A: KEEPING IT GOING

Q.   *I haven't divided my perennials in about six years, and they are all grown into each other. The garden is a rather happy tumble of flowers. Is there any reason I can't leave it like this?*

A.   You have stumbled on a style of gardening that is both old and new. Traditional cottage style gardens are an almost wild hodge-podge of plants. Those who plant cottage gardens aim to combine all of their favorite plants in a way that doesn't look "planted." Lately, this style is being a bit more relaxed into a garden that is somewhere in between a cottage style planting and a wildflower meadow. The *New Perennial Garden* by Noel Kingsbury details this style of perennial gardening very nicely.

There is no reason that you *have* to keep your plants more contained. If you are pleased by this look, by all means continue to let the garden flow as it will. Some plants may be more amenable to this style than others, and you might find that some of the perennials will disappear from the garden over time. Clumps of plants that grow so large that they die in the centers should be dug and divided before this happens. *Iris siberica* is an example of a plant that would benefit from dividing even when planted in such a free-for-all garden.

Plants that are known to spread quickly and self-seed are appropriate for a garden of this type since they are able to either slug it out with each other or cheerfully mingle without being overwhelmed. Examples of vigorous plants include: *Achillea* ssp. (Yarrow), *Coreopsis* ssp. (Tickseed), *Monarda* ssp. (Bee balm), *Physostegia* ssp. (Obedient plant), and all of the *Lysimachias*. Some self-seeding biennials or perennials for this style garden are *Digitalis* ssp. (Foxglove), *Agustache* ssp. (Hyssop), *Gaillardia* ssp. (Blanket flower), and the *Verbasucms*. Every area of the country has different flowers that self-seed with abandon; find out which plants will do this in your locale, and plant them in your almost-wild garden.

Don't hesitate to stick new plants in to this style of garden, filling any bare spots; you will find that any new additions will need to be large enough to compete with their lively neighbors. Bulbs can be placed in and among established perennials in the fall; choose the variety according to which season the garden needs flowers. If there are fewer things blooming in late July, for example, a mix of lilies can be planted in the fall which will add color in that month the following year.

Other garden maintenance, such as the addition of compost every year along with some slow-release organic fertilizer, should be kept up as usual, even though the plants are not being dug and divided. As the perennials spread and seed around the garden, you can either move them around or let nature take its course.

Q. *All of my gardens haven't looked as nice and healthy this year as in previous seasons. Should I have my soil tested?*

A. A soil test couldn't hurt, although it is unlikely that you would have seen a sudden decline due to any deficiency in the soil, or that all of your gardens would be so affected. Before sending samples off for testing, ask yourself if weather conditions might be contributing to the state of this year's garden.

We tend to focus on whatever weather we are experiencing at the present time, and forget that climatic conditions occur in cycles which can affect the plants for months or years in the future. The effects of a severe drought over one summer, for instance, can cause changes in the plants that are not seen until the following season and beyond. A particularly cold winter might cause slight dieback of stems and roots, causing the plant to put its energies toward recovery the following year; such a plant might not look as vital or healthy while it is on the mend. Especially cool and cloudy summers can delay growth and flowering, just as a hot dry summer can dry and reduce a plant's root systems.

Ask other gardeners in your region if they have had a similar experience. Because weather affects the entire area, you can be sure that if that is the cause of your garden's malaise, others will be experiencing it as well. If all other plants in the area are doing famously, try to remember if anything was applied to your property that might be affecting plant growth. Many gardeners on Cape Cod had difficulties with their gardens last year, for example, because a source of bulk manure which had been delivered and placed on their gardens turned out to contain high levels of boron. A soil test pin-pointed the problem in this case, so if you can rule out adverse weather or other causes, sending samples in for testing might give you the answers you seek.

7

SCALING BACK

Even the most avid gardeners may face a time when they can't keep up with the level of gardening that they enjoyed in the past. No matter what precipitates the cutback, reducing the plantings thoughtfully will result in continued beauty, less maintenance, and enduring enjoyment of the garden. Scaling back does not mean a call to the local asphalt company, or the wholesale use of Agent Orange! Sometimes a change in the type or numbers of plants, their locations, or the man-made areas around the garden will give the desired results.

MAKING A PLAN
Before attacking a garden with shovels and spades, or promising plants to all the neighbors, take some time to evaluate what needs to go and what can stay. A perennial border might contain a stand of *Paeonia* (Peony) that is especially beautiful, and since peonies don't need dividing, a little bed of these plants would require little maintenance. Leaving this plant where it is, or moving it to another location, provides a low-maintenance connection with the garden of the past, as well as extravagant, fragrant flowers in the future.

Look realistically at all the plants in the gardens that must be removed. If there are any that require little care they can be moved to a smaller area where they will continue to grace the garden with their beauty. It isn't necessary to have a border filled with many varieties of plants to enjoy perennials; a large stand of a single type of plant can be very impressive and less work.

Gardeners who are scaling down should use the same criteria for the relocation of plants as those who are planning new gardens. Ask yourself where you will see your favorite plants most often. Site the favorites that you want to keep in view of a window, near a frequently used door, or next to a favored porch or patio.

The accessibility of revamped gardens may be a concern; if the gardens are being reduced because physical limitations prevent tending them, it may be possible to construct a new area that is both more manageable and easily maintained. A small raised bed or tall planter allows an experienced gardener to keep his or her hands in the dirt now and then without it being physically taxing. Large containers positioned on either side of a bench can be tended while sitting down, and those on a deck or patio are easily in reach of a gardener who is in a wheelchair.

TEMPORARY HELP

Those who find it necessary to cut back their gardening because of situations that are temporary might want to consider finding someone to assist in garden maintenance, at least until they see if a permanent change is necessary. Assistance can come in the form of a professional landscaping firm, another gardener looking to earn some extra money, or a local teenager. The success or failure of this approach will greatly depend on how well you communicate your desires with the person you've hired.

Even if an experienced, professional landscaping firm is hired, it is important to give detailed instructions. All gardeners have different tastes, and have developed gardening practices that reflect these preferences. I let my perennials self-seed, for example, so I continue to find seedlings that can be moved about or given away; I enjoy watching a plant develop through its entire life cycle, from shoots, to bloom to seed production. Other gardeners cut spent flower heads off before they go to seed so they never have to move or weed seedlings from their gardens, or because they find a plant with wilted flowers to be unattractive. Neither of these practices are any better than the other, but simply a matter of personal style.

Be sure to communicate *your* style of gardening to your helper. Give the person who will be caring for your plants a written plan which details the chores that need doing in each season. If possible, make a sketch of the gardens, marking where each plant is placed. Then walk your property with this individual, talking about what you want done while he or she takes notes; being in the garden may remind you of something that you forgot to write down.

In addition to scheduling the addition of compost or fertilizer, be sure to specify how plants that have passed their bloom period should be treated. I know a gardener who routinely spends a month away at the height of the summer. She hired a professional gardener to tend her extensive gardens while she was away, and every year when she arrived home after her travels she would find that the flower beds looked *terrible* because they appeared so barren and ragged. For three years she assumed that the weather was to blame; those three summers *had* been very hot and dry. If the drought was at fault, then there was nothing to be done.

The following summer this gardener didn't travel as she had in the past, but because other hectic situations pulled her attention away from her property she asked the paid gardener to resume caring for the perennials. It then became obvious that the beds didn't look barren because the plants had dried out, but because it was the landscaper's habit to cut all plants right down to the ground the minute they finished flowering. Naturally, this practice left holes around that garden that were not even filled with foliage.

This frustrating situation could have been prevented had the owner of the gardens not *assumed* that the professional had the same approach to gardening as she did. Always give your helpers specific instructions. "Please spread this mulch 3" deep around the plants, but be sure it doesn't touch the stems" is preferable to "Please mulch the garden." Telling your helper that you want the shrub pruned in a way that retains its natural shape will insure that you will not find your mounding shrub has been reduced to a smooth, green ball.

Those who hire teenagers from the neighborhood will need to give more direction to their helpers than they would if a landscaping firm is hired, although I have heard of professionals mistaking clumps of perennials for weeds just as an inexperienced young person might. When hiring someone to help with the weeding, it might be best to mark annuals and clumps of perennials so it is immediately obvious what stays and what gets pulled. Wooden popsicle sticks, available in stores that sell craft supplies, are good for this purpose. They are inexpensive, not quite as ugly as white plastic markers would be, and if forgotten and left in the garden will weather to an unobtrusive gray before decomposing into the soil. A stick placed in the middle of a clump will tell your garden helper that this plant does *not* get pulled!

Arrangements for the payment of your garden helper should be specific and in writing. If you are paying by the hour, it is easier to add to the list of jobs to done without causing confusion or resentment. If a price is agreed upon for the job as a total, be sure to list all work and the times it will take place in a contract ahead of time. A new agreement should to be written and attached to the first in the event that further tasks need to be added. Taking the time to spell it all out on paper prevents resentments and misunderstandings that would make the relationship difficult or end it all together. If you don't have the time to spend working in your gardens, you don't have the time to find a replacement for help that didn't work out the first time.

When hiring professionals you will want to ask for references and inquire what insurance the company carries. Call the people whose names were given as references to check on the firm's knowledge, performance and reliability. I know that this seems obvious, but it is surprising how few people take the time to do it! An ounce of prevention . . .

REPLACING ANNUALS WITH PERENNIALS

Every spring I speak to people who want to buy perennials to replace the annual flowering plants that have filled their flower beds every summer. "We're tired of spending the time and money on annuals every year!" they say. I explain that perennials may be less work, or may not be, depending on the plants chosen and the care given to them. Even the most care-free perennials require some attention.

In my experience, the amount of time it takes to tend to annuals and perennials is about equal. Both beds require attention to the soil (amendment, mulch and fertilizer), and although you don't spend time planting the perennials every spring, you have to cut the old perennial foliage down in either the fall or spring, and this takes about the same amount of time that planting an annual garden does. For some, filling the annual bed with a flowering or evergreen groundcover or low shrubbery might be a better alternative.

After an annual bed has been planted with something that is more permanent, some people find that they miss the bright, constant flowers that annuals provide. Even those perennials that are said to "bloom all season" don't offer the same abundance of flowers that annuals produce. In this situation a large pot filled with a favorite annual can bring great satisfaction for a minimum investment of time and money.

Annuals planted in pots can be placed more closely together than may be recommended on the tags that come with the plants. Packing them in a pot will give a full, lush appearance right away, and as the plants mature they will cascade over the edge in a pleasing way. Be sure to place such pots of annuals in a spot where you will pass by it frequently; this not only insures that you will enjoy the flowers as often as possible, but that you will be reminded to water it frequently.

REDUCING PERENNIAL BORDERS

Perennials may come up every year, but they are not maintenance-free. If your situation dictates the removal of a perennial bed or border, there are several alternatives to be considered. Such areas can, of course, be planted as lawn. If you need help with the upkeep of your property, it is often easier to find a lawn service or neighborhood teenager to mow and fertilize the grass than it is locate people skilled in the maintenance of perennial gardens. Sections of turf grass can be fairly low maintenance, depending on the area where you live and how meticulous you are about your yard. My personal approach is that anything goes (or should I say grows) in my lawn; if it's green, I mow it and leave it alone. (See the discussion of lawns to follow.) I might as well have a sign on the front yard saying "Weeds Welcome Here." If the sight of creeping charley, clover, or other lawn wanna-bes offends you, the upkeep of your grassy areas will be more time intensive.

Mixed borders can be replaced with a stand of a single variety of perennial plant, as previously discussed. Be sure to choose something such as *Hemerocallis* (Daylily) that can be left untouched for years. Flowering groundcovers such as *Vinca major* or *minor* (Periwinkle) for shade, or *Ajuga reptans* (Bugleweed) for sun or shade, are nice choices since they provide attractive foliage as well as flowers. Such groundcovers are a pretty and practical alternative to lawns and flower beds.

TOP TEN FLOWERING GROUND COVERS

1. *Ajuga reptans* (Bugleweed). *Ajuga* grows well in sun or shade. In addition to the flowers which bloom in mid-spring, many Ajugas have colored foliage which extends their interest past bloom. Bugleweed spreads rapidly and can invade lawns, so plant where edging or other barrier will separate if from the grass. Moderate moisture is required, and old flower heads can be mowed off with the lawnmower if desired. Zones 3-10.

2. *Cerastostigma plumbaginoides* (Dwarf plumbago). Plumbago is one of the few ground covers that blooms in late summer, and the flowers

are a clear, dark blue. It grows in sun or part shade, but does best in hot areas if some afternoon shade is provided. Moderate to moist soil is preferred by this plant. Foliage turns a lovely red-bronze in the fall. Zones 5–10.

3. *Cornus canadensis* (Bunch berry). One of the nicest ground covers for a moist, acid soil with high organic content. Bunch berry requires regular watering as it gets established, and it is a good choice under such acid-loving plants such as pines and broad-leaved evergreens. White flowers in the spring, and bird-pleasing red berries in the fall. Zones 2–6.

4. *Galium odoratum* (Sweet woodruff). Sweet woodruff is a rapid spreading ground cover for moist shade. It has sweet, lacy flowers in the spring and bright green foliage for the rest of the summer and fall. Galium spreads forever in moist situations, so site with care. Zones 4–8.

5. *Gazania rigens* (Treasure flower). Gazania is a trailing groundcover for warmer areas. It likes full sun and is fairly drought-tolerant. Several varieties are available with flowers in white, yellow, orange or bronze, and foliage is either green or silvery gray. This plant looks good cascading over walls and steep banks. Zones 8–10.

6. *Geranium macrorrhizum* (Bigroot cranesbill). This is one of my all-time favorite plants. Growing about a foot tall, it has attractive foliage all season and turns red in cold weather. Flowers are either bright magenta, white or pale pink. The foliage has a scent that I love, although it may not be everyone's cup of tea. *Geranium macrorrhizum* is drought tolerant, grows well in either sun or all but the deepest shade, and spreads by underground roots in a well behaved manner. Zones 3–10.

7. *Phlox subulata* (Moss phlox). In the early spring a ground covered with moss phlox is a carpet of color. Its flowers are either lavender, pink, white or pink and white striped. Low growing and fairly drought-tolerant, this plant likes good drainage. The green foliage looks nice the rest of the summer, and the plant is a fine ground cover for full sun. Moss phlox grows well in rock gardens, and when combined with spring flowering bulbs, satisfies even the most color-starved survivor of winter. Zones 2–9.

8. *Prunella grandiflora* (Self-heal). Prunella thrives in well-drained soils that have some organic matter in them. It will grow in sun or part shade and appreciates some afternoon shade in hot climates. Average moisture keeps Self-heal looking its best although it tolerates some dryness if it is in part shade. Pink or white flowers appear in early summer. *Prunella* is another plant which makes such good ground cover it will cover the lawn, so provide some barrier between it and your turf. Excellent under shrubbery. Zones 4–9.

9. *Vinca minor* or *major* (Periwinkle). *Vinca* has long been a favorite evergreen ground cover under trees. It blooms in the spring with small lavender or blue flowers, and is one of the only plants that will grow well under a maple tree. Both *Vinca minor* and *major* are tough plants that will grow in sun or part shade, but require more organic matter and water if sited in sun. Variegated forms are available. To stimulate new growth on an established patch, mow with the lawnmower and apply a thin layer of compost. Zones 3–9.

10. *Viola labradorica* (Labrador violet). This violet has tiny flowers and lovely foliage that is purplish green. It grows very low and tight, and is happiest in part shade or full shade. Another plant that is, shall we say, very enthusiastic, the Labrador violet should be placed where it can't take over the neighborhood. Mine looks great with variegated hostas, which are large enough to stand up to the violet's vigor. Zones 3–8.

GROUND COVERS AND THE LOW-MAINTENANCE GARDEN

It's a shame that the term "ground cover" causes most people to think of seas of green *Pachysandra*. We have come to think of ground covers as being low and green, but in actuality, any plant that grows together closely enough to cover the ground is a ground cover, and ground covers don't have to be short or all green.

Any perennial that will fill an area well enough to keep out the weeds with its root systems and shade might make a good ground cover. I qualify that statement with a "might" because aside from filling an area and keeping out weeds, we want ground covers to be low-maintenance. The whole point of such plants is to achieve areas that are fully filled with attractive foliage (and perhaps flowers) and do not need to be deadheaded, divided or coddled. Some perennials, such as the previously mentioned *Geranium macrorrhizum* make excellent ground covers, and many shrubs are also practical and attractive when planted en masse.

Ground covers make excellent low-maintenance plantings to replace a portion of lawn, cover the area around shrubs and trees, or fill slopes that are inconvenient to mow. In colder climates, evergreen ground covers are an attractive alternative to turf which turns brown in the winter. And ground covers may need less watering than grass; plants such as junipers, prostrate rosemary, and many of the shorter ornamental grasses are drought-tolerant once established, so they make good alternatives to water-guzzling lawns.

Newly-planted ground covers may look a bit sparse, but most fill in well by the third year. Unfortunately, when many people decide that a ground cover is needed, they often want that ground covered *tomorrow*. Time after time I have spoken with customers at the garden center and heard "I don't care what it is, as long as it grows *quickly*." Americans have been too influenced by fast food I think; we want our gardens to be instantly mature. As understandable as this impulse is, it can create problems down the road.

Plants that fill in quickly must be placed with care, because unless they are contained by physical boundaries of some sort they will just keep on growing. Consider this my plea for patience: choose the most appropriate plant for the location, not one that can be clocked on a speedometer. And as long as you are doing things right, don't forget to prepare the soil!

GROUND COVERS FOR THE LOW-MAINTENANCE GARDEN

1. *Asarum* spp. (Wild ginger). This woodland ground cover needs moist, organically rich soil, and thrives in part or full shade. Evergreen or semi-evergreen, depending on climate, wild ginger is a favorite of slugs and snails, so it is not the groundcover of choice for areas with large populations of mollusks. Zones 9–4. Depending on species. Some wild gingers are hardy to zone 2, others only in zones 7–9.

2. *Archtostaphylos uva-ursi* (Bearberry). This is one of the best low-maintenance ground covers for sun. Because it is nitrogen-fixing, it thrives in poor soils and never needs fertilizing. Evergreen with delicate pink flowers, bearberry likes good drainage and full sun. Does not transplant well, so it is best to buy small container grown plants. Zones 2–8.

3. *Bouteloua gracilis* (Blue grama). This low-growing bunchgrass makes a nice drought-tolerant cover when planted in full sun. Attractive

seed heads are pretty when the light shines through them. Nice on a slope, plant 18"–24" apart. 'Hachita' is a drought-tolerant cultivar for areas such as New Mexico and northern Texas/Oklahoma. Zones 5–8.

4. *Convallaria majalis* (Lily-of-the-valley). Lily-of-the-valley is a favorite ground cover for shade or part shade. It likes soil that is high in organic matter although it manages fairly well in the slightly amended sandbox of my garden. In moist, humusy soils it can almost be invasive. Sweet, old-fashioned and fragrant flowers appear in late spring. The berries of this plant are poisonous. Zones 3–9.

5. *Cotoneaster horizontalis* (Rockspray cotoneaster). Rock cotoneaster is a nice choice for banks and the areas on top of a wall. It grows well in sun or light shade, and is deciduous in the colder zones but evergreen where it is warmer. These shrubs prefer well-drained soil containing organic matter and are tough, adaptable plants once established. Zones 4–7.

6. *Epimedium* spp. & hybrids (Barrenwort). Epimediums are favorite plants for shade or part shade. They do bloom in early to mid summer although the flowers are very dainty, not showy. Barrenwort has heart-shaped leaves and grows between a foot and a foot-and-a-half high. It does not spread rapidly, but forms dense clumps that will grow nicely with other woodland plants or among the roots of trees. Zones 4–9 depending on the cultivar.

7. *Hedera helix* (English ivy). English ivy is a tough, adaptable plant that will grow in full sun or dense shade. It is one of the most popular evergreen ground covers. It grows best in well-drained, slightly moist soils that contain organic matter. Because it grows forever, site this plant with care; ivy scrambles up every wall and tree it meets, so it would require regular pruning in areas where it must be kept in-bounds. Zones 4–9 depending on cultivar.

8. *Hydrangea anomala petiolaris* (Climbing hydrangea). Although usually thought of as a climbing vine, this hydrangea also makes a great deciduous groundcover, especially on slopes. Its bark gets shaggy (exfoliating) as it ages, adding interest even when the leaves are gone. This lovely plant adapts to sun or shade, but keep well-watered for the first two years as it is slow to establish its root system. Once in

place for three years, it grows more rapidly, covering large areas. White lacy blossoms in mid summer. Zones 4–8.

9. *Hypericum calycinum* (Aaronsbeard St. Johns wort). This St. Johns wort spreads rapidly and tolerates poor, sandy soils. It grows one to one-and-a-half feet high and has bright yellow flowers in summer. It may get winter damaged in colder areas, but can be mowed in early spring to stimulate new growth. Zones 5-8.

10. *Juniperus conferta, J. horizontalis, & J. procumbens*. Junipers are probably the most popular ground covers for sunny areas, especially when a drought tolerant plant is necessary. *J. conferta* 'Blue pacific' is a compact, bluish cultivar which is one of my personal favorites. *J. horizontalis* is the most hardy of the junipers, growing in poor, heavy, or slightly alkaline soils as well as seaside conditions. This juniper is available in dozens of cultivars which have foliage ranging from green to bluish, to lime green, and variegated. *J. procumbens* is very low-growing with tight foliage. 'Nana' and 'Nana Californica' are dwarf varieties, the 'Nana' growing taller and wider of the two, and 'Nana Californica' with finer foliage. Zones 6–9, 3–9, and 4–9 respectively.

11. *Lamium maculatum* (Dead nettle). Don't let the common name scare you off; this plant is neither dead nor a nettle. I am conflicted about including it here, however, since I am not convinced that it is as low-maintenance as other ground covers. Lamium does tolerate dry soil and shade to part shade. The flowers are white, pink or lavender, and the many cultivars have variegated foliage which brightens shady areas. In southern areas it is more or less evergreen. So what's not to like? Well, it can get leggy by the end of summer, so it really looks its best if sheared after the first bloom. I have found the variety named 'Beacon Silver' to be less hardy and prone to leaf fungus, but I have had great success with 'White Nancy' and 'Pink Pewter.' Maybe best for covering small areas. Zones 3–10.

12. *Laurentia fluviatilis* (Blue Star creeper). This low, creeping ground cover for warm climates grows in full sun or part shade and needs regular watering. Blue flowers appear in spring and sporadically after that. When planted around 12" apart, young plants will fill the area in one year. Fertilize in spring and midsummer. Zones 9-10.

13. *Liriope muscari* (Lilyturf). This is an especially popular ground cover

in the south for commercial installations, although I am seeing it used more frequently in the Northeast as well. The foliage is grass-like and comes in green or variegated varieties. Tolerant of dry soils when established, lilyturf will grow in sun or shade. The lavender flowers make good blossoms for cutting; the plant blooms in late summer into fall. *Liriope* grows to one and a half to two feet high. In warmer climates it may be useful to mow in the early spring to encourage new growth. The downside? Slugs and snails love it. Zones 5–10.

14. *Pachysandra terminalis* (Japanese spurge). What can be said about *Pachysandra*? In all likelihood the most popular ground cover for shade and part shade, it tolerates full sun but may develop yellowish foliage in such bright light. This ground cover is evergreen; in fact, cuttings of Pachysandra make a nice addition to a holiday wreath. Bees love its white flowers. *Pachysandra* fills in quickly, but may be prone to fungal infections in damp conditions; when watering is necessary, water it deeply in the morning so the foliage will have a chance to dry. Grow Japanese spurge in organically rich, acidic soil that is moist but well-drained. Zones 4–8.

15. *Rosmarinus officinalis* 'Prostratus' or 'Huntington Carpet' (Low-growing Rosemary). Rosemary is a drought tolerant ground cover that you can use to flavor your food. Grow in full sun and lean soil—don't overdo the watering or fertilizer. Zones 8–10.

16. *Schizachyrium scoparium* (Little bluestem). This ornamental grass makes a lovely, mounding ground cover for sun. It will grow in poor, dry soil and doesn't mind heat. Little bluestem grows from one to two-and-a-half feet high, and is, as you might imagine, a bluish green in the summer. Nice fall color is a plus. Zones 3–8.

HEATHS AND HEATHERS

There are other ground covers that are as nice as those listed above, although many of them require a bit more tending. *Erica* ssp. (heaths) and *Calluna* ssp. (heathers) are lovely, low-growing plants that will grow in zones 4-7. Because they are evergreen (some *Ericas* even bloom in the middle of winter!), they are attractive year-round. They require well-drained, acidic soil which contains some organic matter but is generally of low fertility. Foliage colors vary from green to gray to red or yellow, so a planting of mixed heaths and heathers looks like a rich tapestry, even when the plants are not in bloom.

These plants need regular watering their first season as the root systems get established, but after that they are extremely drought-tolerant. Heathers and heaths look best when given a good pruning in early spring, or right after blooming for those which are in flower during this season. (If you plan it right you can have *Ericas* and *Callunas* in bloom year-round.) Cutting them back by as much as a third, and pruning out dead wood, stimulates new growth and results in thick, bushy plants. These plants may be the perfect ground cover for those with a sunny slope of sandy soil, as long as the yearly pruning isn't considered to be an excessive amount of maintenance.

A TALLER ALTERNATIVE TO GROUND COVERS
Ground covers aren't the only suitable replacements when scaling back perennial beds and sections of lawn. Shrub borders and groups of shrubbery are attractive, low-maintenance alternatives. A mixed shrub border will provide flowers from spring into fall and winter beauty in colder areas when combined with evergreen plants. If shrubs are planted where they can grow to their full size, there is little pruning other than the removal of dead wood and a stray branch here and there.

Because the new plants may be so small, mulching the area, then planting a suitable under-the-bushes ground cover will keep the area attractive while they grow. Ground covers help cover the "shaggy bark" look that is less than attractive when an area is newly planted. If the grouping of shrubs is in the sun, choosing a ground cover that grows well in sun *or* part shade will be smart; the bushes will shade the lower plants as they grow larger.

TALLER ALTERNATIVES TO SHRUBS
Scaling back is the ideal time to plant trees. Trees require even less maintenance than shrubs. Planting a varied selection of trees will provide you with year-round beauty, shade in the hot weather, and perhaps even flowers or fruit for the birds. There is an old saying that goes "He that plants trees loves others besides himself."

Because trees take time to grow, placing them on your property is an affirmation of good things in the future. Whether you will be in that location to enjoy the tree twenty years down the road or not, *someone* will be there to appreciate it. As a tree grows it provides beauty for us, homes and perhaps food for wild life, and oxygen for the planet.

Some low maintenance trees you might want to consider planting are:

Abies concolor (Concolor fir). Zones 3–7

Acer buergeranum (Trident maple) Zones 5–9
Acer campertre (Hedge maple) Zones 5–8
Acer ginnala (Amur maple) Zones 2–8
Acer griseum (Paperbark maple) Zones 4–8
. *Acer rubrum* (Red maple) Zones 3–9
Acer triflorum (Three flower maple)
Betula nigra 'Heritage" (Heritage river birch)
Carpinus caroliniana (Ironwood)
Cercidiphyllum japonicum (Katsura tree)
Chamaecyparis pisifera (Sawara false cypress)
Chionanthus virginicus (Fringe tree)
Cornus kousa (Kousa dogwood)
Ginko biloba (Ginko)
Halesia carolina (Carolina silverbell)
Ilex pedunculosa (Longstalk holly)
Koelreuteria paniculata (Golden rain tree)
Maackia amurensis (Amur maackia)
Magnolia x loebneri (Loebner Magnolia hybrids)
Magnolia virginiana (Sweetbay magnolia)
Malus 'Donald Wyman' or 'Professor Sprenger' (Crabapple)
Oxydendron arboreum (Sourwood)
Pinus cembra (Swiss stone pine)
Stewartia pseudocamellia (Japanese stewartia)
Styrax japonicus (Japanese snowbell)
Syringa reticulata (Japanese tree lilac)

CUTTING BACK ON LAWN CHORES

Short of ripping it all up and planting ground-covers, there are several approaches to the lawn that will mean less work for the homeowner. When tended in the traditional manner, lawns can be a great deal of work. The soil must be near neutral on the pH scale, making a yearly application of lime necessary in many areas of the country. Fertilizers need to be used to keep the turf vigorous and green, and unless you let the grass go dormant, large amounts of water are needed in times of drought.

Weeds that invade the lawn need to be dealt with, as do insects and diseases. Unfortunately, in our zeal to combat one problem in our lawns we often inadvertently cause others. Pesticides applied to rid the grass of one insect also kill all the beneficial insects present; some kill the earthworms as well. In doing so, our lawns are then less healthy, and without the beneficial insect populations to defend them, they are wide open to renewed invasions.

Those who decide that the green carpet of grass is worth the bother should keep these general guidelines in mind:

1. *Maintain the proper pH for a lawn* by testing your soil annually and applying amendments if needed. Although spring is the season when most people think to do this, fall is actually a better time because anything you apply to the turf has time to sink in and adjust the pH before the peak growing season the following year.

2. *Plant the type of grass that is hardiest in your area and requires the least maintenance.* There are grasses that are well-suited to each climate; check with your cooperative extension about which is most suitable for you. Ask if endophytic grasses are appropriate in your locale. This type of grass contains beneficial fungus in its tissues that kill or repel common lawn-eating insects. Other grasses are resistant to assorted diseases, and your cooperative extension or local garden center can advise you on which are recommended in your area.

3. *Don't mow your lawn too short.* Keeping the grass at a length suitable for golf is not only stressful for the plant, but exposes weed seeds to the light that they need for germination. A stressed lawn is less able to fight disease or recover from mild attacks by insects. Set lawnmowers to cut the grass to 21/2"–3" in length, and cut frequently enough so you are never removing more than 30%–40% of the length of the blades.

4. *Using organic fertilizers keeps lawns healthy* and helps promote thatch decomposition. Thatch is a layer of un-decomposed dead stems and roots; it is not made of the clippings from mowing a lawn, so there is no danger in using the newer "mulching mowers." Leaving the clippings on your lawn puts nitrogen and organic materials back into the soil. Apply organic fertilizers in the spring and fall.

5. *Lawns planted in areas where the soil is naturally heavy, or those that get frequent traffic, benefit from aeration.* Special machines punch holes in the soil, which allow air and

water into the ground and break up the layer of thatch. Use aerating machines that remove the core of soil and deposit it on top of the lawn. Applications of compost, top soil, seed, and organic fertilizers are appropriate at this time.

6. *Water lawns deeply but less often for maximum health.* Short, frequent applications of water leave plants with shallow root systems and create the ideal environment for the spread of pests and disease.

7. *Monitor lawns frequently for weed invasion and insect or disease attacks.* Such problems are easier to control if caught early. Consult your local cooperative extension, the garden center or a lawn maintenance service for help in diagnosing problems. Two or more opinions are usually advised if the company whose advice you seek has a service to sell. Be sure the treatment makes sense to you, and is in keeping with your general gardening philosophy. Take the time to do your homework before authorizing the use of pesticides, herbicides or fungicides on your lawn.

THE LESS-THAN-TRADITIONAL LAWN

If you have read the above guidelines for healthy lawns, and thought "I don't want to do all that—I'm trying to cut down!" then a non-traditional lawn may be for you. The easiest way to cut down on lawn maintenance is to decide that anything green is welcome in your lawn. Native grasses, wildflowers and other weeds are allowed to grow in with the grass you have planted.

The seeding of white clover into your turf provides a vigorous, green plant in the lawn that is nitrogen-fixing (puts nitrogen back into the soil) which means less fertilizing for you. When white clover is allowed to bloom, it will attract bees, so those allergic to bee stings will want to mow frequently to prevent flowering. Mow in the early morning before bee activity is at its peak, or forego the planting of clover altogether.

Such anything-green-is-welcome lawns still benefit from an application of an organic fertilizer twice a year, and an occasional top-dressing of compost. But it is no longer necessary to use herbicides. A variety of plants in the lawn make the area less vulnerable to insect devastation. I speak from experience though, when I say that you are more vulnerable to solicitations from lawn care companies.

At one house I lived in, my husband and I had our usual generous definition of "lawn." Because anything and everything grew in with the grass, and because we often let it grow a bit longer than we should have, the lawn was often filled with low wildflowers in bloom. I thought it looked rather like an impressionist painting, but others must have had different ideas because our phone often rang with offers of assistance from lawn maintenance companies. One or two even knocked on my door to tell me that my lawn was filled with weeds! My favorite calls were from a fine, but un-needed, company called Lawn Doctor. My standard reply to their offer to have a team tackle my lawn was "Sorry, no need for Lawn Doctor now, but if you see Lawn Mortician, send him over!"

EDGING THE LAWN

One time-consuming aspect of lawn maintenance is edging. Every flower bed and shrub border becomes new territory for the lawn to grow into; in order to prevent the grass from moving into your gardens, it is necessary to periodically weed it out, or chop it off with an edging tool. This not only keeps the grass from spreading into adjacent beds, but provides a space between the lawn and other plants so that the mower does not cut other gardens as it cuts the grass.

Edging can be reduced or eliminated by installing a man-made barrier around the perimeters of the lawn were it meets other gardens. There are many types of edging materials available, from plastic, to metal, to cement. The design of your garden and your budget will determine which you choose.

If flagstones suit the style of your property, installing a narrow path of closely placed flagstones around some or all or your beds is an attractive way to edge a garden. The stones provide a space which creates a narrow path around the plantings; this line of flagstones is easy to run the wheel of a lawn mower over, so the use of a weedeater to trim edges is unnecessary.

Mulching a circle around the trunks of trees, and then placing a flagstone border between the mulch and the lawn, eliminates the need to use the weed trimmer in this area as well. Not only is it less work, but it prevents the accidental scarring of a tree trunk which occurs when the string trimmer gets too close to the tree. Ground covers may be planted in the circle around the trunk to avoid large expanses of bare mulch.

REPLACING LAWN WITH "HARDSCAPE"

Another attractive way to reduce the size of a lawn is to add decks, patios and walkways to your property. Decks and patios create outdoor rooms that can be furnished with an assortment of outdoor furniture and perhaps some containers of plants. Paved areas are attractive when they are planned to complement the architecture of the house and the layout of existing gardens. They allow people to continue to enjoy being outdoors even when they are not physically able to work in the garden or walk over uneven grounds.

In order to maximize the use of the available space, and provide a deck or patio that suits the style of the house, a consultation with an architect or a landscape architect, may be useful. You will want to be sure to include a shaded area, and if a tree is not situated in the perfect spot to perform this function, an architect will help design an arbor or other shade structure that fits nicely with your home.

SCALING BACK IN A NUTSHELL

1. Hire help if you can afford it.
2. Fill annual or perennial beds with ground covers or shrubbery appropriate to the site.
3. Find ways to reduce the lawn by creating areas filled with shrubbery and ground covers.
4. Provide color by planting a few large containers with annuals.
5. Place an edging material between lawns and other gardens.
6. Install an in-ground sprinkling system and automatic soaker hoses for shrub and flower borders.
7. Replace lawn with patios, decks and walkways.

Q & A: SCALING BACK

Q. *I planted bulbs which can naturalize around my shrubs, but they are starting to poke out of the ground even though it is still midwinter. Will the cold damage them?*

A. Bulbs often pop out of the ground long before the calendar says that spring is here, and although gardeners often worry that the final month of cold weather will harm them, usually there is no cause for concern. Only the harshest cold without the insulating benefit of a snow cover might damage the tips of the leaves a bit, and this will not affect the plant or flower overall. Even spring bulbs that are in full bloom seem to come through a cold night or late spring snow just fine.

Those who live in an area of the country where severe cold and windy spells are likely may want to put a loose winter mulch over their bulbs to offer a bit of protection when there is no snow on the ground. Evergreen boughs which have been cut off of the Christmas tree are ideal for this purpose. Most gardeners, however, can rest assured that the bulbs know what they are doing when they start growing in late winter; perhaps they are making it their business to remind us that no matter what the thermometer says, spring is just around the corner.

Q. *My rhododendrons are now large and lovely, but are too big for me to continue to dead head them after they bloom. Can I discontinue this practice?*

A. Leaving the spent flowers on the plant will do no harm. Most people twist off the old blooms because they want to encourage more blossoms the following season, but the growing tips which contain the buds for the next year are already formed by the time the current blossoms fade anyway. At best, those who continue this practice are just cleaning the wilted flowers off the shrub. Relax and enjoy your mature rhodys.

8

How to Make Gardening Time Count

It is a fine day in early spring, and I am determined to get some mulch spread on the perennial bed before the weed seeds start to germinate. I don garden gloves and walk toward the garden shed for the wheelbarrow and pitchfork, passing by the area I want to cover with bark mulch. Hmmm . . . the iris really need to be divided before the mulch goes down . . . better do that first. I get the shovel and head back to the iris, but pass a butterfly bush on the way which reminds me that it needs a hard pruning *now*. Back to the shed for the pruners.

After I cut the *Buddleia* (Butterfly bush) back and put the prunings in the compost, I head back toward the iris, intending to chop it in thirds, only to realize that in order to plant the three clumps which will result, I will need to move some daylilies out of the way. The excess daylilies will go to a friend, but she can't take them for another month so they must be temporarily planted in pots. I head for the garden shed to find containers that will hold large clumps of daylilies.

Once the daylilies are out of the ground and snug in their pots, I dig up the iris, divide it, and plant the three divisions in their new homes in the perennial bed. As I work I spy some *Lysimachia* (Yellow loosestrife) that needs to be removed from the garden before it takes over my entire property, so I dig that out too. I am afraid to put it into the compost, for fear it will *grow* instead of decompose, so I spend some amount of time deciding if it is ethical to send it to the landfill, or if I know someone foolish enough to want it. Finally, I place it in a garbage bag on the deck, its fate uncertain.

Suddenly it is mid-afternoon and my stomach is telling me that I haven't had lunch. There are errands to run and phone calls to return. The tools are put back in the garden shed. I take off my garden gloves, leaving the *Lysimachia* sitting in its garbage bag purgatory, and the perennial bed still unmulched.

Sound familiar? There are so many tasks that cry for our attention in the garden, that it can be difficult to feel that anything ever gets accomplished. Although I *did* get the iris divided, the daylilies dug and potted, the *Buddleia* pruned, and the *Lysimachia* removed, the job that I really needed to get done—the mulching—remained untouched, and I left the garden feeling as if nothing was finished.

Not only was I feeling frustrated, but in the absence of mulch the weed seeds now had a renewed opportunity to sprout. There have been more springs than I care to admit when things would get to the point that the garden couldn't be mulched until it was weeded, and by the time it was weeded the perennials had grown sufficiently to make the mulching more difficult.

I created this problem myself. First, the gardens I tended in those days were too large. When we moved into our house in the foothills of the Berkshire mountains I naively pictured the entire 30' x 50' slope near the driveway planted in perennials. The weeding of this bed alone took three full days.

My second mistake was in not setting priorities before I went out to the garden. In the instance recounted above, for example, I should have spread the mulch first. Once the weed seeds were covered they would be less likely to sprout, so later I wouldn't need spend as much time weeding. If the mulch was disturbed when I got to the dividing of the iris, then so be it; a new layer could be quickly added over any turned soil in the area.

Old dogs can learn new tricks; I am much more focused now. I set a task for myself and am more or less strict with myself about finishing it before I go on to other, equally necessary, garden tasks. When it is time to cut down the old stalks of perennials, I just do that, working until the bed is finished. If I see a plant that needs dividing, the most I will do is take a plastic label from my pouch, mark it "divide," and stick the marker in the middle of the clump. As other jobs occur to me, I may stop and write them down on the pad of paper which is in the pouch with the labels, but I refuse to let myself get sidetracked into other chores.

I am not suggesting that everyone become unbendingly attached to their schedules. Heaven forbid! I am merely suggesting that the timely accomplishment of certain garden tasks saves work in the long run. There is also great satisfaction in finishing a job and crossing it off the things-to-do list. All that is required is a little disciplined focus.

THE BIG JOBS AND THE SMALL

Knowing which chores should be focused on until finished and which can be done piecemeal helps keep your garden sanity. My rule of thumb is that any job that affects the garden *as a whole* should be done in one concentrated effort; tasks that concern a single or small group of plants can be done piecemeal, as your schedule allows.

Mulching, soil amendment, fertilizing and watering are all done to an entire garden bed, so are most efficiently accomplished in one fell swoop. Putting several plants in the garden is also an activity to finish in one session if possible; this includes the planting of large areas of annuals, or a line of foundation plants. Once the necessary tools are assembled, along with soil amendments or other necessities, it is more efficient to place all plants into the garden at that time.

Fertilizing and soil amendment are best completed because if you are anything like me, you will *think* that you will remember which beds were fertilized and which were not, but when you get that bag of nutrients out in two weeks your memory isn't all that solid. Did I stop here . . . or here?

GARDEN WORK AS TEATIME OR COCKTAIL HOUR

Tasks such as dead-heading, pruning or dividing involve single or small groups of plants, and can be done in odd half-hour periods as you get to them. There are those who go so far as to say, "Prune when the pruners are sharp," a euphemism for pruning whenever you get around to it. Most jobs that can be tackled one plant at a time can be done whenever it is convenient.

I have found that these small garden chores can be very relaxing when approached in the right spirit. When you don't expect to *finish* a job, there is no feeling of frustration if only ten minutes of work get done. Weeding, dead-heading and removing leaves with leaf spot fungus can be done in fifteen minute intervals. These small spruce-it-up tasks can be very meditative and calming, as well as helpful to your garden.

Spending fifteen to thirty minutes in the garden is a great way to unwind after work. Taking a cup of tea or a glass of wine into the garden in the evening is one of the most calming cocktail hours I know. You will be surprised at how little time it takes to snip a stray branch from a shrub, pull a few weeds, then wander through, or sit surveying your property. Keep a wide plastic or terra cotta pot near your gardens to drop the weeds and clippings into, and an inexpensive trowel stuck near each flower bed.

GUIDELINES ON TIMING

There are many experienced gardeners who do all garden chores whenever it occurs to them that a particular job needs doing. Many of them have success with that method, which proves that you shouldn't get too rigid about things I suppose. Working with the rhythms of nature whenever possible does make sense, however, and by doing so you avoid creating problems for yourself down the line.

What kinds of problems might you create by doing a job in the wrong season? Plants transplanted in the heat of the summer may go into shock, and their branches may die back because they do not have the root systems necessary to support all the leaves in the heat. The same plant might not suffer such shock if transplanted in early spring.

Some shrubs form their flower buds the season *before* they bloom, so if they are pruned in the fall they won't bloom the following year. Knowing that this particular plant needs to be pruned *immediately* after it blossoms would mean that the gardener won't miss out on a season of colorful flowers. Keep in mind, however, that the worst thing that can happen (usually) from pruning at the wrong time will be diminished flowering. Too radical a pruning might kill certain shrubs, but trimming at the wrong time seldom will.

Successful garden maintenance isn't solely a matter of timing; it is equally important, or maybe more so, to remember that any *large* change stresses a plant. Pruning more than a quarter of a shrub's foliage, or digging and dividing a perennial are all very taxing for the plant. If all other growing conditions are ideal, the plant is better able to recover from the shock, but if such major work is done during a drought, or just before an extremely cold winter, the plant may suffer or die from the combination. Before doing anything that will tax a plant's resources, consider what the weather has been for the past few months, and what the climate is likely to be in the near future.

Below is a rough guide which lays out the best time for certain garden chores. It is laid out season-by-season, since the actual month for these tasks will vary according to your climate. In some areas, early spring is in April, but in other parts of the country spring arrives in February. Check with your local garden center or cooperative extension for the specifics of your area.

EARLY SPRING

Early spring is defined as the time when the temperatures are above freezing in the daytime, but before many plants have broken their winter dormancy. This is the time to:

1. Prune shrubs that form their flowers on new growth. Most of these are not early spring bloomers, but rather are plants that bloom in the summer.
2. Fertilize if necessary. Those using organic fertilizers can do this in the late fall.
3. Check garden tools and watering equipment.
4. Remove dead foliage and stems from perennial beds if it wasn't done in the fall.
5. Pull any weeds that have grown during the winter. (Yes, some weeds grow while everything else is dormant!)

SPRING

Spring is when the night temperatures are *generally* above freezing, and plants are breaking dormancy or beginning to bloom. This is the time to:

1. Plant cool weather annuals such as lettuce, peas, and pansies. Those who garden in warm climates are now removing these "winter" vegetables and flowers to make room for the summer annuals.
2. Divide and transplant established perennials, and plant new ones. Wait to divide spring bloomers until after they flower.
3. Plant new shrubs and move those that may need to be transplanted to another location.
4. Put mulch on beds before weeds germinate.

LATE SPRING/EARLY SUMMER

This is the period right around and after the last expected frost date in your area. This is the time to:

1. Plant remaining annuals and seeds (flowers and vegetables) sown directly in the ground.
2. Begin monitoring rainfall and watering if necessary.
3. Mulch if you haven't done so yet.
4. Prune spring blooming plants immediately after flowering.
5. Begin to check the garden on a weekly basis for insect or disease damage.

SUMMER

The hottest season of the year is the time to:

1. Monitor rainfall and supply water to your gardens when necessary.
2. Keep annuals and perennials which require dead-heading clipped as the flowers go by.
3. If desired, plant annuals to fill in bare spots.
4. Pick flowers, vegetables and fruits as they become available.
5. Cut back herbs (except sage) for renewed growth.

FALL

The frost is on the pumpkin and most plants prepare for either a dormant period or a slow-down in growth. This is the time to:

1. Harvest any remaining garden produce.
2. Plant winter flowers if you live in a warm climate.
3. Plant bulbs if you live in a colder climate
4. Remember to continue watering new plantings until the ground freezes.
5. Clean plants out of beds and borders if desired . (Stems may be left to give winter interest to the garden, and the garden cleaned in early spring.) Mark clumps to be moved or divided in the spring.
6. Spread compost or other amendments on all beds.
7. Add lime to lawns and flower beds if a soil test shows that a change of pH is necessary.
8. Spread organic fertilizers if needed.

WINTER

Winter is a time of rest and planning if you live in a cold climate, and the time to gear up and start spring activities if you live in a warm area. Remember to:

1. Buy seeds
2. Read gardening books
3. Fertilize if needed; those who are too busy in the spring and fall can spread fertilizer in the late winter, spreading it over the snow if desired. If you live in an area that is likely to receive rain *before* the ground thaws, spread fertilizers in

the spring or late fall so that these early rains don't wash the nutrients away before they can sink into the soil.

4. Prune holly and evergreens so clippings can be used for holiday decorations.

THROUGHOUT ALL SEASONS EXCEPT WHEN TEMPERATURES ARE BELOW FREEZING:

1. Pull weeds as they begin to grow.
2. Keep new plantings well-watered their first year.
3. Remove dead wood from shrubs and trees whenever you get around to it.

As you can see from this schedule, spring and fall are the times when the gardens demand the most work. This is the time to plan two or three full days to devote to your garden, although you should give your back a break—the days do not have to be consecutive.

WORK WITH NATURE, BUT REMAIN FLEXIBLE

It is most sensible to work with nature as often as possible. If your time is limited, it is wise to have help in your garden, is it not? Mother Nature can be our best garden assistant, but *she* often sets the agenda. Although we can place new plants in our gardens at any time, for example, when we work with nature as our helper, it helps if we plant in the early spring.

Everything in the plant is geared to grow in the spring, so by putting plants in our gardens at that time, we take the greatest advantage of what the plant is already primed to do. In addition, in most areas spring is the time of most frequent rains. Because new plantings need regular watering, planting in the season when it is most likely to rain in your region saves work.

Although there may be an ideal time for the chores associated with garden maintenance, this is seldom cast in stone. Other than planting, of all the tasks listed in the schedule of garden work, I have found that only three are most firmly tied to a particular season—mulching in the spring, watering (for plants that need it) in periods of summer drought, and amending the soil in the fall. The amending of soil is the most flexible of these three; organic materials don't *have* to be applied to the soil in autumn, it is just most convenient to do so.

Other jobs, such as dividing, fertilizing and pruning *can* be done at other times. There might be some repercussions as I have mentioned before; some flowering shrubs might not bloom if pruned at the wrong time, and plants divided in the heat will need frequent watering. But although a plant may be more stressed if such chores are done in a less-than-ideal season, seldom are such schedule alterations fatal.

PLAN YOUR GARDEN WORK AROUND YOUR ANNUAL RHYTHMS

For some people the months of November and December are the most hectic periods of the year. Those with school-age children often find the fall to be filled with school activities and constant chauffeuring. My fellow employees at the garden center are stressed to the max from April through June. Whether the schedule is crowded because of holidays, family commitments, or the demands of your job, everyone finds that some periods are more hectic than others. The wise gardener plans garden chores *around* these frenzied times of the year.

I try to get my fertilizing and mulching done in late March because by mid-April I will be working extra hours at the nursery. Those who often have company in the summer would want to plan the majority of their garden work for the spring and fall, leaving the summer days free to spend with their guests. If the autumn finds you juggling a teaching job and your own kids' homework, leaving the cutting of old perennials until early spring might be your best shot at maintaining some degree of sanity, at least as far as the *garden* is concerned!

ASSORTED TRICKS AND HINTS

What follows is a list of various ways that garden work can be minimized, or made easier and more efficient.

CREATE NEW BEDS WITH NEWSPAPERS

Those who have decided to cut down on the size of the lawn and plant perennials, ground covers or shrubs do not have to take the turf out first. In fact, that grass is filled with nitrogen that can feed your new plantings instead of the compost—and all it takes is all the news that's fit to print.

Lay out the perimeters of a new garden by using a garden hose, stakes and strings, or by raking fallen leaves into the new area in the fall. If the bed is to be rectangular in shape it is best to measure and mark the edges with stakes and strings. Curved edges are easily marked by curling the garden hose around in the desired shape, then standing back to evaluate the shape and how it blends with the rest of the yard.

No matter which of these methods you use, if the process is done in the fall and you have a yard full of fallen leaves, these leaves can help mark the bed and amend the soil at the same time. Rake leaves into the area defined by the hose or string and leave them on top of the lawn in that area. If it is windy, wetting them with a sprinkler will help keep them in place.

Be sure to stand back at this point and determine if the shape works well in the overall landscape design. If the beds you are planning are to be filled with annuals, perennials or vegetables, remember that it is smart to start small.

Gather as much newspaper as possible and begin laying a stack of open sheets over the lawn or leaves. If your soil is well-drained, the stack can be fairly thick—twelve or more open sheets. If you are not planning on planting right away, you can also use a thick stack no matter what type of soil is under the turf. But if your soil is high in moisture, or is not well-drained, and if you are planning to plant soon after the creation of your new garden, the layers of newspapers should be about four to six sheets thick.

The newspapers decompose after a while, adding their organic matter to the soil along with that of the lawn and leaves. But until the paper breaks down, the soil under the layers is kept a bit more moist than it ordinarily would. This is fine if you are gardening in an area where the soil is sandy or extremely dry, but thick layers of newspapers can keep some sites too wet until the papers start to break apart.

After you have placed several stacks of papers over a small area, fork some bark mulch or manure over the papers to hold them down. Use a layer of mulch or manure that is two to three inches thick. Be sure that the stacks of paper are overlapping at the edges, and work in small sections to keep the papers from blowing away before they are covered with mulch. If the soil is especially dry, water the area well before laying the papers down, and after they are mulched as well. The moisture will help the lawn and leaves decompose, and will please the earthworms that help with this process.

Those who create these beds in the fall can plant in the spring. If the process is done in early spring, the area can be planted later that same season, but you may have to chop a hole in the damp layers of papers in order to stick your plants in the soil.

Raised beds can be built on top of lawn using the same method; after the container has been put into place on the lawn, spread the newspapers over the lawn inside the board or stone walls, and pile manure, top soil and any other organic amendments such as leaves on top of the paper. Do not pack these contents down, but remember that the filled bed will sink somewhat as the organic matter breaks down.

COMPOST RIGHT ON THE GARDEN TO SAVE WORK AND TIME

Fresh manure or leaves can be added to any bed that will not be planted for about six months; non-composted materials can be put on a vegetable plot, an annual flower bed, or a new (unplanted) perennial bed in the fall. It can be left to decompose on top of the bed or you can till it into the soil. The materials break down over the winter and are sufficiently composted right on the site by the time you are ready to plant the following spring.

Those with a vegetable garden or beds where only annuals are planted can save time and work by raking leaves directly onto the garden. If you don't have a fence to prevent them from blowing away, you might need to toss a few shovelfuls of soil on top of the leaves; thoroughly wet them until they are matted down, or cover them with a load of manure or shredded bark mulch. In the spring these beds can be turned or, if they are well mulched and weed-free, your plants and seeds can be placed in the garden as it is.

Kitchen garbage and yard wastes can also be placed directly in the soil or underneath mulch in vegetable gardens. This is the method championed by Ruth Stout, an organic gardener and author of a number of gardening books, including *How to Have a Green Thumb Without an Aching Back*. Composting directly in the garden works best in vegetable gardens, especially those with paths that are heavily mulched.

All kitchen garbage and vegetable waste from the garden itself is placed in a hole dug in a bare part of the garden (again, a path is a good spot for this) or tucked underneath a thick layer of mulch. The mulch hides the garbage well enough so the garden doesn't look like a landfill. This method may attract animals to the garden, however, so if the thought of skunks, raccoons, or other wildlife rooting in your garden bothers you, stick with the compost bin.

COMPANION PLANTS

Most gardeners think of companion plants as those which act to protect each other from insect attack. While this is one type of companion planting there are other combinations that help the gardener save time and work on garden maintenance. Plants can sometimes be combined to hide or help correct an annoying trait that the gardener must otherwise deal with.

Daffodils: floppy foliage in the summer, hidden in the fall

Many people find themselves vexed by the floppy daffodil foliage in the garden after the bulbs have finished blooming in the spring. The foliage needs to remain in the garden until it dies naturally, because this process first feeds the bulb, then signals it to become dormant for the upcoming summer. I have seen gardeners braid the foliage, tie it in knots, and wrap it with twist-ems as though the leaves were a bunch of scallions. These solutions, as ingenious as they may be, are all very time-consuming and are not good for the plant. Besides, macraméd plants look rather out of place in the garden.

A better solution is to plant your daffodils among other perennial plants that are slow to come out in the spring, will hide the wilting foliage by midsummer. *Hostas* are perfect for this purpose if your bulbs are planted in the shade or part shade. Other mid to late summer bloomers such as *Echinacea* (Purple coneflower) are good companions in sunny gardens.

Muscari species (Grape hyacinth) are good companions for daffodils that solve yet another problem for the gardener. Every spring I admire the *Narcissus* in my garden and promise myself that in the fall I will plant more. "I'll remember where I need to fill in." I tell myself. Really. You would think that by now I should have realized that if the phrase "I'll remember . . ." is used, it is almost certain that I really *need* to write it down.

But no . . . I stand in the garden in October, trying to guess where the daffodils are already planted. Once I determine that *this* must be the place where the new daffodils should be planted, I sink in the shovel and find . . . yes, the other bulbs. Now I am smarter, however, and the lovely grape hyacinth is helping me out.

If you have ever planted *Muscari* you might remember that in the fall its leaves pop out of the soil, all fresh and green. Many gardeners panic the first time they see this, certain that the bulbs are confused or mistaken and that they will surely be killed in the winter. Not to worry however, because this is just what *Muscari* do. Knowing this, the grape hyacinth can be pressed into service as daffodil markers every autumn.

Narcissus bulbs get planted at least six inches deep in the ground. Don't skimp—dig the holes deep enough. *Muscari*, being smaller bulbs, are placed three inches below the soil's surface. To mark the location of your daffodils, plant the larger bulbs first, then the grape hyacinths in a layer on top of them. Place the *Muscari* bulbs two inches to the side of the daffodil bulbs, so that the shoots of the emerging *Narcissus* won't grow smack into the little bulbs, but otherwise they can be placed in more or less the same group.

The shorter, blue blooms of the grape hyacinths look lovely below the yellow daffodils that bloom at the same time. If the *Narcissus* are a variety that bloom earlier or later than the grape hyacinths, then the staggered bloom time will extend the flowering period. And best of all, every autumn the *Muscari* will poke up its fresh green leaves just as it's time to plant new bulbs, saying, "Don't plant here... this space is taken!"

The stiff and the floppy

Planting plants that are sturdy and stiff next to those that tend to flop is another way the gardener can have plant companions help each other out. I love oriental lilies, and I have several types in my small cottage garden. The lilies tend to be rather top heavy, however, and they are always in danger of falling over if the weather is especially windy or if a lot of rain weighs them down.

I hate to stake my perennials; I don't like how staked plants look in my casual garden, and besides, I hate taking the time to do it. Top heavy or not, when it comes to staking, I usually pass on staking. A few years ago I did notice that the lilies planted next to the *Boltonia* never fell down. Ah-ha! The perfect match!

Boltonia is a late-blooming perennial that has very straight, stiff stems. Because it blooms in late August, it is still short enough when the lilies bloom that it does not cover or detract from their flowers. After the lilies have gone by, the *Boltonia* foliage grows tall enough to hide the spent lily stalks and their swollen seed-pods. Now many of my lilies have *Boltonia* for neighbors.

Other sturdy, straight perennials can be planted near those prone to flopping. This is most effective when the stiff-stemmed plant is a late bloomer and the floppy plant one which flowers earlier. *Hibiscus moscheutos* (Rose mallow), *Cassia* ssp. (Wild senna), and the taller *Rudbeckias* would also make good, supportive neighbors. If there is a plant that is prone to falling in your garden, look to see if there is another that would lend its stems for the cause.

Early and late bloomers

Placing plants with different bloom times next to each other is another way that plants can be grouped to the gardener's advantage. This is particularly important if an early-blooming plant does not have attractive foliage for the rest of the season. In such cases, placing the earlier bloomer *behind* a plant that blooms later will help to hide any spent foliage. This is especially effective if the plant that flowers later is *taller* then those which came before. A group of tall, late bloomers can hide ugly foliage of a plant that is past its prime.

MAKING GARDEN TIME COUNT

Q. *I occasionally see recipes for home made garden products. Do they work?*

A. One way to save time in the garden is to only treat a problem with a product which you know will work. This might seem simple, but as I will discuss in the next chapter, many people put products in their soils and on their plants without any clear idea if the "cure" is appropriate for the disease.

One impulse home gardeners have is to grab any product out of their cupboards, even though what they are grabbing may not even be intended for the garden. I spoke to a man at the garden center once who was trying to kill insects by poring bleach on them. His bugs were whiter than white, but they were still eating the plants! There are many home remedies and recipes, spread to gardeners by word of mouth and in assorted gardening books. Many of these do work, but others are less reliable.

My concern about any home brew applied to the garden is that often no one has tested it for the best concentration, rate of application, or frequency of use. There are no instructions to refer to, let alone any 800 numbers to call for advice. You might be applying the correct amount for the problem (assuming that the concoction you are using is appropriate for the problem) or you might be using too much or too little.

Sometimes these home recipes seem that they must be less expensive than over-the-counter garden products, but in my experience this is often not the case. And whether homemade or store-bought, any remedy costs too much money when it is used incorrectly. If you are going to put time into making your gardens beautiful, put the time into an accurate diagnosis of the problem, not into mixing an under-the-sink cure-all.

Q.   *Do landscape cloths really work to keep weeds away on a long-term basis?*

A.   Several types of landscape cloths are usually made of non-woven synthetic fibers. They are designed to provide a solid cover over the earth, which allows moisture and air to pass into the soil and keeps weeds from growing by preventing light from reaching seeds and plants. In a word, mulch. Studies show that the denser the fabric, the better the weed suppression. If you can see a great deal of light through the fabric when you hold it up, it is not the product of choice.

Fabric must be covered with a layer of wood chips, shredded bark, or gravel to hold it in place and improve its appearance. Here is one of the places that it gets tricky; if the mulch is organic (such as shredded bark) and the layer is more than 3" thick, weeds will happily grow on top of the fabric. Thick layers of mulch will also cause the trees or shrubs in the area to send roots toward the surface in search of oxygen, and the fine roots can grow into and through the fabric. When the fabric is pulled up and replaced years down road, these roots will tear off needlessly injuring the plant.

Because the mulch holding landscape fabric in place must be kept thin, it must also be renewed periodically as it washes and blows away from the cloth. With attention to the purchase of a dense fabric, proper application and upkeep of the mulch which holds it in place, landscape fabric is a good method of weed suppression for some situations.

9

DEALING WITH PESTS
AND DISEASES

Insects and fungus, wildlife and wilt—these are the sorts of garden problems that make people crazy. It is maddening when we, *Homo Sapiens* and gardeners, have done all that we could for our gardens, only to be challenged—and maybe beaten—by a mere bug! Or worse a fungus that we can't even *see*. It is enough to drive a person to drink. It is no wonder that it does drive many people to use insecticides and fungicides. Usually, however, there is a better way that has nothing to do with the plant, the insect or any microscopic organism. It has to do with us.

Our initial response to a problem in our gardens is to want to fix it . . . *now*. We want our gardens to be beautiful; we care for our plants, and we want to help them be as healthy and lovely as possible. When we see a problem, we want to take action. As understandable as this impulse is, it can start us on a course of action that is ineffective, inappropriate, or causes more problems than it solves. Gardeners should adopt the motto of physicians: we too should pledge to "first, do no harm."

FIRST THINGS FIRST
When it first comes to your attention that a plant is not doing well, take the time necessary to evaluate the situation. There are very few situations in the garden that demand *immediate* action, and seldom will a problem cause the overnight demise of a plant, so don't rush to action. Exceptions might be animals eating your plants, or an exuberant five-

year-old smashing them or pulling them out of the ground; in these cases an instant reaction might save your garden. Covering the plants that are being munched, and diverting the five-year-old, may be enough to stop the damage and save the plant. But most problems in the garden are not as quickly diagnosed or solved.

There are several reasons that a sick looking plant may not be doing well. Insect attacks, diseases, weather, wildlife foraging and human actions can all affect how a plant grows and whether it lives or dies.

It is important to try to determine what is causing the problem in general, and at the same time to ascertain if the damage is continuing. Look over the entire plant with care and evaluate the situation by going through the following steps:

1. *Rule out water stress first;* be sure that the plant has gotten enough, but not too much, moisture. Feel the soil and think about how much rain or watering the plant has received over the last month or two. Too much or too little water can cause a plant to wilt, drop leaves, or die.

2. *Try to determine if the problem is still going on.* If only a few leaves are affected, remove them and monitor the plant to determine if the damage is continuing. If most of the leaves are showing symptoms, find those that are clear and mark them with a twist-em or small piece of string. Look at the plant over a period of four or five days and see if the damage spreads to the previously unaffected leaves that you flagged. Sometimes we notice insect damage after the insect has done the damage and gone; treating the plant in this situation is a waste of time and money. Timing can be important; when caught early, many fungal problems can be stopped simply by removing the affected tissue.

3. *Look at the same plant in other yards and gardens* to see if all plants look the same way at this time. Certain pines, for example, drop needles every fall, but people often assume that something is wrong with their plant when this happens. Ask at your cooperative extension or garden center if the situation you are observing is part of a natural cycle, or if there is a pest that is commonly attacking plants in the area at this time.

4. *Examine the newest foliage on the plant;* is the new growth green and healthy looking? Many plants shed their oldest leaves as they grow, and these leaves often turn yellow and

fall off. Some loss of older leaves is normal, but if many more of the oldest leaves are falling then ever before, suspect water stress or disease. If a plant does not have adequate moisture it is likely to drop the oldest leaves in order to save what water it has for the newest growth. Larger, older leaves lose more water through transpiration, so the plant will let them fall to prevent the excess loss of moisture. Plants that have received adequate water may have a disease. Samples should be taken to your local garden center or cooperative extension office for identification.

5. *Examine the trunk and stems of the plant well.* Are there any holes in the stem? Holes might indicate the presence of a borer. Is the bark or stem tissue cracked or broken? Has the base of the plant been chewed or damaged? Water and nutrients are carried up the plant in the areas under the bark and outer stem tissues, so if this area gets damaged the plant may suffer or die.

   Stems can be damaged by small animals, insects, or mechanical injuries caused by lawnmowers, weed-eaters or other garden tools. If the stem has areas that look depressed and sunken, a virus or fungus may be the cause.

   Single branches that look damaged or diseased should be removed. Follow the stem or branch below any holes or other signs of insects or diseases as discussed above, and cut the branch away from an otherwise healthy plant. Discard all diseased plant materials.

6. *Look for evidence of insect damage.* Some common signs of insect feeding are holes in the leaves, chewed foliage, curling or other distortions of leaves, and yellow stippling. Sticky leaves, or the presence of an abundance of webs, also indicate insect activity, although not all webs are created by insects that hurt plants. See insect damage, below.

7. *Examine plant for signs of diseases.* Fungi, viruses, and bacteria can all injure or kill a plant. Common signs of these diseases are: leaf spots, either round or irregular in shape; yellowing of leaves, either some or overall; sunken tissues that look water-soaked; abnormal growth or plant tissues; and a wilting or defoliated plant. Fungi are the most common diseases which affect plants. See diagnosing diseases, below.

   If you are unable to determine the cause of a problem

yourself, take a piece of the plant to your local cooperative extension or a garden center. Be sure to cut a sample that is large enough to show several damaged areas and some healthy tissues if there are any. Don't take a dead, dried up piece of plant and expect someone to be able to tell what the problem was. Once the stems and leaves are so far gone that they are brown and dried, it will be difficult to get a diagnosis.

DOES THE PLANT NEED TREATMENT?

Once the problem has been identified, ask yourself if treatment is really necessary. Just because a few leaves have chewed edges or spots on them does not necessarily mean that something must be done about it. If over a third of the plant is effected, and the problem seems to be getting worse, you might want to see if intervention will help. Other times, living with an acceptable level of damage is the best response, and if the damage has already been done and is not continuing, then it is too late for treatment anyway. No sense setting the alarm after the thief has gone.

The most low-maintenance approach is to *never* treat a problem— survival of the fittest and all that. This is the approach I usually take in my perennial gardens. If a plant is repeatedly prone to a fungus or insect attack, then out it goes. There are so many plants that do well without the necessity of sprays, potions or prayers that I see no reason that I should have to fuss with ones that do require such treatments. I would rather spend my time building healthy soil than fighting bugs and fungi.

Shrubs and trees, being larger and taking longer to get mature in the garden, demand a *bit* more intervention if they have a problem. A normally healthy plant might have a problem one year because of unusual weather conditions or an abnormally high insect population. There are times when an ordinarily pest-free plant is suddenly covered with insects or fungi. In such cases, it may be desirable to promptly treat the plant in order to maintain its good health. Some insects *do* spread diseases from plant to plant as they suck the juices.

Ultimately, the decision to use an insecticide or fungicide rests with the gardener's good sense. If a woody ornamental is healthy, it will probably survive an unusual attack of insects or fungus brought on by weather conditions. But if a shrub or tree is prone to the same problem year after year, it should be replaced with a plant that does not require such vigilance and intervention to keep it healthy.

WILL THE TREATMENT DO MORE HARM THAN GOOD?

When we work in the garden it is important to remember that our actions affect more than a single plant. The amendments we add to our soils contribute in several ways to keeping the plants in the area healthy, for example. Compost adds organic matter and nutrients, and provides an environment for the many helpful fungi to live and grow. The treatment of insects and diseases usually affects more than the pest we are targeting, so we should take the time to evaluate carefully before any product is used in our gardens.

It is important to remember that in killing off an entire population of insects we cause the predators of that insect to leave our gardens and search for food elsewhere. This creates a wide open field for the return of the pest in greater numbers than before. Nature is filled with checks and balances, and when we artificially destroy a population we don't like, we affect several other populations as well, ultimately to our own detriment.

Insecticides kill all insects they touch, with the exception of the Bt and other biological controls which target single types of insects and larvae. Even pyrethrum, a botanical insecticide which breaks down in a matter of hours, will kill any insects it lands on, good or bad. Insecticidal soaps and horticultural oil sprays work by smothering insects, but these too should be used with caution so that the honey bees aren't smothered along with the aphids. Fungicides will kill the fungus that is harming our plant, but some also destroy the several that help it. All of these products should be used only when necessary, and then *always* according to the directions.

TROUBLE WITH BUGS

Not all bugs are bad bugs. Really. Many of the insects that we cringe from are a great help to gardeners: they eat other insects that munch our plants; they pollinate the flowers that make fruits and vegetables; and they help break down organic matter in our soils. We should greet them with songs of praise, not cans of insecticide. At the very least, our attitude should be one of live and let live.

Many insects get blamed for garden damage because they look creepy, or because they are active in the daylight at the same time we are active in the garden. This bug was next to the plant with the chewed leaves, so it *must* be the one that did the damage, right? Well, maybe yes, maybe no. Just remember that an assumption of guilt might lead to the destruction of an insect that is really working to keep your garden *healthy*, so never assume that an insect is a pest; try to get an accurate diagnosis of the problem.

DIAGNOSING INSECT DAMAGE

If you suspect that the problem is caused by insects, try to find them on or around the plant. Many insects feed at night, so don't be quick to blame the bugs present during the day for damage that may be happening after dark. Go outside with a flashlight to check for night-feeders. Don't look at the most damaged leaves to find the guilty party; chances are that they have moved on. Examine the healthier foliage *next* to the most damaged areas; the insects have most likely traveled on to greener pastures.

Insects that suck juices from a plant

If the plant's leaves feel sticky, a sucking insect has been at work. Such insects suck the juice from leaves and excrete the excess, which makes a tacky coating on the surrounding leaves. Sometimes a dark, gray powder forms on this excreted juice; this is called sooty mold, and although it is unattractive, it is a secondary situation which results because of the damage done by the insects.

Leaves that have been tapped into by sucking insects are often stippled yellow. They may also be puckered or warped because the insect damaged tissues when it sucked out the plants juices, causing the plant to became distorted as it grew. Sometimes a leaf will grow small bumps or tabs out of the places where an insect damaged the leaf. If this is the case, the bumps that are so visible are usually *old* damage; monitor the plant to determine if insect activity is continuing.

Plant pests that are very small, such as mites, can be difficult to spot. Mites suck juices from a plant, but because they are so tiny, gardeners often blame the damage on other bugs in the area. Place a white piece of paper under the leaves of a sick looking plant and knock the branch above it sharply. If mites are present, you should be able to see very tiny dots (almost like dust) moving around on the white paper.

In addition to mites, other sucking bugs commonly found in gardens are aphids, scale, lacebugs, white flies, and mealy bugs.

Insects that chew

Some insects don't suck juices from plants, but chew parts of their leaves, stems, or flowers instead. Because they do not excrete the excess juice (which is called "honeydew") plants attacked by such insects do not get sticky nor develop secondary infestations of sooty mold. It may be obvious nevertheless that the plant is being eaten because most chewing insects take big bites. Even the small flea beetle, which makes tiny holes in leaves, is usually present in such numbers that the plant is riddled with these small holes.

As previously mentioned, chewing insects are often active at night; go into the garden after dark to see if you can spot the culprit. Slug damage is often mistaken for insect chewing, but a flashlight will quickly show if the mollusk is to blame.

IDENTIFYING INSECTS IN THE GARDEN
If you can catch the bugs that you think are harming your garden, put one or two in a jar and take them to your extension service or garden center for identification. Books with color pictures of the most common garden insects can also be helpful. *Rodale's Color Handbook of Garden Insects* by Anna Carr is one I am familiar with, and it is possible that your public library or bookstore has others on hand.

HOW TO RID THE GARDEN OF HARMFUL INSECTS
Most insects with sucking mouth parts are visible during the day. Because you can see them you can also kill them by spraying with a product which smothers them. Insecticidal soap is an easily obtained, safe spray which kills insects in this way. Don't use dish detergent for this purpose, as it usually has other additives which will be harmful to the plants. Insecticidal soaps are available in concentrates which you can mix with water, or already diluted in spray bottles, ready to apply to infested plants.

Horticultural oil may also be used to smother these insects. Sometimes called superior oil, this water soluble oil is highly refined so that it won't harm the plant even though it is smothering the bugs. Do not use dormant oil for this purpose; it is not as refined as the superior oil and is intended for use on dormant (without leaves) plants only. Horticultural oil must be diluted with water, and applied with a pressure sprayer.

Insecticidal soap and superior oil need to be sprayed directly on the insects you wish to kill; spraying the plant itself will have no effect on the insects that arrive in a day or two. Plants should not be sprayed with superior oil if temperatures are above 90 degrees. One of the advantages of these sprays is that you target the mites, scale, or aphids that are on the plant, but you don't harm beneficial insects that may cruise by next week.

Do not use a hose sprayer to spray oils or insecticides on your plants; they are not accurate enough. Hose sprayers may be fine for fertilizers, but they are not made for the application of fungicides, insect killers, and superior or dormant oils.

Chewing insects can be killed by using a product made from pyrethrum. This insecticide is made of the crushed flowers from the painted daisy, and is different from synthetic pyrethrins. The advantage of pyrethrum is that it breaks down very quickly, so it does not linger and poison the soil. It must come into contact with the insect being targeted, however, for it to be effective. There is a time-release pyrethrum available for those who are less than thrilled about wading into their gardens with a spray bottle at midnight.

Other botanical insecticides such as nicotine sulfate, rotenone, and sabadilla can also be effective, and they are available as a dust; these products must be applied with a duster which spreads the product on the underside of leaves where the insects hide. New botanical insecticides are being developed and tested which may be available in the near future. Continue to check with your local garden center and read labels on the products being sold.

ALTERNATIVES TO INSECTICIDES

Gardeners who would like to avoid the use of *all* insecticides do not have to welcome harmful bugs with open arms. A garden filled with flowers will attract beneficial insects to your garden to feed on those you would like to destroy. Placing a birdbath near your gardens will not only attract the insect-eating birds, but will also serve as a watering hole for wasps to eat your problem bugs.

Repellents are also effective when used on plants that are favorite targets for the bugs in your garden. Hot Pepper Wax is a prepared spray of red pepper extract in a wax base that holds it on the plant. A home brew of hot pepper powder mixed with some insecticidal soap or a "sprayer-sticker" product will work as well. Many gardeners make sprays of garlic, or the leaves of other plants that the insects do not attack, but the blending, straining, and bottling of such sprays is a more time-consuming process than most of us want to get involved in.

THE CATERPILLAR CHOMP

Insects may not be responsible for the ragged edges on your plants; remember that caterpillars chew leaves too. Look for frass (caterpillar excrement, usually small, dark pellets) underneath the damaged leaves. Frass is frequently easier to spot than the perpetrator; caterpillars are often similar in color to the plants they eat, so look carefully.

There may be only a few caterpillars feasting on your plant. If the plant is large and able to absorb such damage you may decide to leave well enough alone. If you want them off of your plant, but are reluctant to kill them because they may, after all, turn into beautiful butterflies, it is usually possible to relocate the caterpillars to another plant. Try to find something similar to what they were feasting on in your garden; many caterpillars have rather selective diets. Wear garden gloves when handpicking caterpillars off your plants; I have heard that some people get a rash from the fuzz on certain caterpillars.

Bacillus thuringiensis (Bt) is a parasitic bacterium which kills leaf-eating caterpillars. It is very useful for large infestations of caterpillars because it kills them but *not* any beneficial insects that may be on the plant. Bt is most effective, however, when caterpillars are small. It will kill the gypsy moth larvae when they are small, but Bt is not effective when these creepy-crawlies get over an inch long.

SLUGS AND SNAILS

The most low maintenance way to deal with slugs and snails is to choose plants they do not like to eat. Slugs and snails seem to prefer large and juicy foliage which is like that found on hostas and ornamental kale. They also like moist environments, so they thrive in partly shady areas where there is damp mulch to hide under.

Most gardeners have areas where slugs and snails thrive, and most of us persist in planting *Hostas* or other plants they are found of eating. Once again, it is reasonable to decide that there will be an acceptable level of damage caused by slugs and snails. Some years there are more mollusks around then others, however, so even the most tolerant gardeners get fed up with the holey foliage and decide that intervention is necessary.

I know you have all heard that the best way to trap slugs is to put out a saucer of beer—do yourself a favor, and forget about it. The smell of stale beer isn't great in a bar, and it is even less appealing in a garden. Add to that the sight of several dead, bloated slugs floating in that stale brew, and you have something guaranteed to turn the strongest of stomachs. Do we need this in our gardens? No we do not.

Slugs usually feed at night, so those who wish to hand remove them will find the best hunting is after 10 PM. Early morning, especially on a cloudy day, is an alternative for people who think that a flashlight search is out of the question. Wear garden gloves if you don't wish to be "slimed," and drop slugs in a carton of soapy water, or consider them soil amendments and dig them into the soil, crushing them with a trowel.

Slugs can also be safely killed with a spray of ammonia and water. Mix three parts water with one part ammonia in a bottle that has a direct stream (not a mist) spray. Direct a squirt at each slug you see; the ammonia won't hurt the plants, but it will kill the slugs on contact. This spray might damage fragile flowers, so try not to hit the blooms when you are slug hunting.

Most baits that kill slugs are also poisonous to birds and pets, so they should always be used with caution. Poisons must be hidden in some way so that the slugs can reach the bait but other animals are not able to get to it. Some gardeners create traps out of cottage cheese cartons, cutting holes near the bottom only large enough to accommodate the slug. The carton's lid hides the bait from other animals.

If you are going to go to the trouble of making traps and baiting them, then checking the traps, emptying them, and restocking the poison, I think that you might as well forgo the poison bait and just use a cozy hiding place to trap your mollusks. A smooth board which is placed on top of a couple of rocks and sticks (to hold it *slightly* off the ground—a half-inch to one inch is fine) will be an attractive place for slugs to hide from the sun. Orange and grapefruit halves, pulp removed, are also favored places to spend the day. If you place such traps around the plants most favored by the slugs and snails, the mollusks can be harvested during the day and disposed of.

Attracting predators to your garden will help keep slug populations under control. Many birds and snakes eat slugs, as do toads, shrews, and turtles. Once again we see the wisdom of encouraging a wide variety of wildlife on our properties.

NEMATODES

Nematodes are not insects or mollusks, but are a type of round worms, and are, for the most part, so small they are microscopic. Found throughout the world, these thread-like worms are among the oldest multi-cellular life forms on earth. There are many types of nematodes, most of them beneficial; even those that attack plants are often found in soils but in such low concentrations that they do no appreciable harm.

Gardeners may get confused when it is suggested on the one hand that root knot nematodes are responsible for damage to plants in their vegetable garden, while at the same time, nematodes are sold as *beneficials* which will help control such pests as Japanese beetle grubs. These are two different types of nematodes, one a problem in some areas, and the other a gardener's ally.

Because they are so small, the presence of harmful nematodes is usually something that needs to be confirmed by having soil tested. Those who are having plant problems that they cannot explain may want to seek out such a test. Nematodes seem to be repelled by fish and seaweed emulsions, so the use of these organic fertilizers would be beneficial in areas known to have high populations of these worms.

Large gardens such as annual beds and vegetable plots can be cleared of pest nematodes by planting a solid cover crop of French marigolds over a season, and then plowing the foliage under the soil in the fall. Solarizing the soil by covering it with a clear plastic sheet in the hot weather will also kill excess populations; soil should be turned and dampened before placing the plastic tight against the earth. Both of these methods require a garden to go unplanted for a season.

Beneficial nematodes assist the gardener by killing other insects and larvae and helping compost to break down. The use of compost on the garden encourages the presence of these beneficial, microscopic worms. Beneficial nematodes that attack specific insects are sold at garden centers and through the mail from organic garden supply catalogs.

DIAGNOSING AND DEALING WITH DISEASE

Diseases are best attacked before they happen. It is far easier to plant disease-resistant plants, maintain healthy soil, and practice good cultural practices (see Chapters 2 and 3) than it is to treat a sick plant. Put your efforts into keeping a healthy garden, and you won't have to deal with diseases as often.

Even under the best of cultural conditions, however, plants can be attacked by fungi, bacteria, or a virus, and these problems are often difficult to accurately diagnose. By far the most common diseases found on plants are various fungi, most of which occur at levels that may affect a plant's appearance or vigor somewhat, but won't be fatal.

A fungus in sheep's clothing?

Sometimes the damage done by a fungus resembles an insect's chewing. Shot-hole fungus makes spots on a leaf that dry out and fall away, leaving a hole in the leaf. When these holes join each other they look as if the leaf has been chewed, especially when such areas occur on the edges of the leaves. Examine the entire plant to see if some of the holes still contain dried leaf tissue. If so, a fungus is to blame for the damage, not a chewing insect.

Leafspot

Fungi often appear as spots on the leaves of plants; the umbrella term "leafspot" is used to describe this condition, although many different types of fungi can cause spots on leaves. These spots usually start small, and are often yellowish or yellow surrounding a dark spot. The spot may grow in size, and the center may be dry and dead. Sometimes several of the spots combine together to form an irregularly shaped area on the leaf.

If only a few leaves are affected, removing those leaves promptly may be enough to control the problem. Spraying the plant with organic fungicides (used according to the directions) is most effective at this point, *before* the fungus gets a good hold on the plant. Organic fungicides include Bordeaux mix, copper compounds, and sulfur sprays. Other organic formulations that discourage fungal growth are anti-transpirants (many brand names including VaporGard and Wilt-pruf), and a mix of baking soda and superior oil.

Plants prone to fungus attacks (including roses that routinely get blackspot and mildew) can be sprayed with a mix of one gallon water, 21/2 Tablespoons of superior oil (also called ultra-fine or horticultural oil), and 1 Tablespoon of baking soda. This mix is put into a pressure sprayer and applied to plants *before* evidence of a fungus is seen, and every two weeks throughout the growing season. Low maintenance? Don't be silly. But if you have one or two plants that routinely need protection from fungus, it *may* be worth it.

Mildew
There are several plants that often get mildew on their leaves, which is a different form of mildew than that which grow on the walls in a damp house. There are two types of mildew fungus which form on plants: downy mildew, which is a downy mass attached to the underside of leaves; and powdery mildew which is a fine, grayish, dusty-looking substance found on the surface of leaves and stems.

If you find such a substance on your plants, examine it closely. I have known gardeners who have assumed that they had downy or powdery mildew, when in reality it was an insect infestation which coated their plants. Cottony scale, mealy bugs, and euonymus scale are all white and fuzzy looking, and could at first glance be confused with a fungus.

Downy mildew is most common in the deep South when the nights are cool and damp and the days warm and humid. This fungus gets down into the plant's tissues, and the plants leaves wilt or drop. Because the fungus is growing throughout the plant, it is more difficult to control with fungicides, and the infected plants usually need to be removed and destroyed.

Mildew occurs on plants when the air is damp and circulation poor. Plants that have become overcrowded so that their leaves are too close together are prone to mildew in climates were the air is damp. Paradoxically though, these plants are *more* prone to powdery mildew when rainfall is scarce. It is thought that the action of a steady rain running over the leaves washes mildew spores off before they get attached.

Plants that have not gotten enough rain are stressed, and a stressed plant is more prone to mildew as well. I have always had less of a mildew problem on *Monarda* (Bee balm) that is grown in part shade than that grown in a very hot, sunny spot. Bee balm wilts in the heat of the day, and that action of losing so much moisture that the leaves wilt, then reviving again in the evening, is stressful for the plant. Some plants are more prone to mildew in the shade because the air around them remains moist, and the circulation poor. Other plants never get mildew at all, no matter where they are planted.

Mildew can be controlled by spraying with sulfur, or the anti-transpirants described in the section dealing with leafspot. My approach to mildew is to ignore it, and clean up mildewed foliage in the fall. If mildewed leaves are left on the garden, the spores overwinter in the soil and are conveniently located to infect the plant next season. Cleaning the garden in the fall helps prevent continued spread of fungi.

This fungus is not only unattractive, but as it takes the juices of a plant to live, mildew weakens its host. Usually mildew alone is not enough to kill a plant, however, so you might decide to ignore it as I do. I know a gardener who has just decided that her zinnias will get mildew every year, and so what? She grows them for cutting anyway, and always removes the leaves before arranging them in a vase, so why worry? This gardener has determined that a certain level of "damage" is acceptable.

Lilacs often get powdery mildew on their leaves late in the season, but it is more of a cosmetic problem than a threat to the plant's health. A weekly spraying with the garden hose may help wash mildew spores off before they get attached, but why spend the time "painting the roses red?" If you want red roses, don't plant white ones, and if you don't like mildew, don't plant lilacs...or zinnias, bee balm, crape myrtle, or asters!

Fungus in the vegetable garden
In addition to mildew on squash leaves, other fungi and diseases cause gardeners to tear their hair in frustration. Most common are the several fungi which attack tomatoes. Symptoms on tomato leaves usually take the form of leaves yellowing from the bottom up, with or without the presence of dark spots. The prompt application of a copper or sulfur fungicide can help slow the spread of such fungi, but certain cultural practices will help prevent diseases in the tomato patch to start with.

One of the first pieces of advice given to vegetable gardeners is to rotate their crops. If you plant tomatoes in the same spot each year, any spores left from the previous year don't have to work very hard to infect plants the next year. This makes good sense, but the reality is that most people don't have large vegetable gardens these days because they don't have the space for them, or the time to tend to the plants and harvest the produce.

Those who simply cannot rotate where vegetables are planted can help prevent the spread of disease by cleaning all old foliage and produce out of the garden. Dump any diseased foliage into a brush pile or the trash, not into your compost. When in doubt, throw it out.

Placing a fresh layer of mulch on your garden immediately after it is planted helps prevent the movement of disease organisms from the soil to the plants. Rain and sprinkler water can splash the soil near a plant, carrying fungi or bacteria along with it. A layer of mulch, whether plastic, cardboard, or straw, prevents this splash of water and mud. Watering your garden with soaker hoses also cuts down on the splashing, and, therefore, on the spread of disease.

Because tomato stems are usually buried to create strong, deep root systems, many plants can end up with their lower leaves touching the dirt and exposed to fungal spores. Tomatoes are one of the few plants that have the ability to grow roots from the stem, and a deep rooted plant is a stronger plant, so this practice is always a good idea. Snipping off any lower leaves which might otherwise touch the ground will prevent the transmission of fungi from soil to plant, even when the stem is deeply buried.

TOP TEN TIPS FOR THE PREVENTION OF
DISEASE IN THE GARDEN

1. *Don't overfertilize:* plant growth that is put on too quickly is weak and prone to both insect attacks and disease.

2. *Keep soil healthy* by adding compost annually.

3. Wherever possible, *use organic mulches* on the soil's surface.

4. *Don't crowd* disease-prone plants in the garden; give them room to breathe.

5. *Water early in the day*, and avoid repeatedly wetting the foliage. Use soaker hoses when possible.

6. *Clean any diseased plants out of the garden* promptly, and destroy the stems and foliage.

7. *Clean tools regularly;* disinfect pruners and other tools with bleach every month, and dry them well. Oil them to prevent rust.

8. *Don't work in the garden when the foliage is wet*; your hands, tools, and body can spread fungi just as the rain can.

9. *Treat plants* that are prone to fungal attacks before you see symptoms.

10. *Plant disease-resistant varieties.* Find out which diseases and insects are most common in your area, and use plants that resist such pathogens and pests.

Bacterial and viral diseases

Fungal diseases are the most common in a garden, and this is probably good because they are more easily prevented, dealt with, and often cured. Bacteria also occasionally attack plants, usually entering a plant through a wound or tiny openings in the plant stems or leaves. Various bacteria can cause stems and leaves to rot, and a plant's vascular tissues to collapse. Plants that have been attacked by bacteria will sometimes have a disagreeable odor.

Viral diseases are most commonly spread from plant to plant by insects that suck a plant's juices, although they may also be spread by the gardener's hands or tools, and by infected seeds. Some plants show little sign that they are infected with a virus, but others may turn a blotchy yellow, be stunted or deformed, or suddenly die.

There is no cure for a plant with a virus or bacterial disease. Infected plants should be dug and discarded so that the disease won't spread into the compost or other parts of the garden. Once a plant has died and you have had a diagnoses made that it was due to viral or bacterial disease, it is wise to place a different type of plant in that location. Most gardeners don't go to the trouble of having a plant analyzed when it dies however, and a lab analysis is necessary to determine the presence of a virus or bacteria. Those who are not sure how a plant died may want to dispose of it, and sterilize all tools just to be on the safe side.

THE CALL OF THE WILD

Anyone who has had wildlife foraging in the garden instantly appreciates insect attacks. Insects are small, so they usually eat small amounts; they chew edges or leaves, suck some sap, or make a few holes. Rarely, however, will a bug make off with the entire plant. Woodchucks and deer are another matter all together; they will eat a plant down to the nubs or beyond! One plant only serves to whet their appetites, and an entire vegetable garden or landscape can be destroyed in two or three evenings.

Every year, suburban gardeners who formerly dealt with the occasional skunk and an abundance of gray squirrels, find themselves facing extensive damage caused by the Bambi clan. Others may garden for years without so much as a glimpse of a groundhog, only to have them appear in large numbers out of nowhere. As more and more wild country becomes developed, the wildlife that lived in rural areas is now commonly seen in the suburbs, and gardeners everywhere need to find ways to cope.

There are all kinds of hints and tricks given to gardeners with animal problems: get hair from a beauty salon or barber and scatter it around the garden; put scented soaps in your shrubs and trees; spraying plants with a mixture of eggs and water will keep away deer; scattering bloodmeal around the garden repels rabbits. The list of items said to repel animal pests stretches from fox urine (I don't even want to think about the inhumane way they must collect that!) to lion dung.

These suggestions are all ways to fill the garden with smells that the foraging animals will shy away from. While all of these methods do work to one degree or another, the chief disadvantage of them is that they must be re-applied every week, or more often after heavy rains. Often, an odor will keep an animal away for awhile, but after a few weeks it no longer repels them as it once did. I guess that after smelling lion dung for a month without seeing the lion, even an animal with a brain the size of a marble will figure out that it is being duped.

Now let's all be honest; gardeners who find it difficult to find the time for the *enjoyable* aspects of gardening certainly don't have the time to drip fox urine around the shrubbery, or spray egg-emulsion on the perennials. As clever or entertaining as all those suggestions are, they don't solve the problem on a long-term basis.

Short of systematically killing off the wildlife (and we *know* that if deer have eaten your perennials, it *has* crossed your mind) there are two ways to make your garden more animal-proof. The first is to erect fencing, and the second is to fill your garden with plants that the wildlife won't eat.

Erecting a barrier

Fences can provide the barrier needed to keep animals on one side of your property, and your gardens on another. Specific areas, such as vegetable gardens, can be enclosed, or entire properties may be fenced in where it is feasible. The type of fence required will depend on what sorts of animals you have for neighbors, what type of garden you are enclosing, local zoning restrictions, and the style of your gardens.

The least expensive way to protect a garden is to group the plants that are most appealing to the wildlife in one area and put a barrier around it. This barrier can be as simple as a low electric wire that keeps out small animals, to a tall wooden or electric fence that blocks off the deer. Because it might be necessary to install barriers to keep out a variety of animals, gardeners should have a clear idea of the type of critters they are fencing out before planning the enclosures.

Keeping out small animals

Groundhogs (also called woodchucks) and rabbits are the two most destructive small animals are in the garden. Those who plant corn would also add raccoons to that list, but since these masked creatures don't usually bother much else, they are not of prime concern when planning a fence.

Electric fences are very effective at keeping out small animals, but they must be installed close to the ground. Running a wire four to six inches from the ground, and another at around fourteen inches will keep small animals out of the garden. Electric fences can be placed on a timer so that the current will be running in the evening, through the night, and into early morning, the times when most small animals are out feeding.

In order for electric fences to work, the weeds underneath them must be kept trimmed so the plants don't come in contact with the electric wire; anything that touches the wire will short out the current, making the entire fence ineffective. Plants inside the garden will also need to be placed far enough away from the wire so that they won't touch it as they grow. Weeds grow quickly, so the area around the fence will need to be trimmed weekly; if this sounds like too much maintenance, another style of fence should be chosen.

Small animals can also be kept out of contained areas by a fence which is buried in the soil, and flops on the top. Such a fence is buried at least 12" (the deeper the better), and is bent at the 12" mark to extend away from the garden at almost a ninety degree angle. This buried angle prevents an animal from digging under the fence to get at the garden. It will not defeat the most determined of groundhogs, however, because they can start their tunneling four or five feet away from the garden and go under the buried fence.

The middle of this wire fence is attached to the poles which hold the fence in place, but the top eighteen inches is left unfastened. Once the fencing is all in place, the top portion should be slightly bent away from the garden. This creates a part of the fence which will flop away from the garden if an animal tries to climb over the fence. It may not be the most attractive fencing in the world, but is one of the best ways to discourage both the diggers and the climbers.

This style of fence can be made more attractive by placing it around a standard wooden style fencing. Wire becomes almost invisible when placed in front of wood boards or a picket-style fence, and from a distance the fencing all but disappears from view. Be sure that the gate which is installed is a tight one which is always kept closed.

Keeping out deer

The good news is that deer do not dig; they never tunnel under a fence. The bad news is that deer jump over tall fences with ease. Many homeowners have found that an eight-foot fence is necessary to keep the deer out of their property. This is especially true in areas where the ground slopes up, moving away from the garden. The rise in ground level helps the deer sail over a six-foot fence in some cases.

Electric fences do not need to be as tall to discourage these lovely, but hungry, creatures. I successfully kept the deer out of a 30' x 50' perennial bed in the Berkshires with a single strand of electrified wire placed about three feet from the ground. Other gardeners find that adding an electric wire to the top of a standard wooden fence, four to six feet tall, is successful at keeping deer out of the garden and makes an attractive enclosure for the garden at the same time. As mentioned previously, electric fences can be put on timers so the current is off when the people are around the gardens, and is turned on when the deer are looking for breakfast or dinner.

Those who consider fencing off their entire property will need to solve "the driveway problem" in the planning stages. Gates will keep out the deer, but they need to be opened every time a car comes in and out, which can get to be a real annoyance. Be realistic about your willingness to get in and out of the car in all types of weather before you sink the big bucks into a large fence. Cattle grates can be installed at the end of the driveway, but I have heard reports of deer jumping them on occasion. Cattle grates are metal grids which have holes large enough to be slippery and unstable for hoofed animals to walk on. Cows won't cross them, but they don't have the ability to jump that a deer does.

When given lemons, make lemonade
Once it becomes a necessity to fence a garden in, use it as an opportunity to give a structure to your gardens that wasn't there before. Europeans have long understood that walls and fences are desirable for aesthetic *and* functional reasons; walls provide the "bones," or framework for the garden in all seasons. In addition to keeping out animals, fences shelter plants from the elements, give privacy in crowded neighborhoods, and provide support for vines and espaliered shrubbery. If you have to fence out the wildlife, use it as an opportunity to create a lovely, walled garden.

Filling a garden with plants they won't eat
Whether the furry visitors to your garden are rabbits or deer, there are plants they love to munch on, and those they will never touch. If fencing the garden is out of the question, or for those gardens outside of fenced areas, it is only sensible to grow plants your animal neighbors won't eat. This might seem disappointingly limiting at first, but it is important to remember that in many situations, larger stands of a few plants can be even lovelier than a mixed group. Necessity may restrict your choices, but a beautiful simplicity can be the result.

Smell the foliage, but don't eat it!
In general, most animals don't eat plants with smelly foliage. This is not a hard and fast rule, but it will give the gardener a place to start. Animals will usually leave sage and *Alliums* alone for example, as well as *Stachys byzantina* (Lamb's ears), *Geranium macrorrhizum* (Bigroot cranesbill), and *Santolinas*. Unfortunately, although *Achillea* (Yarrow) has scented foliage, groundhogs seem to love it anyway.

Poisonous foliage is also avoided by animals—they may be hungry, but they're not suicidal! *Aconitum* (Monkshood), *Digitalis* (Foxglove), and *Rheum* (Rhubarb) are all lovely plants which fall into this category. *Agrostemma* (Corn cockle), *Aquilegia* (Columbine), *Arum* (Jack-in-the-pulpit), *Colchicum* (Autumn crocus), and *Paeonia* (Peony) are also poisonous and avoided by animals. Keep in mind that *all of these plants are also poisonous to humans*; don't plant them if there are adults or children who are likely, for some reason, to nibble on your plants.

Looking to nature can be a good way of determining which plants will be passed over by local wildlife. If a wild stand of goldenrod goes untouched, for example, then you might want to plant some of the many lovely varieties of *Soladago* in your gardens. One of the problems many gardeners face is that plants which are ignored by the wildlife in one part of the country are favorites of the same animal in another area! Because this is the case, recommendations from local gardeners or your extension service are especially valuable.

Before investing in an entire border filled with a particular perennial or shrub, plant one or two as a test crop to determine if the animals in your area have a fondness for it or not. Investing in larger plants is worthwhile since animals will often eat the foliage of a younger plant, but pass over the same plant when it is more mature.

Be aware that even after successfully testing a plant in the garden, there are no guarantees. I had *Berberis thunbergii* (Barberry) growing on my deer-populated property in the Berkshires for years, and for years the Bambi Gang ignored it. One particularly long and snow-filled winter, however, they must have been desperate for food, for they ate the barberries down by two-thirds—stems, thorns and all.

In the plant lists that follow, I haven't included many animal-resistant annuals because few sources agree on which annuals won't get munched, and my experience has varied from year to year. In general, deer are said to avoid *Ageratum* (Floss flower) and *Impatiens*, as well as other plants grown as annuals that are included in the perennials list.

RABBIT-RESISTANT PERENNIALS

Achillea spp. (Yarrow)
Aconitum spp. (Monkshood)
Artemisia spp. (Wormwood)
Arum spp. (Jack-in-the-pulpit)
Aster spp. (Aster)
Astilbe hybrids (False spirea/Astilbe)
Baptisia australis (False Blue indigo)
Campanula pericifolia (Peach-Leaved companula)
Cimicifuga spp. (Snakeroot)
Colchicum spp. (Autumn crocus)
Digitalis spp. (Foxglove)

Doronicum spp. (Leopard's bane)
Epimedium spp.
Filipendula vulgaris (Meadowsweet)
Geranium spp. (Cranesbill Geraniums)
Hemerocallis hybrids (Daylily)
Hosta hybrids (Hosta/Plantain Lily)
Iris spp.
Kniphofia uvaria (Red Hot poker)
Papaver orientale (Oriental poppy)
Paeonia spp. (Peony)
Salvia spp. (Sage)
Stachys byzantina (Lamb's ears)
Trollius spp. (Globeflower)
Yucca filamentosa (Yucca/Adam's needle)

DEER-RESISTANT PLANTS

Plants that the deer are *less likely* to eat, especially when the plants are mature.

Trees

Abies spp. (Fir)
Acer spp. (Maples)
Cedrus spp. (Cedar)
Cercis spp. (Redbud)
Chamaecyparis spp. (False Cypress)
Ginko biloba (Ginko)
Ilex spp. (Hollies)
Magnolia spp. (Magnolia)
Picea spp. (Spruce)
Pinus spp. (Pines)
Podocarpus spp. (Podocarpus)
Quercus spp. (Oaks)
Umbellularia californica (California laurel)

Shrubs

Abelia grandiflora (Glossy abelia)
Berberis thunbergii (Japanese barberry)
Buddleia spp. (Butterfly bush)
Buxus spp. (Boxwood)
Calluna vulgaris (Heather)

Calycanthus floridus (Common sweetshrub)
Cotoneaster spp. (Cotoneaster)
Cytisus scoparius (Scotch broom)
Erica spp. (Heath)
Escallonia cultivars (Escallonia)
Gaultheria shallon (Salal)
Juniperus spp. (Junipers)
Kerria japonica (Kerria)
Leptospermum cultivars (Tea tree)
Mahonia (many species and cultivars)
Myrica spp.
Nandina domestica (Heavenly bamboo)
Nerium oleander (Oleander)
Potentilla fruitcosa (Cinquefoil)
Rhododendrons hybrids excluding Azaleas
Spiraea spp. (Spirea)
Syringa spp. (Lilac)
Viburnum spp. (Viburnums)

Ferns, Vines, and Ground covers
Ajuga reptans (Bugleweed)
Althyrium filix-femina (Lady fern)
Arctostaphylos uva-ursi (Bearberry)
Carex spp. (Sedge)
Ceratostigma plumbaginoides (Dwarf plumbago)
Clematis spp. (Clematis)
Dryopteris spp. (Wood ferns)
Festyca spp. (Fescues)
Hedra helix (Ivy)
Liriope muscari (Lilyturf)
Miscanthus sinensis (Maiden grass)
Pachysandra terminalis (Japanese spurge)
Vinca minor (Vinca/Periwinkle/Myrtle)
Wisteria spp. (Wisteria)

Perennials and Bulbs
Acanthus mollis (Bear's breech)
Aconitum carmichaelli (Monkshood)
Adenophora confusa (Ladybells)
Agave spp. (Agave)
Allium spp. (Ornamental onions)

Aster spp. (Asters)
Aquilegia spp. (Columbine)
Baptisia australis (False blue indigo)
Begonia (tuberous, many cultivars)
Boltonia asteroides (Bolton's aster)
Campanula porcharskyana (Serbian bellflower)
Cassia marilandica (Wild senna)
Centranthus ruber (Red valerian)
Chrysanthemum frutescens (Marguerite)
Chrysanthemum parthenium (Feverfew)
Convallaria majalis (Lily-of-the-Valley)
Coreopsis grandiflora (Tickseed)
Dahlia cultivars
Dicentra spectabilis (Bleeding heart)
Echinacea purpurea (Purple coneflower)
Echinops ritro (Globe thistle)
Eschscholzia californica (California poppy)
Eupatorium purpureum (Joe Pye weed)
Euphorbia spp. (Euphorbia/Spurge)
Gaillardia grandiflora (Blanket flower)
Helichrysum spp.
Iberis sempervirens (Candytuft)
Iris sibirica (Siberian iris)
Lysimachia clethroides (Gooseneck loosestrife)
Monarda didyma (Bee balm)
Papaver spp. (Poppy)
Peony lactiflora (Peony)
Phlox subulata (Moss phlox)
Pulmonaria spp. (Lungwort)
Santolina spp. (Lavendar cotton)
Salvia officinalis (Garden sage)
Stachys byzantina (Lamb's ears)
Solidago hybrids (Goldenrod)
Thymus spp. (Thyme)
Verbena spp.
Yucca filamentosa (Yucca/Adam's Needle)

Bulbs
Cammassia esculenta
Colchicum spp.
Crocus spp.

Chionodoxa spp. (Glory of the Snow)
Galanthus nivalis (Snowdrops)
Hyacinthus orientalis (Hyacinth)
Narcissus spp. (Daffodils)
Scilla spp. (Squill)

Small animals causing big problems

Sometimes gardeners are plagued by the presence of small critters such as shrews, chipmunks, mice and squirrels. Animals that tunnel through the soil cause plant roots to dry up; shrubs and trees can be girdled by tiny teeth chomping on the bark; and curious squirrels often dig freshly planted bulbs. Even birds, a joy for gardeners most of the time, can cause headaches by eating newly planted seeds, and ripping the petals off of flowers.

Repelling moles and voles

Many gardeners report that tunnelers such as voles and moles are repelled by castor oil. Commercial castor oil-based mole repellents are available, but gardeners can also make their own by mixing one tablespoon of castor oil with one tablespoon of dish soap and a cup of water. Beat these well with a whisk or in the blender, then stir the mix into a gallon of water.

Spray this brew on lawns or gardens where moles and voles are a problem. Be sure that the grass or garden has been watered well before spraying the repellent on, so that it will penetrate the soil quickly and completely.

Small animals tend to avoid open spaces, so clearing an area where they are likely to travel under cover might discourage them from traveling to your flower beds. Making your property attractive to natural predators is also advisable.

Keeping small animals away from shrubs and trees

Young shrubs and trees are most vulnerable to mice and voles. Although the woody bark isn't the food of choice in the summer, they will eat away at the base of shrubs and trees in the winter when food is scarce. Keeping the area around shrubs and trees clear of high grass and weeds, especially when the plants are young, is the best way to prevent them from being girdled by small animals. Be sure that any mulch stops well away from the plant as well since mulch can provide a place for small critters to hide.

There are plastic guards for the base of shrubs and trees which will cover the area of bark near the ground. These are useful in the winter when the plant is most vulnerable to small animal appetites, but it is important that they be removed in the spring. Anything that covers the bark of shrubs and trees provides a place for insects to hide and breed. Plastic around stems and young trunks keeps them moist and dark, a perfect place for diseases to grow as well. Unless the guard is made to be expandable, forgetting to remove it will result in the girdling and death of the tree.

Squirrels and bulbs

Has this ever happened to you? You *finally* get the bulbs planted, and you feel so good because they had, after all, sat in the garage for a month after you bought them. But yesterday you got them in the ground, and you can freely dream of the lovely show of spring flowers you will enjoy next year. Your dream dissolves as you look out to the garden and see the bulbs you tucked into the ground with such care are now lying over the surface of the garden. Something dug up the bulbs you so carefully planted!

In most cases, squirrels are to blame, although other animals occasionally dig newly planted bulbs as well. Adding bonemeal to the planting area along with the bulbs can attract skunks, dogs, and other animals. It has been common practice for years to throw a handful of bonemeal into the hole before the bulb is put in place. But the smell of bonemeal attracts animals that eat meat.

Gardeners who wish to use organic fertilizers should put the bonemeal in the ground three weeks before the bulbs are planted. Superphosphate, or a complete fertilizer formulated for bulbs, will nourish the plants without attracting wildlife; mix it into the entire area where the bulbs will be growing. Placing it in the hole with the bulb keeps it in that small space, but the plants roots will soon grow beyond where the nutrients are. Because research shows that phosphorous does not travel quickly through the soil, it is most available to plants if it is placed in the soil where the roots will be growing, not directly under the bulb.

If bonemeal is worked into the soil ahead of time, any animals who are attracted to the smell and dig in the area out of curiosity will have come and gone before the bulbs are planted. Squirrels, however, will show up any time bulbs are planted, whether bonemeal is used or not. This is because they are attracted to the freshly turned earth, not what is in the soil.

If a squirrel senses that the soil has recently been disturbed, it thinks that there must be something of interest at the bottom of that hole. Other squirrels bury nuts and seeds, so it is possible that it is another animal's treasure. Large insects dig into the soil as well, so perhaps there is a tasty treat at the bottom of that hole. I am sure that most squirrels are profoundly disappointed when they find a mere bulb instead of something delicious. In some cases the bulb is gnawed a bit before being rejected; other times the bulb is left intact, and occasionally it is carried away completely.

Once the soil covering freshly planted bulbs has settled, squirrels will no longer dig in the area, so gardeners can protect what they have planted with a temporary covering, and by watering the area well. I usually plant bulbs in groups, and when I have finished putting a cluster in the ground, I place a piece of chicken wire on top of the area, holding it in place with a rock or small log. Once the ground settles, usually after two weeks or three good rains, I remove the chicken wire and save it for the same use the following fall. Watering the area well will also help to settle the soil, so running a sprinkler over newly planted bulbs will speed the process along.

When bulbs are planted more deeply than normal, it discourages animals from taking them out of the ground. It is usually recommended that large bulbs, such as tulips and daffodils be put six inches under the surface. Let's admit the truth; most gardeners skimp on this depth. The average gardener digs the hole to the depth of the blade of the trowel and calls it done, right?

A slightly smaller hole is usually not a problem, but if animals are prone to taking the bulbs out of the holes, a shallow depth puts the bulb right into their paws. Taking the time to dig an eight-inch deep hole may mean *not* having to take the time to plant more than once; squirrels will usually give up after digging down four or five inches.

Did I really see a bird rip the petals off my petunias?
I have spoken to many people who have watched in amazement as a bird flies into their garden and rips a flower right off a plant. The nerve! You feed them all winter, change the water in the birdbath *daily*, and this is the thanks you get! Fortunately, such attacks are usually short-lived.

Flowers seem most attractive to wildlife in the early spring and summer. Perhaps the petals contain a nutrient they need. Or maybe the animal, like the humans who planted the flowers, are so starved for color after a long winter that they just have to grab a piece of it for themselves.

All right, I admit that I'm reaching here. But we often say "It looked so beautiful I could have eaten it up!" about something which isn't even *remotely* edible.

Last spring some sadistic animal neatly cut the heads off of all my early purple tulips. I never discovered if it was a bird or a squirrel, but every morning I would find five or six new tulip heads on the ground. I sprinkled hot pepper on those still intact, and they were left alone. This leads me to blame the squirrels; hot pepper repels them, but doesn't seem to bother birds in the least. (I am told that mixing red pepper in your birdseed helps to keep squirrels out of the feeder.) I didn't have to use the red pepper on the tulips that came into bloom later; whatever had attacked the earlier group had either seen the error of its ways, or gone on to cause mischief elsewhere.

If an animal is suddenly destroying a plant or flower, try spraying that area of the garden with something smelly, such as a garlic spray mixed up in your blender, or a sprinkling of hot red pepper. The sweat-soaked T-shirt you wore yesterday in the garden or the gym can be hung on a stick for a few days in the garden as well. It is often enough just to place something unfamiliar in the garden, whether that object is smelly or not.

Like the human beings they share the neighborhood with, animals in the garden are great creatures of habit. Once an animal finds something attractive in one part of your property, it will keep coming back to that area either until the object of its affection is gone, or something happens which changes the pattern.

If the gardener places an unusual object near a plant that has become a target for attack, this can often be enough to force the animal to change its habits. This is most effective in situations such as the petal-ripping birds, when an animal's actions are a bit out of the ordinary and not long-lasting. As I mentioned earlier in this chapter, putting smelly objects and liquids in the garden in an attempt to keep a hungry animal away from a food source is a time-consuming, and often frustrating job. On an occasional basis, however, it helps to take the homeopathic way to solve the problem: treat like with like. Responding to an animal's infrequent, idiosyncratic action with an unexpected action of your own often stops the behavior.

It is important that we recognize the wisdom of providing for other places where wildlife can live. Gardeners everywhere have a vested interest in preserving wild spaces; we are not only inspired by the beauty of undeveloped areas and native plants, but such places provide a home where the wildlife can live without invading our gardens. Those who love their gardens are well advised to work to preserve wild areas in their region. We need to preserve habitats for predators that keep otherwise pesky animals in check.

PLANTS HELPING PLANTS

Occasionally, gardeners can grow a plant that wildlife normally eats by surrounding it with plants the animals avoid. This is most effective in informal gardens where plants are more likely to knit and tumble together. It should not be used as a foolproof method of keeping an entire garden from being eaten, but it might be worth experimenting with a plant or two. There has been much experimentation with placing plants that are usually insect-resistant next to those that are often insect-ridden. Gardeners who have tried this report mixed results.

Planting certain vegetables together has gotten a great deal of attention lately; every gardener hears things such as "plant marigolds around your tomatoes," or "beans don't like onions." Most of this information is either based on someone's experience in their own gardens, or their general intuition about what *should* be happening. I have yet to read of any controlled studies that prove one combination of plants *repeatedly* does better than the same plants placed in other areas.

Placing some crops near each other makes sense in terms of their size or when they mature. Early crops such as spinach and radishes can be planted in the same rows as produce that matures later, such as broccoli and brussel sprouts. Short plants that tolerate part shade (or those with shallow root systems) make good companions for larger sunlovers. Thus, lettuce is a natural companion for cabbage or broccoli. And while there is no data that says that the tomatoes will grow better with marigolds as their neighbors, there isn't any that says they harm each other either.

It has long been thought that plants with smelly foliage, such as marigolds and feverfew, will repel some insects. There is no hard data to confirm this belief; studies on companion planting have had mixed results. It has been proven that a solid planting of marigolds will reduce populations of harmful nematodes, although placing a few marigolds around other plants does not have the same result. Marigolds may repel some pests, but they are a favorite food of others; Japanese beetles and slugs *love* marigold foliage! Unfortunately, companion planting alone won't keep a large population of insects at bay.

Q & A: PESTS, DISEASES, AND PROBLEMS

Q. *My shrub hasn't bloomed this year; it was always covered with flowers in the past. What could be wrong?*

A. There are several reasons why an otherwise healthy plant—whether a shrub, annual, or perennial—does not bloom. Consider whether any of the following apply in your situation:

1. *The weather.* If the previous winter was extremely harsh, flower buds formed the year before may have been damaged. Drought may stress a plant sufficiently to cause it to put it resources solely into survival, and not into flower production for a season. Weather can affect plants other than shrubs and trees; an especially cold summer might delay the flowering of heat-loving annuals. Flower buds on many types of plants can be injured or even destroyed by a heavy frost in the late spring or early summer.

2. *Too much nitrogen.* If a plant is getting excess amounts of nitrogen, it will grow many green, lush leaves, but produce no flowers. Gardens that have been given large amounts of manure, bloodmeal, cottonseed meal, or other sources of nitrogen will produce plants with large amounts of foliage and no flowers. Shrubs and trees that are surrounded by lawns may get too much nitrogen from the nutrients put on the grass. Fertilizers formulated for turf are very high in nitrogen because we want our grass to be all leaf and no flowers. If your shrubs or trees are close to a well-fertilized lawn they may be getting too much nitrogen.

3. *Changes in light.* Sometimes the light in our yards changes over time; a shrub might have gotten sufficient sunshine when it was planted, but as surrounding trees grow, or additional houses are built in the neighborhood, the amount of sun the shrub receives is greatly reduced. If a sun-loving

plant does not get the light it requires, the flowering will be affected.

4. *Pruning at the wrong time.* Some plants form their flower buds a year in advance. This is especially common in shrubs that flower in the spring; these plants commonly produce buds (which will be flowers the following season) immediately after they bloom. If such plants are pruned after these buds are formed, next year's flowers will all be cut off.

5. *Attack by insects or the stress of disease.* Check to be sure your plant is indeed healthy. Insects might have chomped off flower buds, or the plant may be in the beginning stages of a disease. If something is attacking the roots of a plant, it won't produce flowers or new growth in a normal fashion. Monitor your plant over time to be sure it isn't in the beginning stages of an infestation of insects or disease.

6. *Immature plants.* Your shrub has bloomed before, but other plants may not flower because they are just too young. Some vines, shrubs, and trees need to mature for a few years before they will bloom. Frequently, perennials will not flower their first year; some grow for two years before blooming.

When the weather is to blame, gardeners don't have many options for helping a non-blooming plant except maybe to water it in periods of drought. Sunlovers can be moved to the sun, fertilizer amounts can be reduced on lawns near blooming plants, pruning can be done at the proper time, and insects and diseases dealt with. Bloomers can be encouraged with an extra dose of phosphorous from bonemeal, superphosphate, or other fertilizer formulated for flowering plants.

In certain cases, it behooves the gardener to be creative. The owner of a local bookstore asked me for advice about her morning-glory vine which was still without flowers in September. This type of annual vine had been grown for years on a post in front of the bookstore, and regular customers were used to the flowers being spectacular. Because our summer had been so cool, it was beginning to look like the vine would never have flowers this season. I advised the owner to go to the local discount store, buy the artificial flowers that appealed to her the most, and fasten them in and among the morning-glory foliage. Instant color, guaranteed to be amusing.

Q.   *If I'm unsure if my plant is being attacked by a fungus or an insect, can I put a fungicide and an insecticide in my sprayer to kill whatever is hurting the plant?*

A.   Mixing up an all purpose brew is tempting, but in doing so you might be doing more harm than good. Fungicides and insecticides may cancel each other out when mixed, resulting in a spray that is completely ineffective against anything. Worse, combinations of treatments may harm or kill the plant.

There is another danger in using a product when it isn't needed. Repeated use of insecticides and fungicides can result in the mutation of insects and fungi that are immune to these treatments, much as the overuse of antibiotics has resulted in strains of bacteria that are no longer killed by the usual medications. We need to be very careful to use fungicides and insecticides sparingly, and always according to the directions. Although it is more of a bother, obtain an accurate diagnosis of a problem and find the appropriate cure before anything is mixed in your sprayer.

Q.   *My neighbor thinks that the Japanese Beetle traps do more harm than good. How could this be possible?*

A.   It isn't that the traps are harmful per se, but they will attract more Japanese beetles to your property than they will catch. Any trap which works by attracting an insect draws more into the area. Although some do end up in the bag, many more remain free to feed on your plants, breed, and overwinter as grubs in your lawn. You have considerate neighbors; it is actually to their advantage to have you hang such a trap on your property, since it would draw the beetles away from their yard and into yours.

If Japanese beetles are a problem for you, the most effective treatment is to apply one of the many biological controls on your lawn in order to kill the beetles when they are in the larval stage. Milky spore disease, beneficial nematodes, and a new form of Bt are effective in treating beetle grubs when used according to the directions.

Keeping lawns on the dry side can help keep beetle populations down as well because the adult Japanese beetles prefer to lay their eggs on soft, moist soil. Watering the lawn deeply, but less often makes good sense for insect control as well as general lawn health and reduced water consumption.

Although it is a gross, time-consuming job, beetles can be hand-picked off the plants they are attacking. The easiest way to both collect and kill them is to knock them into a jar which contains an inch or two of water, covered by an inch of salad oil. The insects quickly drown in the oil, and can be fished out with a spoon and disposed of. The same jar of water and oil may be used all season in this manner.

The most sensible approach to Japanese Beetle control is not to put those plants they are particularly attracted to on your property. Japanese beetles are especially fond of the following plants:

Acer spp. (Japanese and Norway maple)
Alcea rosea (Hollyhock)
Betula spp. (Birch)
Hibiscus syriacus (Rose of Sharon)
Kerria japonica (Japanese kerria)
Ligustrum spp. (Privet)
Malus spp. (Apple)
Malva spp. (Mallow)
Parthenocissus spp. (Boston ivy, Virginia creeper)
Prunus spp. (Cherry, peach, plum)
Rosa spp. (Rose)
Tagetes spp. (Marigold)
Vitis spp. (Grape)
Wisteria spp. (Wisteria)

10

THE GARDEN AS A SOURCE
OF REFUGE AND RELAXATION

Sometimes a gardener can be doing everything right in the yard, and it all looks lovely, yet it still seems to be a frustrating place. Other people may be breaking all the rules, yet they enjoy their yards and gardens tremendously. One gardener may only be happy when every plant is doing well, while another enjoys the process of tending the garden whether it is beautiful or a disaster. All of the horticultural information in the world won't make the garden a source of refuge and relaxation, because this has more to do with the person who tends the garden than it does with the soil, plants, or the weather.

Once we know some basic information about establishing the garden and keeping it healthy, finding satisfaction instead of frustration in the garden is often a matter of turning our attention to the gardener. Although it might not be immediately obvious, as we care for plants, we are cultivating something in ourselves as well. Even the most mundane of garden chores can be relaxing; as we tend our gardens, we ourselves can be nourished and recharged. Often, however, we miss the opportunity to experience garden chores as refreshing. This has less to do with the chore at hand than it does with the attitude we bring to the job.

FEELING OVERWHELMED BY THE GARDEN
Gardens drive people crazy when they feel overwhelmed by the amount of work which needs to be done there. Once you have determined that

your gardens are appropriately sized and planted, however, this may be more a matter of perspective than anything else. It is helpful to remember that a *garden is never finished*. Because gardening is an ongoing process, there will *always* be things that need to be done, and, because a garden is a living thing which is always changing, that is the way it is supposed to be. We need to change our *expectations* that garden work can and should be completed somehow.

When we make the decision to cultivate the areas around our dwellings, we also need to accept the fact that in doing so we are committing to a continuing interaction with our plants. Without this involvement the garden would go wild, and we would eventually be living in a native landscape of grassland, desert, or woodland.

While there is nothing wrong with this—indeed, it has a great deal of appeal on many levels—a native landscape is not the surrounding most people choose. A contented gardener first accepts that by cultivating the land he or she accepts an ongoing involvement with the garden.

TAKING SATISFACTION IN WHAT YOU ARE GETTING DONE

Given that we accept some ongoing maintenance of our landscapes, it is helpful to remember that all work in the garden is done one task at a time. When you are amending the soil, you can't be dividing a perennial and pruning a shrub at the same time. But somehow while working in the garden, the gardener's mind is all too willing to rattle off all the jobs that remain, all the other things you should also be doing.

I know I am not the only gardener whose thoughts carry me away from the task at hand. After a while I realize that tune which is playing through my head is running something like this: "I've *got* to remember to move that shrub before it gets any larger . . . but the peony's location has to be changed first . . . I need to get some other colors of peonies . . . where can I plant them? Maybe over near that lilac, which I *really* need to lime . . . when did I last check the pH in the perennial gardens...maybe they need lime too, and organic matter as well . . . I never added manure to the back beds last fall . . ."

This chatter goes on and on, robbing me of any satisfaction I feel about what I *am* doing in the garden. For most gardeners, it often becomes easier to pay more attention to the chatter of the mind then to the task at hand; instead of leaving the garden with a feeling of contentment about the work that *was* completed, the gardener is left feeling defeated about all that *wasn't* finished that day.

And where did the sense of frustration come from? Were the plants yelling at the gardener because he or she wasn't working fast enough?

No, the plants were growing as well as they possibly could in the current situation. Were the tools complaining that the work was less than adequate? No, the tools were performing the jobs they were designed to do. Even the gardener's body was doing its best to get the garden chores done. It is the gardener's own mind that is causing the discontent.

I saw a new garden ornament advertised recently. A smooth rock is engraved with a word or simple saying, such as "peace" or "welcome." It is a nice idea, and I have always wanted one which borrows the title from a book by Ram Dass—I would like to have a rock in my garden that says "Be Here Now."

If all gardeners had such ornaments in the garden, as their minds carry them away and begin to scold about all the work which remains to be done, a glance at the rock would remind them to focus on what they are presently doing.

GARDENS OF THE PAST AND FUTURE

Our minds not only remind us of all the work which remains to be done, but they constantly carry us into the gardens of the past and the gardens of the future. Seeing a plant that has not grown very well this year might start us thinking about how it looked in previous seasons. We are then reminded of other plants that were once placed next to it, and we wonder what ever happened to that perennial or shrub. Before you can say *Geranium macrorrhizum* we are swept away from the present to a garden of the past.

In the same way we often forget to admire and appreciate the garden right in front of our eyes, because in an instant we travel to the garden of the future. "This perennial bed would really look better if that phlox was taken out and replaced with something blue . . ." and the mind is off and running, thinking about how much better it will look once the phlox is gone. Whether the phlox is dead or blooming and gorgeous, our attention has been carried away to some future garden, and we don't fully appreciate what we currently have.

At each moment our gardens are full of great beauty, mysteries, and miracles, if only we can keep our attention in the here and now. There is a saying, "Yesterday is history, Tomorrow is a mystery, but Today is a gift, and that's why they call it the present." Our gardens are full of gifts for us, but we have to be *present* to receive them.

COMING BACK TO THE PRESENT MOMENT

Anyone who has tried meditation knows that for a long time it is next to impossible to quiet the chattering mind. One of the first lessons of meditation is that the mind has a life of its own, and much as we might occasionally want silence, it chatters merrily away, uncaring about any quiet we are seeking. When I first started to meditate, not only did my mind continue to chatter, it got *louder*!

Whether you meditate or not isn't important. Doing anything in a focused, concentrated way is a type of meditation, and gardening can be a lovely form of such contemplation. All gardeners will find that they get greater satisfaction from their gardens and garden work if they try, as much as possible, to stay in the present moment as they work.

Even though the mind seems determined to rattle on, spinning its tales whether you want to hear them or not, just becoming aware that this is what goes on will be a help. Often, just taking notice of a situation will stop what would otherwise automatically proceed. Once I became aware that my mind was carrying me away from the garden, I found that although it was difficult to stop that babble all together, it became easier and easier to cut it off mid-stream.

Don't scold yourself when your thoughts take you out of the present moment. The mind is very, very useful tool, so it does not do to regard it as an enemy. It helps instead to think of your mind as a dear, but sometimes pesky child—a chatterbox to be sure. Just remind yourself where your body is and what you are doing. As you work in the garden and become aware that you have once again been swept away, simply say to your mind "Yes, yes. That's all very interesting, but right now I'm planting annuals."

BE WILLING TO SEE WITH NEW EYES

In addition to bringing our attention back to the present garden, it also helps if we are willing to see our gardens, and the work required for its maintenance, with new eyes. This often happens to us when another gardener admires a plant we have always dismissed as a weed. "Look at that dark green foliage," our friend might say. "And those flowers! How can you *not* like this plant?" and before you know it you are looking at the leaves and flowers with new eyes, deciding that you won't pull it out of the garden after all.

In such cases we borrow someone else's eyes for a moment, and see the plant from a different point of view; and just as we can see an object from another perspective, so too can we change our opinion about garden maintenance. A man I know tells of how he used to rush through the planting of his annuals and vegetables, anxious only to get them in the ground and get the mulch laid down. "I was completely focused on how those flowers would look in July, when they were tall and in bloom. When

I planted the vegetable garden I was wanting only to get it done early enough so that I would have a ripe tomato before my neighbors did."

This gardener started looking at these tasks with new eyes after reading about some monks who grew all their own food; the tending of the gardens was viewed as a time of meditation and prayer, as sacred as the time spent in the sanctuary of the church. My friend started thinking about what the monks had that he didn't. They had a garden, and he had a garden. They had chores to do and so did he. All that was different was their *attitude* about the work which they did in the garden.

"I wouldn't go so far as to say I'm meditating—I don't really know about all that stuff. But I do know that when I plant I am more peaceful, and I enjoy it more. I've learned to regard the time I spend in the garden as a quiet time for myself, and I don't get too many of those."

This gardener learned to appreciate the time he spent planting in a new way, but I can attest that it works for less pleasant garden jobs as well. Many gardeners hate weeds, but looking at weeds with new eyes helped me to cherish (yes, cherish!) this garden chore.

When we moved to our house on the New York/Massachusetts border years ago, I optimistically—or should I say naively—decided that the entire slope of land next to the driveway should be a large perennial garden. This area was about 30' by 50', and the land there had been a field of weeds growing in clay for years. Since weed seeds can remain viable for thirty years or more, I had my work cut out for me.

Every time I turned the earth to add the much-needed amendments to the soil, and every time I dug a hole for a new plant, I would expose a whole new batch of seeds to the light, which would then trigger their germination. Consequently, though I spread a four-inch layer of mulch on the garden every spring, I spent a great deal of time weeding.

The garden was so large that it would take me three days to get it weeded, and this process needed to be done twice during the season. In order to get the garden weeded I needed to first clear my calendar for three days, pray the weather would cooperate (I hate to weed in sunny, hot weather) and hope my back would hold out. But despite all the hoops I had to jump though to make it happen, I soon learned that those weeds were a gift.

Nothing else would have taken me into that garden in quite the same way. Moving through the perennials on my hands and knees, I was forced to see the garden from a different angle; I was sitting nose to nose with my plants, enjoying their company for an extended period of time. I saw details that I would have otherwise overlooked.

I experienced my garden, and all that went on there, over a large stretch of time. Birds flew overhead and perched on nearby trees; I learned that their songs were different in the early spring from the tunes they would sing in late summer. Rabbits and snakes would sometimes pass by, more startled by my presence than I was by theirs. So many bees, hummingbirds, and other insects were coming and going from plant to plant that the airspace over that garden was busier than O'Hare.

Those weeds took me into my garden in a way that I *never* would have otherwise taken the time for. Although I am glad that the flower beds which I now tend aren't quite so large, I still cherish my weeds and look forward to the time it takes to pull them out of my garden.

LOOK AT YOUR VEGETABLES WITH NEW EYES

Ask vegetable gardeners for extra zucchini and watch their eyes light up. We stick six little squash seeds in the soil once the ground gets warm, and it seems impossible to believe that in two months we will be overrun with zucchini. After making stuffed squash, zucchini bread, and even zucchini cake, many a gardener has threatened to toss the extras into any open car window on Main Street.

When a garden starts producing, it is often a case of overabundance. This should be a cause for celebration, but many people just feel badly about the vegetables that they don't have time to pick, let alone cook and freeze. For some, the regret they feel about the unused produce makes a trip to the vegetable patch an unpleasant prospect; they can't enjoy their gardens because they feel guilty about the waste!

In a perfect world no food would be wasted and all gardeners would have time to pick their vegetables. In a perfect world the excess from all gardens would be easily disseminated to those who need it. We all wish it was a perfect world, but we all know it is not. What a shame it is though, that because such things don't run smoothly, we deny ourselves the pleasure of appreciating the abundance that is there. It seems a double waste; not only is some of the produce not being used, but the gardener isn't getting the maximum amount of pleasure from what they have grown.

I urge all vegetable growers to look at their gardens with new eyes of celebration. If you have the time to pick the extra vegetables and give it to your co-workers or the local food pantry, it's terrific. But when life is so hectic that you feel lucky to pick a handful of beans for dinner, or when the unexpected occurrences in life make frequent trips to the garden impossible, relax and be thankful that the garden is so abundant. A garden filled with flowers never makes us feel bad if we can't get them all picked and put into bouquets, does it? There are times when the best thing to do is to think of our vegetables as ornamentals, then add them to the compost so that they will enrich future gardens.

AS OUR PLANTS GROW, SO DO WE
Our gardens are constantly challenging us to stretch and grow, just as our plants are growing. For many gardeners, the routine maintenance of their landscapes isn't the hard part. Gardens constantly challenge us to do two things that are difficult for us—embrace change, and admit that we aren't in control.

Gardens are places of constant change: a plant develops from day-to-day and season-to-season. Shrubs and trees grow larger, perennial clumps spread, and many plants self-seed around the garden. One plant might occupy the same spot in the garden for years, while another moves about or disappears all together. In order to fully embrace our gardens, we must also welcome this constant change.

Our feelings about the fluctuations in the garden are usually mixed; we celebrate the arrival of first tulip or strawberry, yet we want perennials that bloom all summer. It is exciting to discover and plant something new in the garden, but we don't want a plant that we love to die. What it comes down to is that we accept that change is an integral part of the garden when the changes please us, but we resent changes which are inconvenient, or that don't fit into our plans.

We are not in control of our gardens, and those who recognize this and accept it graciously will find more satisfaction in their gardening than those who continue to think that they are in charge. We may be the directors of our gardens, but Nature is the producer and the plants are the stars of the show. Without the support crew (soil, insects, weather etc.) we are nothing.

As directors, we help arrange the stage so that it shows off the talents of plants; we strive to create an environment where all work in harmony to produce the best possible show. But we are not in charge. We can only do *our* job to the best of our ability, recognizing that we do have the responsibility to orchestrate things so that all of the other participants in the garden have an opportunity to grow to the best of *their* ability as well.

Novice gardeners are often most frustrated by their gardens because they are under the illusion that they are in control. Those who have gardened for some time learn the wisdom of going into every season without expectations; it isn't that they have become pessimistic. Quite the opposite. They are just more content to let the garden lead; they are more willing to *be surprised*.

GIFTS FROM THE GARDEN

Anyone who stays involved with gardening for any length of time realizes that it is one of the most life-affirming things we can do. When we place a plant in the landscape, we are demonstrating hope for the future because we look forward to the maturing of what we have planted; at the same time, we are expressing appreciation for the garden in its present state. We make a commitment to helping our plants, and given even a minimum amount of care, they respond wholeheartedly.

Cultivating a garden encourages generosity and teaches us about the connectedness of all things. Most gardeners respond to the abundance in their gardens with the desire to share it with others. I have time and again been overwhelmed by the willingness most gardeners have to share their gardens, knowledge, and plant cuttings. Even those who are competitive enough to care who has the first ripe tomato are eager to share exactly how they did it, so it seems less a competition than a good-spirited celebration of technique.

It is no surprise that there is a renewed interest in "healing gardens," and that many hospitals, prisons, and nursing homes are adding horticultural programs or garden areas for the benefit of clients and staff. Gardeners see firsthand that all is connected in their gardens, and the pleasures experienced there, as well as the lessons learned, grow into the rest of their lives.

WHAT GOES AROUND COMES AROUND

There was a period of time when all the artwork I did looked like garbage to me. I spoke with a friend, who is also an artist, about how discouraged I felt about it, and he gave me this advice; "Just start looking at things. Look at other artwork, at nature, at things that you love . . . all I know is, if you put enough inside, something has to come out."

Over time I have found this to be true as an artist, and as a gardener. Gardening is a way of putting beauty into ourselves, and as my friend said, if you put enough in, it has to come out. The splendor of a garden inspires our generosity, encourages our appreciation of beauty, and stimulates our creativity.

GARDENING AND CREATIVITY

Artists have long been stimulated by gardens. Monet might be the most famous artist/gardener, but all creative people are inspired by their gardens. Landscapes don't just provide subject matter for an artist's works, however, but are creative pieces in themselves.

For many people, the work that they do around their homes and properties is their primary creative and artistic outlet. Because we live a culture where art and commerce are very closely tied, gardens are not widely thought of as art forms; they cannot be exhibited in galleries, bought by collectors, or purchased by museums. Gardens are *never* considered to be good investments! But when a person plants a garden, he/she is putting together color, texture and form as surely as any painter or sculpture.

We all lead busy lives, and for many people there isn't much time for creative activities, so the work that they do on their properties combines the desire to beautify their yard and the need for artistic expression. Any artist will tell you that one creative act feeds another. Thus, in planting a garden the gardener not only gains a lovely landscape, but stimulates the "creative juices" at the same time. I believe that this is one of the reasons that gardeners and artists are often good cooks.

Gardens can supply us with both the food for our dinner and the creative inspiration which helps turn that produce into a wonderful meal. But gardens don't just feed us physically and creatively; they feed us spiritually as well.

GARDENING IN THE SPIRIT

I read an article in a gardening magazine years ago that reported the results of a survey asking gardeners *why* they enjoyed gardening. An overwhelming number of those surveyed responded that the garden was the place where they felt closest to God. Even people who don't consider themselves to be religious report feeling a part of "something greater" when they are in a beautiful garden or lovely natural setting.

I think this is why so many people find gardening to be so deeply satisfying; it is an activity that communicates with our deepest selves. Spirit speaks to us in our gardens, and our hearts and souls are nourished there.

RECEIVING WHAT IS THERE

The many benefits of gardening are there for us whether we seek them out or not, but the attitude with which we approach our work in the garden can enhance our awareness of all that we gain. Often, all that is required is a reminder to focus on the garden, just as it is at the moment, for a few minutes. We sometimes can get so focused on being *productive* in our gardens that we forget to simply *enjoy* them.

Instituting a habitual tour of the grounds can be a way of insuring that you enjoy the benefits of your garden on a regular basis. A ten minute walk around the property as you drink your coffee or tea is a lovely way to start the morning. The meditative calm we absorb in the garden at such times can stick with us throughout the next few hours. In his book *Time Shifting—Creating More Time to Enjoy Your Life*, author Stephan Rechtschaffen talks about the wisdom of consciously choosing the rhythms we are exposed to early in the day.

Most people have experienced one of those hectic mornings when something goes wrong, and then the entire day is colored by that early frantic period. We understand that a crazy morning can set us "off" for several hours, but we seldom stop to remember that the opposite is also true. A calm, peaceful spell in the morning can get us in sync with rhythms which set an even tone for the day to come. The garden is a natural place to allow this to happen.

I am sure you have had the experience of going to the supermarket and being seemingly unaware of the music which is playing as you do your shopping. Later you find yourself humming the song that played as you stood in the checkout line—you might even find that it is impossible to get it out of your head for the rest of the day. The sights and sounds of the garden can stay with us in much the same way, but we are often less aware of them.

I worked in my garden for ten minutes one morning as the chicka-dees sang in the trees near the bird feeder. The crows sat above my compost bin, each crow claiming the contents as its own. Later in the morning, I realized that the songs of the chickadees and the cawing of the crows still echoed in my mind, much like the tune from the super-market repeats itself all day. But unlike the melody from the food store, the bird songs recalled some of the feelings of being in the garden on that summer morning, even though I was now at my job and the pace was rather hectic.

In the evening, a walk around the garden, or fifteen minutes spent sitting on the patio and gazing at the yard, can clear a great deal of mental static left from a busy day. Those whose schedules don't allow a daily period of contemplation in the garden might want to make it a weekly habit—Friday evening, Saturday morning, or whenever it works best.

CELEBRATING THE SMALL THINGS

The garden provides a wonderful opportunity to celebrate the small. If something in the garden is looking especially lovely, it does not take much time to move dinner out of doors, the better to appreciate whatever is in bloom. Children in particular are pleased with a spontaneous meal on a cloth on the ground; as adults, we often forget to make room for such simple celebrations.

I spoke to a woman once who had friends over for lunch every year when the daffodils were in bloom. Another man I heard of had a party every time a particular orchid was in blossom. Such gatherings need not be elaborate or even planned very far in advance; we need only to turn off our televisions and remember that such minor celebrations are possible.

THE GARDEN AS CLASSROOM

For a great segment of the population, the time spent working in yards and gardens is the only time they spend outdoors in an average week. During the work week it is not uncommon to go from home-to-car-to-work and then back again, the trips between building and auto being the only time spent outside. Gardening, then, becomes the main activity which keeps people connected with nature.

The lessons we learn in our gardens tell us far more about the environment then any program we might see on the Discovery Channel, as interesting as those programs might be. Any elementary school teacher will tell you about the value of "hands on" learning, and it is just as valuable for those out of the traditional classroom. I think that the garden is the adult's main classroom where the curriculum is the natural world.

Because we are a part of this environment, our gardens not only teach us about our home, but we also learn about ourselves. Entering the garden with willing hands and open eyes, mind, and heart becomes the wisest attitude for maintaining a healthy landscape *and* a healthy gardener. When approached in this manner, our gardens will *not* drive us crazy, but will bring us great joy.

DON'T JUST TALK TO YOUR PLANTS; LISTEN TO THEM!

I tend to be a fairly concrete, grounded person; I don't have crystals buried in the corners of my property, nor do I see fairies in my perennials, although I don't deny that they may be there. I haven't ever channeled information from a rose bush or heard secrets whispered from tree to tree. But I can say with great certainty that *there is* a communication that occurs from plants to people, and when I became aware that this was the case, I became a better gardener.

Remember when the press was filled with interviews with people who espoused talking to house plants? It was thought that this one-sided conversation made the plants grow better. I have no idea if this is true or not, but I am sure that *listening* to your plants will help you in the garden. In order to hear them, however, you need to be quiet enough yourself to hear something which not expressed with language.

Most people have had the experience of suddenly "knowing" something in a flash of intuition. This knowledge comes not by having the subject at hand explained with words, but rather in an instant understanding. Insights sometimes come when, although we have only a small "piece of a puzzle," we are able to suddenly see the whole. Communication with plants happens in much the same way.

The paradox is that once you have learned some basic information about the proper care of the garden, it can be helpful to empty your head of all of that learning and simply "hear" your plants. Focus your entire attention, as much as you are able, on one of your plants and just listen. The key is to approach the communication with your garden without expectation. If you expect to actually *hear* something, or if you are trying to receive information, say, about why the plant is not thriving, your mind will start spinning tales around your pre-conceived notions about what should be happening.

I first became aware that there was a communication with plants when I was visiting my mother in Wisconsin. I walked into her A-frame house, which is filled with many large plants, and absent-mindedly said "Your plants are thirsty." Her houseplants were not wilted nor showing any signs of distress, and I hadn't given them any more then a glance from across the room, but without thinking about it I knew that they were dry. I only became aware that some sort of communication had gone on when my mother's response to my comment was "Oh! You can do that too!" I learned that she could also sense when a plant needed watering, even though there was no visible sign that this was true. After our conversation I resolved to cultivate this ability, along with my plants.

Gardeners do not *have* to be able to sense what their plants need nor have any desire to do so. It is certainly not necessary to have beliefs or opinions that agree with mine in order to have lovely gardens and positive experiences in them. But any gardener who is willing to focus his or her attention completely on the garden for even small periods of time will find great rewards there. Who knows? You might even hear secrets passed from tree to tree. Whether you hear plants whispering or not, as you care for your garden I am sure that you will find yourself nourished physically, emotionally, spiritually and creatively.

I wish you good gardening.

GLOSSARY

Acidic: Soil with a pH that measures lower than 7.

Alkaline: Soil with a pH that measures higher than 7.

Annual: A plant that lives for one year, germinating, growing, flowering, and producing seed in that period of time. Annuals are further classified using the following terms:

Hardy Annual: An annual plant that tolerates some cold temperatures. The seed from such plants will withstand cold winter temperatures, so they often self-sow around the garden. Such plants can be planted in the fall for winter or spring flowers in regions where winter temperatures dip below freezing but do not remain there for long.

Half-Hardy Annual: An annual plant that does not withstand frost but produces seed that will remain viable through cold temperatures.

Tender Annual: An annual that will be killed by a light frost. Such plants should be started indoors from seed and planted outside after the last likely date for frost in your region.

Bed: An area where plants are intensively grouped together for mass effect.

Biennial: A plant that requires two years to produce flowers and seeds; foliage grows the first year, flowers and seeds the second season.

Clay: Fine particle of soil that measures less than .002 mm. across.

Compost: A natural soil conditioner and fertilizer made of decomposed animal and vegetable materials such as manure, fruit and vegetable peels, leaves and lawn clippings.

Crown: The base of a plant where the stems meet the roots and new stems are formed. Also, the top of a tree.

Cultivar: A plant variety that has been cultivated by people. Cultivars have a name which begins with a capital letter, is not italicized, and is enclosed by single quotation marks. Example: *Itea virginica* 'Henry's Garnet.'

Cultural conditions: The growing conditions that determine how healthy a plant will be. Includes natural elements such as the soil and humidity, as well as how a plant is placed in the ground, watered, fertilized etc.

Cultural requirements: The growing conditions a plant needs to thrive. Particular amounts of sunlight, water, soil pH, and organic matter are things which plants need in order to grow.

Damping off: A fungus that kills young seedlings; discouraged by the use of sterile potting soil, good air circulation and prudent watering.

Dead-heading: Removing wilted flower heads promptly.

Deciduous: Dropping when no longer needed, usually applied to shrubs and trees which lose their leaves in the fall.

Determinate: A plant whose stem growth is halted by the growth of a terminal flower; most commonly seen describing types of tomatoes that stop growing after one set of flowers are produced. Such tomatoes produce one large crop of fruits that all ripen at about the same time.

Division: Separating plants into smaller clumps or pieces in order to produce more plants or to revitalize older ones.

Dormancy: A time when a plant is not growing because conditions such as winter weather or drought do not support growth.

Edging plant: A plant used to mark the edge of a bed between the garden and a walk or patio. Often used in formal style gardens, the entire line is planted in a single variety of plant.

Espalier: A way of training trees or shrubs to a flat surface using a combination of supports or wires and regular pruning.

Evergreen: A plant that retains some of its older leaves as newer ones are formed, thus remaining leafy all year.

Exfoliating: Bark that pulls and peels away from the stem or trunk in a highly ornamental manner.

Foundation plant: Plants originally placed around the base of a building to hide ugly concrete foundations, now applied to landscaping around the perimeter of a building.

Fungicide: A chemical used to kill or control the growth of fungus.

Genus: A group of plants that share similar characteristics. The genus gives a plant its generic Latin name, such as *Quercus* for all oaks.

Girdling: Any process which removes the bark, cambium and sapwood of a shrub or tree resulting in the death of a branch or the entire plant. Girdling is sometimes done mechanically, by leaf-eaters or an animal's teeth, or by strangulation of ropes, wires, or the roots of the plant itself.

Ground cover: A group of plants, often but not always low-growing, that cover and protect an area of ground. Perennials and vines are most commonly used for ground covers, but grasses and shrubs often serve the purpose as well.

Hardening off: The process of gradually adjusting plants that were started indoors to the difference in temperature, sunlight, and wind in the out-of-doors.

Hardpan: A layer of compacted soil, usually clay, below the topsoil.

Heaving: The pushing of plants out of their soil by the action of alternating warm and cold temperatures causing the soil to expand and contract. Most harmful to newly planted plants with new or poorly established root systems.

Herb: Usually a plant grown for use in cooking, or for its scent or medicinal properties.

Herbaceous: A plant that does not have woody stems and dies to the ground in the winter.

Humus: Organic matter in the soil which is fully or partly decayed.

Hybrid: A plant that has been bred by from genetically dissimilar parents. The name often is preceded by the multiplication sign (x).

Indeterminate: A plant that does not stop growing as flowers or a terminal leaf is formed. This term is often seen describing a type of tomato which continues to grow and produce new flowers and fruits throughout the season. The tomatoes on indeterminate plants grow and ripen at different rates, over a long period of time.

Insecticide: Something toxic to insects.

Leaf mold: Decomposed (composted) leaves.

Leggy: Describes a plant that has grown tall with little foliage at the base. Usually used to describe annuals and perennials which have been grown so close together that they have stretched toward the light, growing tall and thin instead of compact and bushy. Also used to describe older annuals with the same appearance.

Lime: A white substance that contains calcium oxide which is used to neutralize acidic soils.

Loam: A fertile soil made of mineral particles of varying sizes (sand, silt, and clay) along with a great deal of organic matter.

Mulch: A material placed over the surface of the soil to retain moisture and retard weed growth.

Pathogen: Any disease-producing organism.

Perennial: A plant that grows for three seasons or more. Most commonly used for herbaceous plants that die to the ground and regrow from the roots.

Pesticide: A substance that targets and kills specific garden pests such as fungi, weeds, bacteria, and insects.

pH: The measurement of soil acidity. The pH scale measures the hydrogen ion concentration from 0 to 14. A reading of 7 is considered neutral, and is the best for growing many plants.

Pip: The bud on a root crown which will grow to be a new shoot. Some plants such as lily-of-the-valley are sold in groups of pips instead of in pots.

Planting zones: Regions determined by the average minimum temperatures. Zones are separated by 10° F differences in temperature and have been determined to help gardeners know which plants will survive in their area of the country. See the USDA map on page 238.

Reversion: Return to the original state; flower colors of hybrids may revert to the original color, or variegated plants may revert to solid green foliage.

Rhizome: A type of horizontally-growing rooted stems from which leaves and flowers grow. Rhizomes typically grow under the surface of the soil, or just on top of the soil as in iris plants.

Runner: A trailing stem which usually roots at the nodes. Plants with runners are often invasive.

Scarification: Scratching, nicking, or filing a hard seed coat to hasten germination.

Self-seeding: The tendency of some plants to drop seeds around the garden which germinate and grow.

Slow release: Fertilizers that dissolve slowly or require bacterial decomposition in order to be absorbed by a plant's roots.

Species: A group of similar plants which are interfertile individuals; the subdivision of a genus. Species name is the second italicized name in a plant's Latin name.

Sport: A mutant part of a plant that is different than the rest. New varieties of plants often begin from cuttings of a sport from another plant.

Stoloniferous: Growing by runners, which are trailing stems which root by the nodes to create new plants. A plant that is described as stoloniferous is often invasive.

Subshrub: A shrub that may die back to near the ground in cold winters, such as the *Buddleia* (Butterfly bush). Also used to describe any small, woody plant that is commonly grown as a perennial, such as lavenders, heathers, or thyme.

Sucker: Vigorous, vegetative shoots arising from shrub and tree roots.

Thatch: The build-up of decaying roots, stems and leaves at the base of grass plants.

Topdressing: Adding fertilizer, compost, lime or other soil amendments onto the surface of the garden.

Trace elements: The micronutrients necessary for plant growth but only required in minute quantities. They include boron, copper, iron, manganese, molybdenum, and zinc.

Viability: The capacity of seeds to germinate.

Vermiculite: A lightweight, expanded mica product used in potting soils. Often used for a medium to root cuttings in, for the storage of bulbs, and to lighten heavy soils.

Water sprout: A rapidly growing shoot on a limb or trunk of a tree. Often produced in response to over-pruning.

Zone: see Planting zone

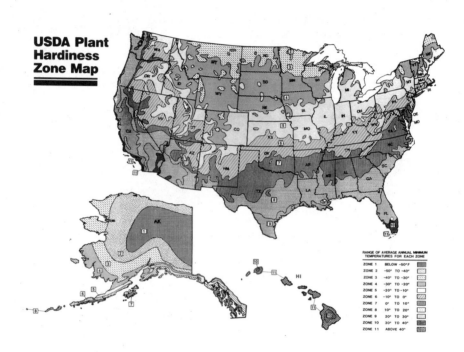

USDA Plant Hardiness Zone Map

RANGE OF AVERAGE ANNUAL MINIMUM TEMPERATURES FOR EACH ZONE

ZONE 1	BELOW -50°F
ZONE 2	-50° TO -40°
ZONE 3	-40° TO -30°
ZONE 4	-30° TO -20°
ZONE 5	-20° TO -10°
ZONE 6	-10° TO 0°
ZONE 7	0° TO 10°
ZONE 8	10° TO 20°
ZONE 9	20° TO 30°
ZONE 10	30° TO 40°
ZONE 11	ABOVE 40°

Chart courtesy of the U.S. Department of Agriculture

238

BIBLIOGRAPHY

Armitage, Allan M. *Allan Armitage on Perennials.* New York: Prentice Hall, 1993.

Armitage, Allan M. *Herbaceous Perennial Plants.* Athens, GA: Varsity Press Inc, 1989.

Ball, Jeff and Liz Ball. *Landscape Problem Solver.* Emmaus, PA: Rodale Press, 1989.

Bush-Brown, Louise and James. *America's Garden Book.* New York: Macmillan, 1996.

Clausen, Ruth R. and Nicolas H. Ekstrom. *Perennials for American Gardens.* New York: Random House, 1989.

Daniels, Stevie. *The Wild Lawn Handbook.* New York: Macmillan, 1995.

Dirr, Michael A. *Manual of Woody Landscape Plants: Their Identification, Ornamental Characteristics, Culture, Propagation and Uses.* Champaign, IL: Stipes Publishing, 1990.

Duffield, Mary Rose and Warren D. Jones. *Plants for Dry Climates.* Los Angeles: HP Books, 1992.

Ellis, Barbara W. and Fern M. Bradley (eds.). *The Organic Gardener's Handbook of Natural Insect and Disease Control.* Emmaus, PA: Rodale Press, 1992.

Hudak, Joseph. *Gardening with Perennials Month by Month.* Portland, OR: Timber Press, 1993.

Kingsbury, Noël. *The New Perennial Garden.* New York: Henry Holt and Company, 1996.

Köhlein, Fritz and Peter Menzel. *Color Encyclopedia of Garden Plants and Habitats.* Portland, OR: Timber Press, 1994.

Nollman, Jim. *Why We Garden.* New York: Henry Holt and Company, 1994.

Olkowski, William, Sheila Daar, and Helga Olkowski. *Common-Sense Pest Control.* Newtown, CT: Taunton Press, 1994.

Olwell, Carol. *Gardening From the Heart.* Berkeley, CA: Antelope Island Press, 1990

Pirone, Pascal P. *Diseases & Pests of Ornamental Plants.* New York: John Wiley & Sons, Inc., 1978.

Rechtschaffen, Stephan. *Time Shifting.* New York, NY: Doubleday, 1996

Sunset Magazine. *Sunset Western Garden Book.* Menlo Park, CA: Sunset Publishing Corporation, 1995.

Taylor's Guide to Perennials. Boston: Houghton Mifflin,1986.

Taylor's Guide to Annuals. Boston: Houghton Mifflin,1986.

Taylor's Guide to Shrubs. Boston: Houghton Mifflin,1987.

Taylor's Guide to Natural Gardening. Boston: Houghton Mifflin,1993.

Taylor's Guide to Roses. Boston: Houghton Mifflin,1995.

Titchmarsh, Alan. (1996) Tales From Titchmarsh, *BBC Gardeners' World.* October 1996

Turnbull, Cass. *Landscape Design, Renovation, and Maintenance.* Cincinnati: Betterway Books, 1991.

INDEX